WE·THE PEOPLE

HOUGHTON MIFFLIN
Share Our World

WE·THE PEOPLE

Share Our World

Sarah Bednarz

Catherine Clinton

Michael Hartoonian

Arthur Hernandez

Patricia L. Marshall

Pat Nickell

McGregor, Iowa

HOUGHTON MIFFLIN · Boston
Atlanta · Dallas · Geneva, Illinois · Palo Alto · Princeton

Sarah Bednarz
Assistant Professor
Texas A&M University
College Station, TX

Arthur Hernandez
Associate Professor
Division of Education
College of Social and
Behavioral Sciences
University of Texas at
San Antonio
San Antonio, TX

Catherine Clinton
W.E.B. Du Bois Institute
Fellow
Harvard University
Cambridge, MA

Patricia L. Marshall
Assistant Professor
Department of Curric-
ulum and Instruction
College of Education
and Psychology
North Carolina State
University
Raleigh, NC

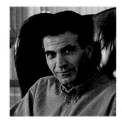

Michael Hartoonian
Professor and Director
Carey Center
Hamline University
St. Paul, MN

Pat Nickell
Director
High School Curriculum
and Instruction
Fayette County Schools
Lexington, KY

Susan Buckley General Editor

Acknowledgments appear on page 371.

Printed in the U.S.A. ISBN: 0-395-76542-0   56789-VH-99 98

CONSULTANTS

Felix D. Almárez, Jr.
Department of History
University of Texas
San Antonio, TX

Manley A. Begay, Jr.
John F. Kennedy School
of Government
Harvard University
Cambridge, MA

William Brinner
University of California
Berkeley, CA

Phap Dam
Director of World
Languages
Dallas Independent
School District
Dallas, TX

Philip J. Deloria
Department of History
University of Colorado
Boulder, CO

Jorge I. Domínguez
The Center for
International Affairs
Harvard University
Cambridge, MA

Kenneth Hamilton
Department of History
Southern Methodist
University
Dallas, TX

Charles Haynes
Freedom Forum First
Amendment Center
Vanderbilt University
Nashville, TN

Shabbir Mansuri
Founding Director
Council on Islamic
Education
Susan Douglass
CIE Affiliated Scholar

Roberta Martin
East Asian Institute
Columbia University
New York, NY

Acharya Palaniswami
Editor
Hinduism Today
Kapaa, HI

Linda Reed
Department of History
Princeton University
Princeton, NJ

Dahia Ibo Shabaka
Director of Social Studies
Detroit Public Schools
Detroit, MI

Ken Tanaka
Institute of Buddhist
Studies
Graduate Theological
Union
Berkeley, CA

Ling-chi Wang
Department of Asian
American Studies
University of California
Berkeley, CA

TEACHER REVIEWERS

Kindergarten/Grade 1: Wayne Gable, Langford Elementary, Austin Independent School District, TX • **Donna LaRoche,** Winn Brook School, Belmont Public Schools, MA • **Gerri Morris,** Hanley Elementary School, Memphis City Schools, TN • **Eddi Porter,** College Hill Elementary, Wichita School District, KS • **Jackie Day Rogers,** Emerson Elementary, Houston Independent School District, TX • **Debra Rubin,** John Moffet Elementary, Philadelphia School District, PA

Grade 2: Rebecca Kenney, Lowery Elementary School, Cypress-Fairbanks School District, TX • **Debbie Kresner,** Park Road Elementary, Pittsford Central School District, NY • **Karen Poehlein,** Curriculum Coordinator, Buncombe County School District, NC

Grade 3: Bessie Coffer, RISD Academy, Richardson School District, TX • **Shirley Frank,** Instructional Specialist, Winston-Salem/Forsyth County Schools, NC • **Elaine Mattson,** Aloha Park Elementary, Beaverton School District, OR • **Carmen Sanchez,** Greenbrier Elementary, Fort Worth School District, TX • **Irma Torres,** Galindo Elementary School, Austin Independent School District, TX

Grade 4: Patricia Amendariz, Lamar Elementary, El Paso Independent School District, TX • **Lenora Barnes,** Duncan Elementary, Lake County School District, IN • **Dianna Deal,** Park Hill Elementary, North Little Rock School District, AR • **Karen Dodson,** Martin Elementary, Alief Independent School District, TX • **Linda Johnson,** Memorial Drive Elementary, Spring Branch School District, TX • **Marina Lopez,** Hillside Elementary, El Paso Independent School District, TX • **Becky Murphy,** Butler Elementary, Springfield School District, IL • **Ann Powell,** Austin Independent School District, TX • **Sumner Price,** Legion Park Elementary, Las Vegas City School District, NM • **Sara Stultz,** Richland Elementary, Richardson Independent School District, TX • **Jim Wilkerson,** Glenoaks Elementary School, Northside Independent School District, TX

Grade 5: Pat Carney-Dalton, Lower Salford Elementary School, Souderton School District, PA • **Janice Hunt,** Dearborn Park Elementary, Seattle Public Schools, WA • **Debbie Ruppell,** Dover Elementary, Dover Union Free School District, NY • **Jon Springer,** Bethany Elementary, Beaverton School District, OR • **Nancy Watson,** Weeks Elementary, Kansas City School District, MO • **Gloria Wilson,** Forest Park Elementary, Little Rock School District, AR

Grade 6: Marcia Baynes, The Longfellow School, Middlesex County Schools, MA • **Diane Bloom,** Steelman School, Eatontown School District, NJ • **Hillary Callahan,** Coordinator of Language Arts, Roanoke City Schools, VA • **Tom Murphy,** Carusi Elementary, Cherry Hill School District, NJ • **Mark Newhouse,** A.T. Morrow School, Central Islip School District, NY • **Dot Scott,** Meadow Creek Elementary, Hurst-Euless-Bedford Independent School District, TX

CONTENTS

UNIT 1 How We Learn About Communities
THEME: PICTURING PLACES

UNIT 2 American Communities in History

UNIT 3 Communities and Their Geography

THEME: ENVIRONMENT

UNIT 4 Earning a Living

THEME: DEPENDING ON ONE ANOTHER

UNIT 6   Governing Ourselves

THEME: COOPERATION

VOTE
for your
MAYOR

FEATURES

★ CITIZENSHIP ★

THINK LIKE A GEOGRAPHER

MAPS

We·the·People

American Voices

" *As long as the sun shines and the waters flow, this land will be here to give life to men and animals.* "

Blackfoot Chief

" *I lift my lamp beside the golden door.* "

Emma Lazarus

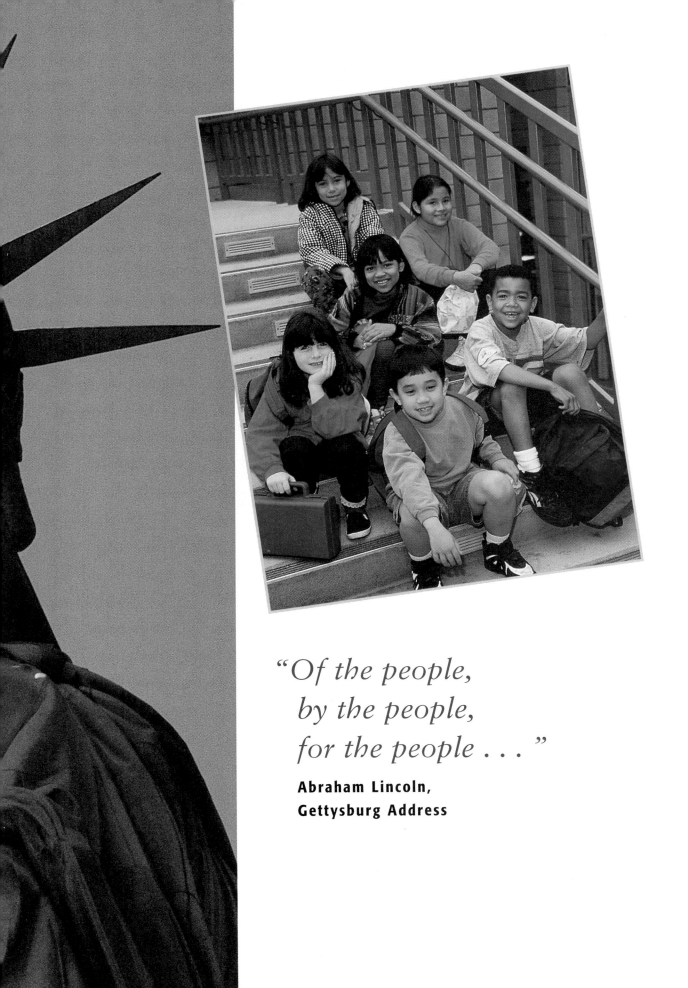

"Of the people,
by the people,
for the people . . . "

**Abraham Lincoln,
Gettysburg Address**

"*If there is no struggle, there is no progress.*"

Frederick Douglass

We are the

Spirit of America!

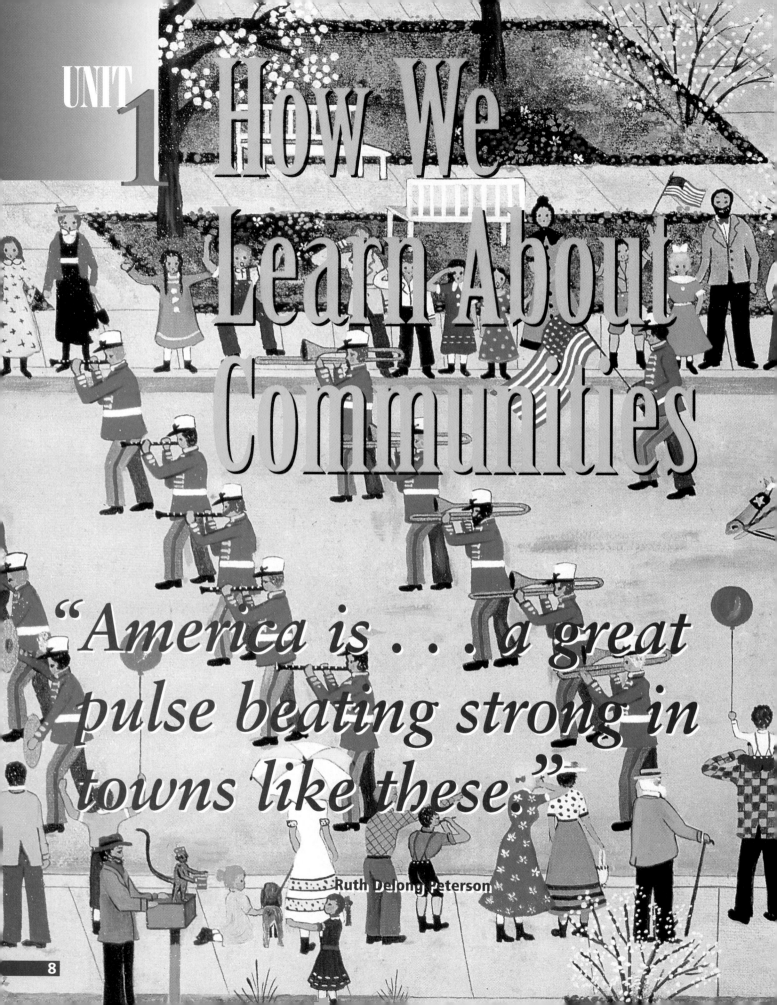

How We Learn About Communities

"*America is . . . a great pulse beating strong in towns like these.*"

—Ruth Delong Peterson

· THEME ·

Picturing Places

> ❝We study about communities to learn how to work as a group, to make a better living, and to build a better world in the future.❞
>
> Albert McGee, Austin, Texas

What is a community? A community is a location and a natural setting. It is the things that have happened in that place. It is the jobs and work of people in that place. It is the way people in that place celebrate. It is the way people in that place make rules for living together. Social studies gives you many ways to look at communities. You'll be learning to look at communities in this unit.

Theme Project

Create a Bulletin Board

Collect information about your community. Show what you learn on a bulletin board. Find out:

- What kinds of land forms are in your community?
- When was your community started? What are some important events that have happened there?
- What kinds of work do people do?
- What celebrations are important to the people in your community? Why?
- Who are the leaders of your community?

◀ Parades bring people in a community together.

WHEN & WHERE
ATLAS

 Look at the map of North America. Within this huge land are thousands of communities, large and small. These communities share many of the same features. Each of these communities has its own special character, too.

In this unit, you will learn more about communities. You will also read about some of the ways social studies can help you understand communities better. You will learn to look at communities to learn about their geography, history, work, culture, and government.

Unit 1 Chapters

Chapter 1 What Is a Community?

Chapter 2 A Community Close-Up

ALASKA
(United States)

PACIFIC
OCEAN

HAWAII
(United States)

Unit Timeline

1800	1840	1880

A Learning Place

These students found out that you can learn something almost anywhere. *Chapter 1, Lesson 1*

Through Time and Space

This man lives in the present, but works in the past. *Chapter 1, Lesson 2*

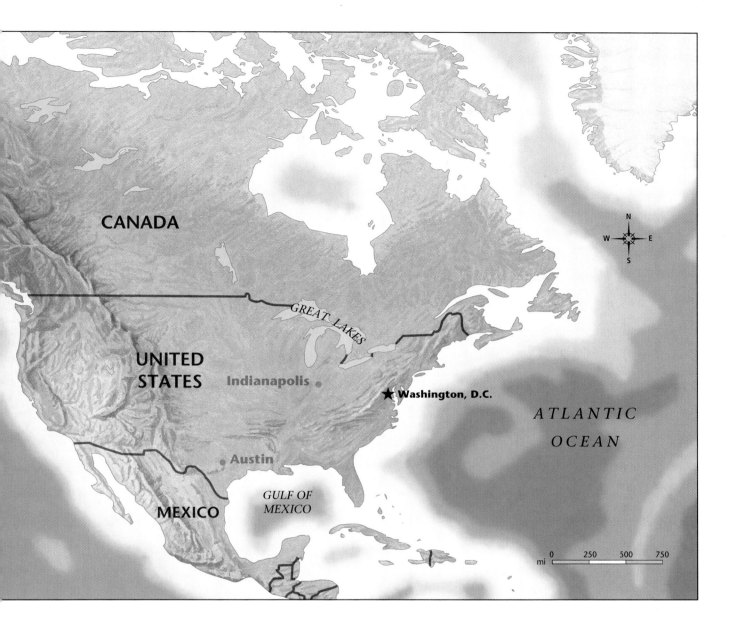

CANADA

GREAT LAKES

UNITED STATES

Indianapolis

★ Washington, D.C.

ATLANTIC OCEAN

Austin

GULF OF MEXICO

MEXICO

| 0 | 250 | 500 | 750 |
mi

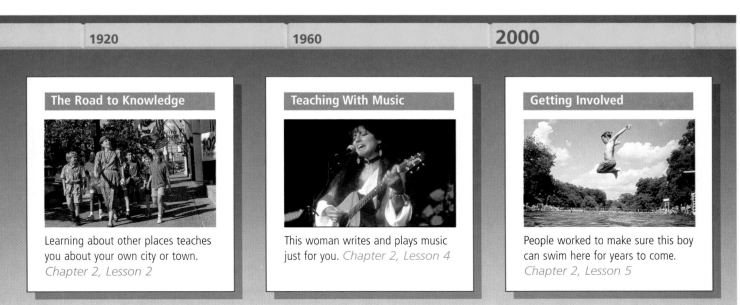

1920

1960

2000

The Road to Knowledge

Learning about other places teaches you about your own city or town. *Chapter 2, Lesson 2*

Teaching With Music

This woman writes and plays music just for you. *Chapter 2, Lesson 4*

Getting Involved

People worked to make sure this boy can swim here for years to come. *Chapter 2, Lesson 5*

What Is a Community?

Chapter Preview: *People, Places, and Events*

1760	1810	1860

A Learning Adventure

We're going to follow these students on their trip. *Lesson 1, Page 16*

Serving and Protecting

How would you like to step on his toes? *Lesson 1, Page 17*

Working Hands

This man makes a living handling fire. *Lesson 2, Page 21*

Let's Look at a Community

Main Idea A community is a group of people who live in the same area and who share the same laws and rules.

Key Vocabulary

community
law
route
canal

A dab of color here. A piece of tape there. Mrs. Hatcher's third graders are hard at work. They are hard at work learning about social studies.

These students in Fox Hill Elementary School are making pictures of places in Indianapolis, Indiana. This is the city where they live. The class will also learn about people and other places in the United States and around the world. They will study how people live and work together. You will, too.

Soon the students will take a bus trip. They will use social studies to explore Indianapolis. You can plan your own adventure in the area where you live.

Mrs. Hatcher's class is ready for their adventure in social studies.

◀ In communities like Indianapolis, people need places to come together.

1910	1960	2010

Connecting Across the Ocean

Let's spend a day at the races! *Lesson 3, Page 24*

A Building for You

This train station helps make Indianapolis a crossroads. *Lesson 2, Page 23*

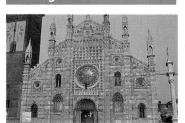

Sharing Your Beliefs

Find out what this building has to say about Monza, Italy. *Lesson 3, Page 26*

Exploring a Community

Focus *What are some features of a community?*

"Before we leave on our trip, what can you tell me about communities?" Mrs. Hatcher asks her class. *You* probably know something about communities already. A **community** is made up of people who live together in the same area. Communities come in different sizes. A community can be a town in the country or a large city.

People in a community work together. They also share the same laws. A **law** is a rule that people must follow to keep order. Laws help people live together peacefully and safely. Just think what would happen without traffic laws. Cars and trucks could go too fast. Traffic would not have to stop for red lights. You would have a hard time crossing a street safely.

Mrs. Hatcher's third grade students are learning new ways of looking at communities. One way they will learn more about their community is by taking a trip to different

Are you ready? Get set! Go! Mrs. Hatcher and her third grade students are all set to go on their field trip around Indianapolis. They are taking notebooks along. Now they can write down what they learn along the way.

places in it. Mrs. Hatcher and her students need to plan their trip. They look at a map of Indianapolis. The map shows them different routes. A **route** is a road or street that the students can follow to find their way around the city.

What kinds of things would you take with you to explore a city? Look on the right. These are things that Mrs. Hatcher's class will take. They will carry notebooks to write down what they learn along the way. They can use a camera to take pictures of what they see. In the picture below, you can see the class is ready to go.

Why don't we join Mrs. Hatcher and her students? Let's see what we can learn about a community. The bus is waiting. Let's go!

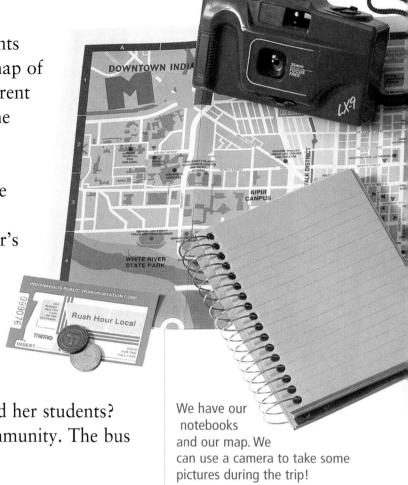

We have our notebooks and our map. We can use a camera to take some pictures during the trip!

Say "cheese!" These picture-perfect students pose with Tom. He is a firefighter at Fire Station 13.

Indianapolis looks very different when you're on the 31st floor.

Back on solid ground, students talk to Wilma Gibbs.

A Closer Look

Focus *What are some things that people do in Indianapolis?*

First stop: the Indiana State Library and Historical Building. This place has information about past times. There, students talk to Wilma Gibbs. Her job is to help people learn what Indianapolis was like in the past. Long ago, Indianapolis was laid out to be one mile square. That's about 10 blocks long and 10 blocks wide. The city has grown a lot since then!

To find out where the students go next, answer this riddle. How can you walk underneath cars? By walking through a tunnel! The students walk under the street through a tunnel to get to the Indiana State Capitol. State leaders meet in the capitol building. It's their job to make laws for the whole state.

Let's follow the class to Fire Station 13. There, we can learn how city leaders keep people safe. That is part of their job. The city provides a fire department to protect the community.

When a fire alarm rings, firefighters slide down poles to get to their fire trucks. Tom, a firefighter, shows the students his uniform. Outside, children climb on a fire truck.

Would you like 20 people to jump up and down on your toes? Firefighters wear shoes made with steel to protect their toes. Students jump on Tom's toes to see just how strong his shoes are.

In any community, people need places to rest and have fun. The Canal Walk in Indianapolis has gardens and fountains. It is built around a canal. A **canal** is a waterway built by people. People who work nearby go to the Canal Walk to exercise or rest. Molly chose this spot for Mrs. Hatcher's class to eat lunch. Ian pointed out the big goldfish swimming in the canal. Don't fall in!

On to the Indianapolis City Market. People can buy fruits and vegetables there. A community has places where people can buy what they need. The students pick out apples, grapes, and fruit salad.

Back to school we go! Mrs. Hatcher's students used social studies during their trip. They discovered how people work together in ways that make Indianapolis a community. How do people work in your community?

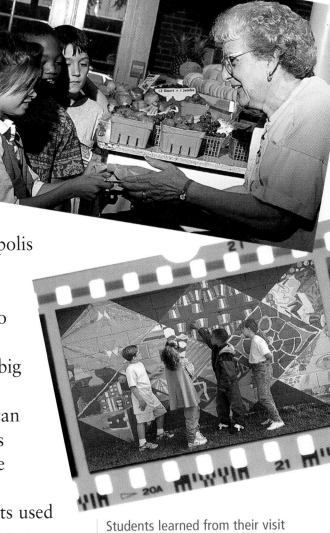

Students learned from their visit to the market and the canal. Economics: *Why is the City Market important to people living in Indianapolis?*

Lesson Review

1. **Key Vocabulary:** Describe Indianapolis using these words: **community, law, route, canal.**

2. **Focus:** What are some features of a community?

3. **Focus:** What are some things that people do in Indianapolis?

4. **Critical Thinking/Interpret:** Why is it important for people in a community to do different jobs?

5. **Geography:** How would you use a map if you were taking a trip around your community?

6. **Citizenship/Writing Activity:** The city provides police officers and firefighters for the community. Write a story about a police officer or firefighter. Your story should tell why police work or fighting fires is important.

Workshop

Making Maps

It's a Snap to Make a Map

Suppose you move to Indianapolis. You write a letter about your new community to your best friend back home. You talk about your new house, the school, and the playground. How can you show your friend how your new neighborhood looks? Draw a map! A map is a special kind of drawing of a place. It can show streets, buildings, rivers, lakes, parks—any place you want. You can use a map to show how to get from one place to another. A map is also a good way to show your friend where everything is in your new neighborhood.

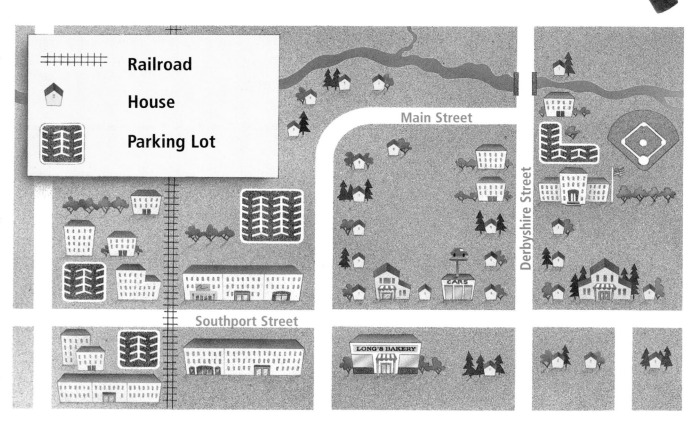

Railroad

House

Parking Lot

Main Street

Derbyshire Street

Southport Street

LONG'S BAKERY

1 Here's How

Let's find out what the maps on these two pages show about the community of Indianapolis.

- Look at the first map of a neighborhood in Indianapolis. Read the street names. What buildings do you see on the map? Is there a school? Is there a post office?

- A student drew the map on this page. What places do you see on this map? How is this map like the other one? How is it different?

- Now, make your own map of this neighborhood. Trace the outline of the neighborhood on a sheet of paper.

- Find the school and the park. Instead of drawing each of them, make up a symbol that stands for each place. You could use a book for the school and a tree for the park. What other symbols could you use?

- Look at the map on this page to decide where to draw the symbols for the school and the park.

- Don't forget to make a map key, so other people will understand your map.

2 Think It Through

How do you think people get the information they need in order to make a map?

3 Use It

1. Draw a map of your own neighborhood, showing streets, buildings, bridges, or other places.

2. Pick some important places, and decide what symbols you'll use for them.

3. Write the symbols in the correct locations on the map.

4. Write the symbols and what they stand for in the map key.

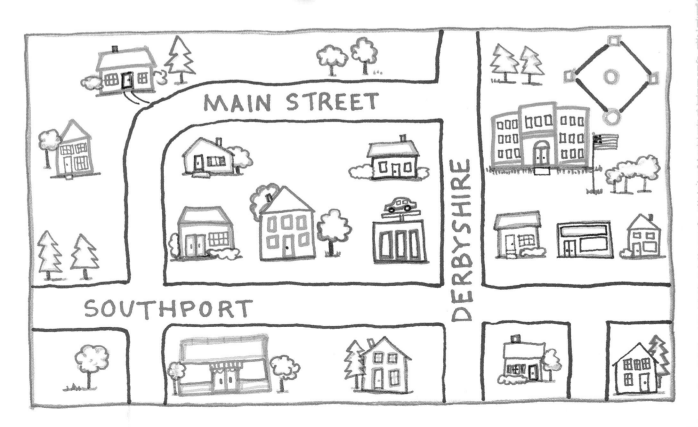

Log Cabin Days

Main Idea Long ago, in Indianapolis, people worked together in ways that make Indianapolis what it is today.

> **"I**t was the custom for neighbors and kinfolk for miles around to lend a hand clearing land, or building a cabin, or sharing food.**"**

Oliver Johnson had many memories from his childhood. In 1822, Oliver's family moved to Indianapolis. His family called him Ollie. Ollie and his family were early settlers of Indianapolis. A **settler** is a person who moves to a new place to make a home.

Long after Ollie grew up, he shared his memories with his grandson Howard. You can find Ollie's stories about growing up in a book called *Log Cabin in the Woods*.

The Indianapolis of Ollie's boyhood looked much like this picture. Mrs. Hatcher's class may have seen a picture of Indianapolis like this one at the Indiana State Library and Historical Building.

Things that happened in a community's past helped the community become what it is like today. To understand your own town or city, you need to learn about its past.

In 1825, Indianapolis streets had many stumps and trees. **History:** *How can pictures teach about life long ago?*

1825

Helping Hands

Focus *What was life like in Indianapolis long ago?*

Native Americans had lived in the area before settlers moved to Indianapolis. These settlers moved west from different parts of the United States. Then the settlers worked together to build their communities.

Ollie's stories about his childhood show how sometimes, work and fun went hand in hand.

At a logrolling,

> **"T**here would be good things to eat...and storytelling by the men.**"**

A logrolling took place after settlers chopped down trees. They chopped them down to make room for cabins and farms. Men rolled logs into piles while women cooked. For Ollie, logrollings weren't work — they were fun!

People also helped each other by sharing food and seeds to grow crops. They helped each other in times of sickness, too.

Settlers couldn't borrow or grow everything they needed. Sometimes they bought what they needed at the general store. General stores sold sewing needles, flour, clothes, and other things. Settlers also went to blacksmiths to buy tools.

Blacksmiths were important to the community. They made tools from metal by heating the metal over fire. Then they twisted or hammered the metal to make axes, horseshoes, and other tools that the settlers needed.

These people work in a museum, showing how people lived long ago. The man on top is repairing his cabin. This blacksmith is heating metal. Below, the women are making a material called flax.

Crossroads of the Nation

Focus *How did trains change the way people traveled from place to place?*

What has four wheels, 16 legs, and goes very fast? If you had lived in Indianapolis around 1847, you would have known the answer. It's a stagecoach pulled by four horses! A stagecoach is a four-wheeled carriage. Many people traveled by stagecoach on the National Road at this time.

This road stretched from Maryland to Illinois. It passed through Indianapolis.

As time went on, transportation changed. People use **transportation** to travel from one place to another. Fewer people rode stagecoaches when they had to go a long way. Instead, they took trains. Soon, miles of railroad tracks connected American communities.

Each of these trains had its own route — and there were many different routes. Train travelers often had a hard time switching from one train to another.

Then, in 1853, Indianapolis became the first city to connect all its railroad lines at one place: at Union Station. There, people could easily switch from one train to another without ever leaving the city or station.

The map below shows why people call Indianapolis the "Crossroads of America." **Map Skill:** *Name two states people could travel to on the National Road.*

Indianapolis, the Crossroads of America: 1853

WISCONSIN

MICHIGAN

Michigan City

South Bend

ILLINOIS

I N D I A N A

OHIO

Indianapolis   National Road

Terre Haute

Madison

KENTUCKY

Each day, about two hundred trains roared into Union Station. Steam puffed out of their engines. Whistles screeched. The voices of thousands of people traveling to and from Indianapolis filled the air. No wonder people call Indianapolis the "Crossroads of America." A **crossroad** is a place where two or more roads meet.

Today, people still visit Union Station. However, Union Station isn't a train station anymore — it's a shopping mall! Now, people go there to shop or eat.

Indianapolis is still an important crossroads. It is a center for airplane travel. Planes leave Indianapolis and carry people, packages, and letters all over the world. People use many types of transportation to get from place to place. How do people travel around your community?

The top picture shows how Union Station looked in the 1800s. As you see above, the station has changed since then.

Lesson Review

1. **Key Vocabulary:** Write a sentence for **settler, transportation, crossroad.**

2. **Focus:** What was life like in Indianapolis long ago?

3. **Focus:** How did trains change the way people traveled from place to place?

4. **Critical Thinking: Interpret** A crossroads is where two or more roads meet. Why can you use this word to describe Indianapolis after 1853?

5. **Geography:** How did settlers use the land to get the things they needed?

6. **Theme: Picturing Places/Research Activity:** Today, people visit Union Station for different reasons than they did more than 100 years ago. Find out how a business or place in your community was used long ago. Compare the way it was used and looked then with the way it is used and looks today.

Sister Cities

Main Idea People in communities can work with and learn from people in other communities.

Key Vocabulary

sister city
culture
custom
religion
worship

And they're off! When they wave the checkered flag below, the race begins. On the right, a car races around the *Autodromo* in Monza, Italy.

VROOOMMM! The red race car speeds around the track. Children and their families jump to their feet. They wave and shout, "Alesi!" (ah LAY zee) They are cheering for the driver in the red car, Jean Alesi. This is the *Autodromo* (OW toh DROH moh) in Monza (MOHN zah), Italy. People say that the *Autodromo* is the fastest racetrack in the world.

Like Monza, Indianapolis has a famous racetrack, the Indianapolis Motor Speedway. People in Indianapolis like to watch auto races. The races bring people together. The races have also brought these two communities together.

Communities around the world are different in many ways. But they can still reach out to one another.

Sharing Across the Miles

Focus *What do sister cities share?*

Monza and Indianapolis are sister cities. A **sister city** is a city that shares its ways of living and doing business with another city. Monza and Indianapolis became sister cities because both cities have famous automobile races. Both also have special children's hospitals. Doctors in both cities hope to share information to help sick children. Students and teachers from Indianapolis may go to Monza to work and learn. Workers from an automobile plant in Monza may share ideas with automobile workers in Indianapolis.

These two cities also share information about each other's culture. **Culture** is everything that makes up the way of life of people in a community. Your culture explains why you do things the way you do. It is a part of how you eat and dress. It includes the arts, beliefs, and past of the people in a community. Culture includes so many things you can't list them all!

The globe shows that an ocean separates Indianapolis (1) and Monza (2). The picture below the globe shows a street in Monza. **Map Skill:** *Is Indianapolis on the ocean?*

Different Ways of Doing Things

Focus *What are some ways in which the cultures of Monza and Indianapolis are alike? How are they different?*

"*Parla italiano?*" means "Do you speak Italian?" If you move to Monza, you need to learn Italian. Most people speak Italian in Monza. In Indianapolis, most people speak

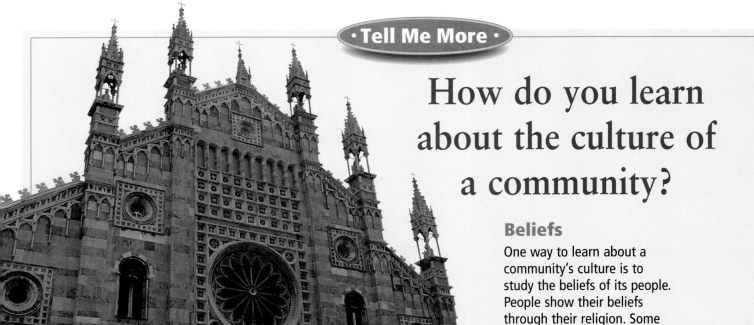

How do you learn about the culture of a community?

Beliefs

One way to learn about a community's culture is to study the beliefs of its people. People show their beliefs through their religion. Some people in Monza worship at this Roman Catholic church.

?

Ask Yourself

Suppose you were to talk to a student from Monza.

What would you like to know about Monza's culture? What would you share about your own community's culture?

? ? ? ? ? ? ? ? ? ? ? ? ? ? ?

English. Language is an important part of culture. Customs are, too. A **custom** is a way of doing things.

What did you eat for breakfast this morning? In Indianapolis, it is the custom for children to eat many different things for breakfast. They may have a glass of orange juice and a bowl of cereal. They may eat eggs, bacon, and toast. After breakfast, they pack their lunch and head for school.

It is the custom for children in Monza to eat a quick breakfast of hot milk, cookies, and a sweet roll. They don't take a lunch to school. In Monza, children go to school six days a week. School in Monza ends at 1:15 P.M. Then, children go home to eat with their families. This midday meal is the biggest meal of the day. People eat foods like noodles, vegetables, and fish or meat.

Children in Italy dress like the students we met in Mrs. Hatcher's class. Many wear blue jeans and T-shirts. Children in Monza also have fun kicking soccer balls and scoring goals. Soccer is the national sport of Italy. Some children also play basketball.

Religion is another part of culture. **Religion** is the way people show their beliefs. When people **worship**, they take

Customs

A community's culture is also made up of its customs. Customs include the way people greet one another and how they celebrate holidays. These two people are sitting in the Piazza Duomo (pee AHT zah DWOH moh). This is a common place for people to meet and greet in Monza.

Language

Another way to find out about another culture is to study its language. People use their language to sing, to write, to tell stories, and just to talk to one another. In Monza, most people speak Italian. The newspaper or magazine the man is reaching for is written in Italian.

part in religious services. Most of the people who live in Monza are Roman Catholic. People who live in Indianapolis have many different religions.

Culture is a part of the Indianapolis community. It is a part of your community, too. When people share ideas about how to talk, sing, tell stories, and have fun, they share their culture. When people in Monza and Indianapolis share ideas, they share their cultures too. Does your city have a sister city? Why don't you find out?

Lesson Review

1. **Key Vocabulary:** Write a paragraph about Monza using these words: sister city, culture, custom, religion, worship.

2. **Focus:** What do sister cities share?

3. **Focus:** What are some ways in which the cultures of Monza and Indianapolis are alike? How are they different?

4. **Critical Thinking: Generalize** How can sister cities help each other?

5. **Citizenship:** Sister cities share information about their laws. What can you tell a person from another country about some of your community's laws?

6. **Geography/Research Activity:** If you chose a sister city for your city from others in the United States, where would it be? Why would you choose that city? Find the state it's in on a map of the United States.

Chapter Review

Summarizing the Main Idea

1 Copy the chart below. Fill in the blank boxes of the chart with the names of people and places found in Indianapolis.

What Makes Indianapolis, Indiana, a Community?	
People	**Places**
firefighters	*Indiana State Capitol*

Vocabulary

2 Use the words below in a paragraph. Compare what it was like living in Indianapolis long ago and living there today.

community (p. 14) **culture** (p. 25) **canal** (p. 17)
settler (p. 20) **route** (p. 15) **religion** (p. 26)
law (p. 14) **crossroad** (p. 23) **worship** (p. 26)
transportation (p. 22) **custom** (p. 26)

Reviewing the Facts

3 What are some things that people in a community share?

4 What did visiting the capitol building and the fire station teach Mrs. Hatcher's class about city leaders?

5 How did early settlers get the things they needed?

6 What changed the way people traveled by train? Why did this make train travel much easier?

Turn back to the map on page 18.

7 Draw or trace the outline of the map. Suppose you were traveling to this community. Draw symbols to show the places you plan to visit. Include a map key for your symbols.

8 Draw the route you plan to use to get around the neighborhood pictured in the map. Write a letter to a friend. Give directions for how to use your map.

Critical Thinking

9 **Identify Main Idea** Read the section in Lesson 2 called "Helping Hands." Write one or two sentences that explain the title and the main idea of the section.

10 **Comparing Then and Now** How was living in Indianapolis in the past different from living there now?

11 **Problem Solving** Suppose a doctor in a children's hospital in Monza, Italy, needed some help with a problem with one of his or her patients. How do you think the people in Indianapolis and Monza could work together to solve the problem?

Writing: Citizenship and Economics

12 **Citizenship** What new law does your community need? Write to a lawmaker. Explain why he or she should make your new law.

13 **Economics** People visit the City Market to buy what they need. List other places in a community people can visit to find what they need.

Activities

Economics/Language Arts Activity
Make a word web using the word "blacksmith." Include things that a blacksmith made and who might have bought each of these things. Make a poster to show your work.

History/Drama Activity
Reread the information about Oliver Johnson's life. Write a play about Oliver Johnson that shows what life was like in Indianapolis in the past. Act out your play with a friend for the class.

Internet Option

Check the **Internet Social Studies Center** for ideas on how to extend your theme project beyond your classroom.

THEME PROJECT CHECK-IN

Have you used what you've learned about communities in your theme project?
- What places are in your community? Who would you find there?
- How many people lived in your community long ago? How many live there now?
- Does your community have a sister city? What information can you include in your theme project about your community's sister city?

Chapter Preview: *People, Places, and Events*

1760	1810	1860

Field Trips

How are they protecting the land in their community? *Lesson 1, Page 34*

Keys to the Past 1854

What can these people tell us about their community? *Lesson 2, Page 38*

A Walk into the Past

These students are walking back through time. *Lesson 2, Page 40*

Geography Close-Up

Main Idea Geographers learn about communities by looking at different features of the land.

Key Vocabulary

geography

geographer

pollution

habitat

car-pool

How well do you know your community? Let's take a closer look. Are there mountains nearby? What was it like living there long ago? How do people earn money? Do people from other countries live there? What kinds of laws does your community have? These are all social studies questions. To find answers, you must look at your community in different ways.

This year you will "travel" to many communities. You will learn how people live and work. Let's go to Austin, Texas! You will discover five ways to look at Austin. You can then look at your own community in those same ways.

◀ You can look at communities around the world in some of the same ways.

1910	1960	2010

Big Business

He is working on his recipe for success. *Lesson 3, Page 49*

To Live and Learn

Tune into music and learn about your community. *Lesson 4, Page 54*

People Growing Together

He is working to make his community healthy. *Lesson 5, Page 59*

Just like you, Lee Hoy spends some days taking field trips. When he plans a road or trail, he must go out to the land to see if his road or trail will work there.

Lee Hoy uses tools like maps and computers to plan his roads and trails.

AUSTIN METROPOLITAN AREA TRANSPORTATION PLAN

From the Ground Up

Focus *How do transportation planners collect information about the land?*

To find out about Austin's land, you use geography. **Geography** is the study of people, places, and the earth. **Geographers** study where things are located on the land. They look at the earth's natural features, like its rivers, hills, plants, animals — and the earth's people, too.

Geographers study how the land affects people. For example, the shape of the land affects the way people travel. Lee Hoy is a transportation planner in Austin. Transportation planners design roads, trails, and railroads. They use geography to help them decide where the road, trail, or railroad should be located.

If you asked transportation planners what their most important tool is, many would answer maps. When Lee Hoy plans a road, he uses maps to find out what the land looks like. Below, you can see a map of some trails in Austin. Then Lee uses computers to plan the road. Computers will show him the kinds of roads that can work on the land around Austin.

After Lee chooses the best place to build the road, he goes out to visit the land. He makes sure the road or trail can be built there. This is part of "ground truthing."

Transportation planners aren't the only people who work on the road. Scientists check to see what is under the soil. Other people build the road. Boom! They blast rocks and dirt out of the way. They smooth the ground and lay down the pavement. All of these workers use geography.

Lee Hoy knows that planning roads, trails, and railroads is a lot of work. He says, "It can take 10 years and $50 million before you have an actual road."

Workers smooth the ground so roads will be safe for bicycle riders and others who use them.

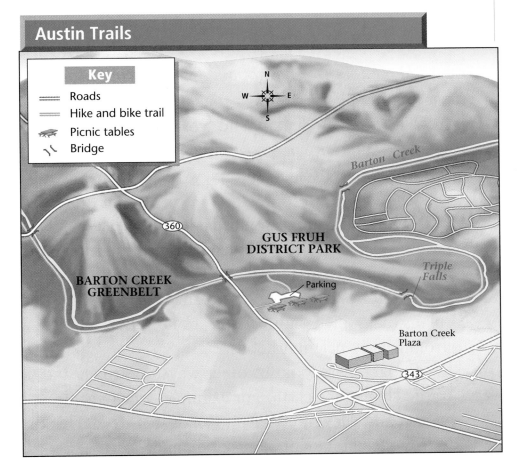

Austin Trails

Key
==== Roads
―― Hike and bike trail
Picnic tables
Bridge

N
W E
S

Barton Creek

360

GUS FRUH
DISTRICT PARK

BARTON CREEK
GREENBELT

Parking

Triple
Falls

Barton Creek
Plaza

343

This is a map of some of the trails in Austin. **Map Skill:** *What do the curving lines say about some of the trails?*

Who can use the trails in Austin?

Everybody can! A lot of work goes into building the trails in Austin. Leroy Click works for the Austin Metropolitan Trails Council. He plans trails that everyone can use: bicycle riders, walkers, people on roller skates, and also people who have to use wheelchairs.

Leroy looks for land that is flat when planning a trail. Flat land makes safer trails because it is easier to walk or ride on a flat trail. He also wants people to feel welcome to use the trails. When he looks at a map of some trails, he thinks about the children who will walk on them. He says,

> **"K**ids love trails. Getting kids involved is important. They're the future.**"**

Share the Road

These are "tools" that a walker might carry with her while on a trail or road. The pedometer tells you how far you've walked.

Focus *How does transportation affect the land in Austin?*
Transportation planners design roads to get people to the places where they live, shop, and work. As communities grow, more and more people use the roads. As a result, people need more roads built. New roads change the community.

New roads can mean more pollution. **Pollution** is harmful things in the water, soil, or air. Pollution harms plants, animals, and people. Austin tries to stop pollution from reaching its streams and rivers. It also plans high, thick "noise walls" to keep traffic noises from nearby neighborhoods.

Geographers look for other ways that roads and traffic change the earth. For example, when people build roads, they often have to cut down trees. This can destroy the habitats of plants and animals.

A **habitat** is the place where a plant or animal lives. Some animals move to new habitats. Other animals may die out completely.

The city of Austin also tries to cut down the number of cars on roads. The city asks people to walk, ride bikes, or take buses instead. Austin has also planned more sidewalks. This makes it safer to walk along busy streets. People are asked to **car-pool,** or to form groups in which people take turns driving. If you've ever ridden your bike to school or ridden in a school bus, you were helping to cut down on pollution in your community.

Today, cars must share the road with everything from joggers to dogs! **Geography:** *How can car-pooling help the plants and animals that live on the land around Austin?*

Transportation planners help people get to places they need to go. They use geography to pick the best and safest places to build roads, trails, and railroads. They try to protect the people, the animals, and the land. How have people changed the land in your community?

Lesson Review

1 **Key Vocabulary:** Use these words to describe the work of a transportation planner in a community: **geography, geographer, pollution, habitat, car-pool.**

2 **Focus:** How do transportation planners collect information about the land?

3 **Focus:** How does transportation affect the land in Austin?

4 **Critical Thinking: Interpret** How do transportation planners help the community?

5 **Citizenship:** What can you do to keep the land in your community from being damaged or polluted?

6 **Geography/Writing Activity:** What are some different land features around your school or home? Describe some of the features you see. To get started, answer the following questions: Is the land flat or hilly? What kinds of plants grow there? What animals live there?

THINK LIKE A
GEOGRAPHER

The World in Spatial Terms

How Can You Tell It's a Park from the Map?

Have you ever saved something special because you knew you couldn't get any more? That is what the United States does with some natural areas. National and state parks save special features of the land, like forests, caves, lakes, or mountains. This land is also set aside to give people the chance to enjoy nature. In National Parks, people can hike, bike, boat, swim, and do other outdoor activities.

The map on this page shows the Great Smoky Mountains National Park. When you look at the map, how can you tell that this land has been set aside? Notice that there are more roads outside the park than inside the park. What does the key tell you about the roads in the park? Are there cities or towns inside the park? The land inside the park is colored green on the map. What color is the land outside the park? Why show it this way?

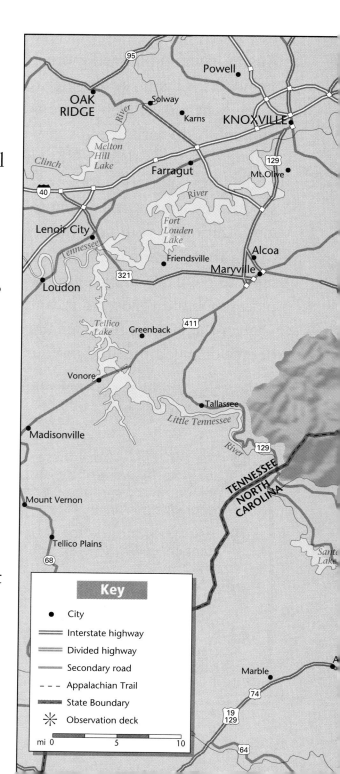

Key
- City
- Interstate highway
- Divided highway
- Secondary road
- Appalachian Trail
- State Boundary
- Observation deck

mi 0   5   10

Art Connection

Yellowstone National Park, the first National Park, was created in 1872 by Congress after William Henry Jackson brought back beautiful photographs of the wilderness. Can you find some pictures of the outdoors?

Research Activity

1 Find a map of the area where you live. What areas are set aside for specific uses, like parks or playgrounds?

2 Using the map and the map key, make a list of the information which shows you the different purposes for the different areas.

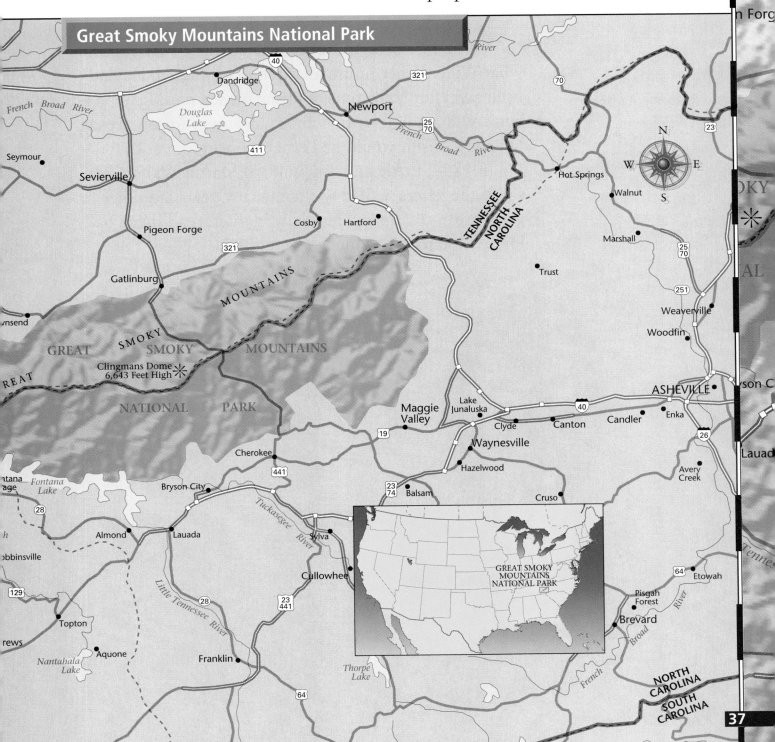

Great Smoky Mountains National Park

History Close-Up

Main Idea Historians learn about communities by studying the past.

Key Vocabulary

history
historian
research
landmark
architecture

Lettie tore open the letter. She couldn't wait to read what William, her future husband, had written. He had been away for some time, and she missed him. Lettie read what William had written about his life in Austin, Texas. One day Austin would be Lettie's home too.

In 1854, Lettie married William Martin Walton. She saved the letters he had written. Many years later, her great-great-granddaughter, Sally Hunter, read them. Sally loves those letters as much as Lettie did.

Sally used those letters as her keys to unlock Austin's past. William's letters make Austin in the 1850s come alive.

Lettie and William Walton posed for this picture and wrote these letters more than 100 years ago.

Unlocking the Past

Focus *How do historians find out about a community's past?*

Sally Hunter wants to learn about Austin's history. **History** is the study of the past. Every community has a history. Learning about your community's history will help you understand how it began. History also shows you how the community has changed and how it has stayed the same. A community's past makes it what it is today.

Sally looks at Austin through the eyes of a historian. You may have guessed that a **historian** is a person who studies history. Historians use different keys to unlock the past. Letters are one of those keys.

Sally Hunter uses a computer to explore what happened many years ago.

These are some other "keys" Sally Hunter uses. They include old pictures, letters, and other information that helps her study the past.

These students are looking at a cornerstone on a building in Austin. A cornerstone usually has a date that tells when the building was built. It is located at a corner where two walls meet.

Looking for Clues

Sally Hunter's study of Austin's history included reading the letters of her great-great-grandmother. Sally says these letters gave her "a real feeling of the way things were." In those letters, her great-great-grandmother described what Austin was like when she arrived.

Historians also talk to older people, asking them what they remember about the past. Sally Hunter talked to her grandmother, Louise Parmele Johnson. Her grandmother was born in 1893. She knew people who had lived in Austin long ago. She told Sally stories about Austin in the old days.

When historians do **research**, they study a subject very carefully. They look for information in many places. They might look in libraries or museums. Sally did research in the Austin History Center. There she found some old photographs. These pictures showed her how businesses and streets in Austin looked long ago.

Off we go!

We'll start our tour at the capitol building. History: *What could a tour teach you about your community?*

Walking Around

In downtown Austin, Sally and her students see buildings that have stood in Austin for many years.

Sally read old newspapers, too. The papers described events in Austin's past. Old advertisements also helped. They told her what people in Austin used to buy and sell.

Community records are information that communities write down to save. Communities keep records such as when people are born and when they buy houses. Such records help historians. Old records told Sally how many people lived in Austin in the 1850s.

Passing It On

Focus *How do historians share what they learn?*

Historians want to share what they find out. Luckily, Sally Hunter knows a group of people who will listen to her talk about history: her students! Sally Hunter teaches third grade in Austin.

Sally thought of different ways to teach her students and others what she knows. She created a walking tour of Austin. People can walk around different parts of the city. They can look at city landmarks. A **landmark** is a place or building that is important to the city.

Landmarks

What landmarks can you see and touch where you live?

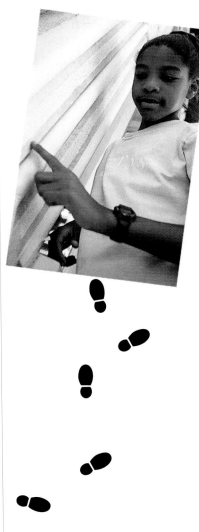

Wow!

They can learn a lot by reading what is written on a plaque outside of one of the buildings.

Austin, Texas, has changed in many ways since 1850. One thing that has changed since then is the number of people that have made their home there. In 1850, there were only 629 people living in Austin. By the year 2000, there will be more than 600,000.

Walkers learn about the community's past by looking at old street names. The walking tour also teaches people about Austin's architecture. **Architecture** is the design of a building, such as a house. Houses and other buildings show the time period in which they were built. You can guess the age of a house by looking at its architecture.

Historians look for new ways to share what they know. To a historian, the past is just as exciting as what is going on now. Sally Hunter created a computerized tour of Austin. By pressing a few computer keys, people "walk" around Austin without ever leaving their seats! She even takes her third graders to an old cemetery. There, children read the gravestones of people Sally has talked about. Sally says,

"Everyday people play a part in the community. You can show that through history."

Does your library keep old newspapers? Can you find old pictures of your community? These may be the keys that unlock the door to your own community's past.

Lesson Review

1 **Key Vocabulary:** Write a sentence for each of the following words: history, historian, research, landmark, architecture.

2 **Focus:** How do historians find out about a community's past?

3 **Focus:** How do historians share what they learn?

4 **Critical Thinking: Compare** What things about the past could you learn better from photos than from letters?

5 **Geography:** Suppose one community is located near a river and another community is not. How might their histories be different?

6 **Theme: Picturing Places/Research Activity:** What was it like living in your community 20 years ago? Ask someone who was living there at the time. Visit your local or school library to find newspaper articles or information about what life was like then.

Preparing for an Interview

Getting To Know You

Sally Hunter asked her grandmother questions about life in Austin long ago. This is called an **interview.** Suppose you wanted to find out more about the history of your community. Who could you interview? These steps will show you how to plan and do an interview.

1 Here's How

- What do you want to know? You might want to learn how your community has changed in the last 50 years.

- Find someone to interview. You can talk to your teacher, older people in your family or friends of the family, or ask at the library.

- Think of some questions you want to ask, such as the following: What types of businesses were there? Have more people moved to your community during this time? What did people in school do for play? Work? Write your questions down.

- Write a letter to the person, asking for the interview. During the interview, write down his or her answers to your questions. After the interview, don't forget to send a thank-you letter!

2 Think It Through

What kinds of information can you learn in an interview? How is an interview different from just talking with a person?

3 Use It

1. Think of something you want to learn that someone in your class might know about.

2. Make a list of questions.

3. Interview someone in your class. Did you find out what you wanted to know?

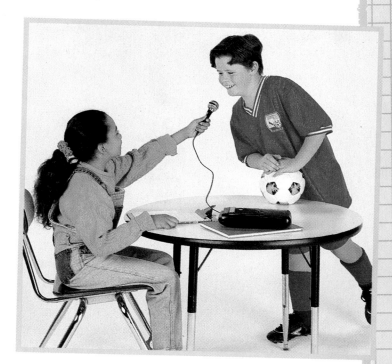

HOME PLACE

Realistic Fiction

by Crescent Dragonwagon,
illustrated by Jerry Pinkney

The past is never far away. We can discover a lot about ourselves and our neighbors by looking back. If we learn to notice things, even a walk in the woods can take us back to a different time.

But once,
someone lived here.
How can you tell?
Look. A chimney, made of stone,
back there, half-standing yet, though honeysuckle's
grown around it — there must
have been a house here. Look.
Push aside these weeds — here's
a stone foundation, laid on earth.
The house once here was built on it.

And if there was a house, there was
a family.
Dig in the dirt, scratch deep, and what
do you find?

honeysuckle –
*a vine that has yellow,
white, or pink flowers
shaped like tubes*

foundation –
*the base on which a house
or building is built*

A round blue glass marble, a nail.
A horseshoe and a piece
of plate. A small yellow bottle. A china doll's arm.

Listen. Can you listen, back, far back?
No, not the wind, that's now. But listen,
back, and hear:
a man's voice, scratchy-sweet, singing "Amazing Grace,"
a rocking chair squeaking, creaking on a porch,
the bubbling hot fat in a black skillet, the chicken frying,
and "Tommy! Get in here this minute! If I have to call you
one more time — !"
and "Ah, me, it's hot," and "Reckon it'll storm?"
"I don't know, I sure hope, we sure could use it,"
and "Supper! Supper tiiiiime!"

dusk –
*the time of day that
is just before dark*
vacant –
empty

If you look, you can almost see them:
the boy at dusk, scratching in the dirt with his stick, the
uneven swing hanging vacant
in the black walnut tree, listless in the heat;
the girl, upstairs, combing out her long,
long hair, unpinning,
unbraiding, and combing, by an oval mirror;
downstairs, Papa washing dishes
as Mama sweeps the floor

and Uncle Ferd, Mama's brother,
coming in, whistling, back
from shutting up the chickens
for the night, wiping the sweat
from his forehead.
"Ah, Lord, it's hot, even late as it is,"
"Yes, it surely is."
Someone swats
at a mosquito.
Bedtime.

Meet the Author

Crescent Dragonwagon is the author of more than 24 books and novels for young people. She and her husband also own a country inn in Arkansas called Dairy Hollow House. Many of her children's books are written in poetry, like *Home Place*. She likes taking readers to explore special times and places.

Additional Books to Read

Our Flag
by Eleanor Ayer
The story of America's flag.

Everybody Cooks Rice
by Nora Dooley
Suppertime around the neighborhood.

Response Activities

1. **Interpret** The author asks you to "listen back, far back." Sally Hunter also asks you to look back into the past. What do you think this writer and Sally Hunter really mean?

2. **Descriptive: Write a Word Picture** The words "squeaking, creaking" describe the rocking chair. Write down the words that describe "marble," "a man's voice," "swing." List other ways to describe them.

3. **History: Looking for Clues** Write down some clues you found about the old house and the family who lived there. What do they tell you?

LESSON 3

Work Close-Up

Main Idea Economists learn about communities by studying how businesses work.

Key Vocabulary
- economics
- economist
- manufacture
- high-tech

Do you think you're too young to have a business? Well, you're not! Many seven- and eight-year-olds have opened lemonade stands on hot summer days. They have scrubbed dirty cars or cut the neighbor's grass. To plan a business, you have to decide what you want to sell. Then you have to decide how you want to sell it.

To plan your business, you have to use economics. **Economics** is the study of how things are made, bought, sold, and used. You can learn a lot about a community like Austin by looking at the kinds of businesses that people run. An **economist** studies how businesses change a community.

Thirsty? These children have started a business that depends on thirsty people. They know that people will buy a cup of ice-cold lemonade on a hot summer day.

Setting Up Shop

Focus *What kinds of questions should a business owner ask when planning a business?*

What do you like to do? What are you good at doing? These are important economics questions to ask yourself before starting a business. When people do work that they like, they usually do a good job.

O. C. Houston owns and runs a pharmacy in Austin. A pharmacy sells medicines and other things that people need for their health.

O. C. had always liked science. He liked working with people, but he wanted to be his own boss. He opened a pharmacy so that he could do things that he liked doing.

O. C. also thought about the best place for his business. He opened his pharmacy in a neighborhood where people knew him. He felt it would be easier to find and keep customers.

At his pharmacy, O. C. Houston can do work he enjoys. Below are some tools he uses to get his job done.

He also hoped the patients of a doctor he knew would buy medicine from him.

O. C. thought about one more economics question: What is the most important thing I will give my customers? He decided, "Service is the most important." When a grumpy customer comes in, he and his workers make a bet. They bet each other one mint to see who can make the person smile.

O. C. Houston makes sure his customers are satisfied.
Economics: *How will having happy customers help his business?*

> **"C**all a customer by his or her name. If you make a mistake, apologize. Treat someone as you want to be treated.**"**

These are O. C.'s ingredients for success in business.

Everybody's Business

Focus *Why do businesses move to certain places?*
Each business has its own recipe for success. Some companies **manufacture** what they sell. They make things by using machines. These companies may be high tech companies. **High tech** companies make up-to-date machines like computers and computer programs. In 1974, one of these high tech businesses moved to Austin.

Gordy Davies works at that high tech company. He says that "the number one reason we moved here was the highly educated community and work force." Austin is home to many colleges, such as the University of Texas at Austin. Many people in Austin learned to do the things

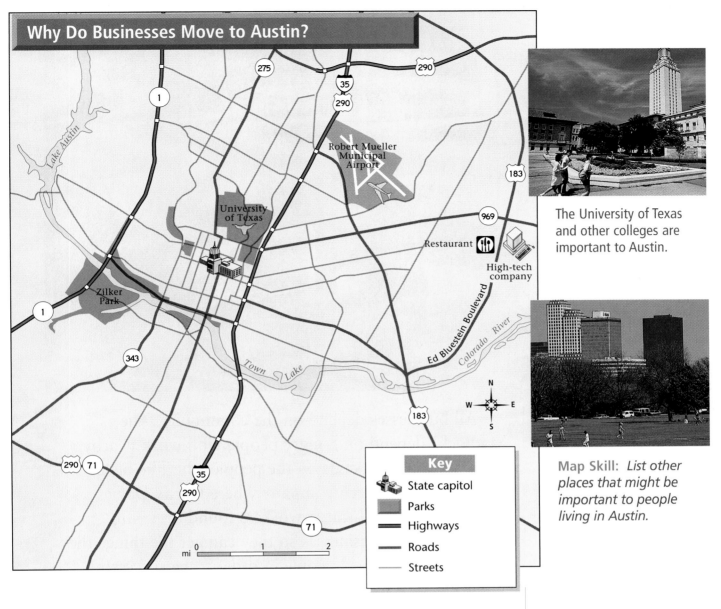

Why Do Businesses Move to Austin?

Key
- 🏛 State capitol
- Parks
- Highways
- Roads
- Streets

The University of Texas and other colleges are important to Austin.

Map Skill: *List other places that might be important to people living in Austin.*

that high tech companies need. High tech businesses move to places where they can find educated workers easily.

All businesses need good workers. Sometimes they also get help from other businesses. Matthew and Jessie Madlock are a husband and wife who serve food from a trailer in Austin. They park it across the street from a big company. Matthew used to work for that big company.

Matthew Madlock left his old job to start his own business. He made a deal with a store owner to park his red food trailer at the edge of the store's parking lot. Jessie says, "We were in the right place at the right time." The delicious smell of food travels far. At lunchtime, it draws hungry workers from nearby businesses.

If you lived in Austin, maybe you would be one of Matthew and Jessie Madlock's customers. Their business depends on the hungry people who work nearby.

All businesses depend on the community. The Madlocks depend on hungry people who work nearby. O. C. Houston depends on the people who like his good service. The high tech company where Gordy Davies works needs the educated workers found in Austin.

People need businesses so they can get the things they need. Businesses need people in order to be successful. What kinds of businesses are a part of your community?

Lesson Review

1. **Key Vocabulary:** Write a paragraph about Austin, using **economics**, **economist**, **manufacture**, **high tech**.

2. **Focus:** What kinds of questions should a business owner ask when planning a business?

3. **Focus:** Why do businesses move to certain places?

4. **Critical Thinking: Conclude** Why is location so important to a business?

5. **Citizenship:** Businesses often help community organizations, like sports teams and scout troops. How might this help the businesses too?

6. **Theme: Picturing Places/Math Activity** Many families move when parents change jobs or when the business they work for moves. Find out how many new students started at your school last year. How many new students are there this year? What is the difference in these two numbers?

Culture Close-Up

Main Idea Folklorists study the special music, stories, arts, and customs of a community.

*"**M**aggie, Maggie, where is Jiggs?*
Down in the cellar eating pigs.
How many pigs did he eat?"

You can hear that rhyme on playgrounds in Austin. Children chant it as they jump rope. Every year, new children learn that rhyme. Then they teach it to other children.

Jump-rope chants are a part of the folklife of a community. A community's **folklife** is its special music, stories, arts, crafts, and other customs. Let's take a closer look at the folklife of a community.

How many pigs did Jiggs eat? Let's count as they jump. While you count, think of other chants and rhymes you know.

Above is Pat Jasper. She may not use hammers or nails, but she does use the "tools" below. **Technology:** *Name some tools you see. How do you think Pat uses each of them?*

Heard It Through the Grapevine

Focus *How does a folklorist learn about the customs of a community?*

How do you learn about a community's folklife? You might take pictures of the clothes people wear. You might ask a woman how she learned to weave blankets. You can even listen to songs on the radio! A person who studies folklife is called a **folklorist**.

Pat Jasper is a folklorist in Austin. She takes pictures of examples she finds of folklife. She writes things down, too. Like a historian, she also does research in libraries. Folklorists keep records of everything they find.

The man on the left creates artwork from what other people throw away.

Folklorists also think it's very important to talk to people in the community. Pat Jasper calls this "fieldwork." She says,

"Folklife is something people carry in their heads."

Pat Jasper might knock on the doors of every house in a neighborhood. She talks to people to learn about Austin's traditions. A **tradition** is a custom or belief that is passed down from parents to children. For example, one family's tradition might be to eat black-eyed peas every New Year's Day.

What examples of folklife are you carrying around in your head? Write them down! Does your family celebrate special holidays each year? This is all part of your family and community folklife.

The woman above carves animals and other objects from wood. She carved this cow.

Austin's Music

On the left is Tish Hinojosa (ee noh HOH sah). She uses her music to share stories about her family and their customs. Santiago Jimenez (sahn tee AH goh hee MEH nehz), Jr., is on the right. He plays conjunto (cohn HOON toh) music. This kind of music is played by a group of three to six people. Both Tish and Santiago sing in English and Spanish so that all Texans can learn from their music.

Tish Hinojosa

Santiago Jimenez, Jr.

Sharing Folklife

One of the members of Santiago's band plays a guitar like this. These guitars are often used for conjunto music.

Focus *How do folklorists teach people about the folklife of a community?*

Mexican culture is an important part of Austin's folklife. Meet Christine Granados, who calls herself a "Mexican Texan." Her great-grandparents moved to Texas from Mexico. She says, "They brought with them special holidays to celebrate, foods to eat, and a way of speaking and thinking about things."

Long ago, Texas was part of Mexico. Texas is still right beside Mexico. Today, more than 100,000 Mexican Texans live in Austin. Their customs and traditions began in Mexico. Christine Granados says, "Some of these customs and traditions are enjoyed by all Texans."

While Pat Jasper records examples of Austin's folklife, Christine Granados shares and teaches part of it. She works at the Terrazas Library in Austin. Sharing customs can be as much fun as telling a story! At the library, storytellers tell children stories about Mexico.

What are other ways to learn about a community's folklife? Christine plans parties to teach people about Mexican culture. Let's have a party! We can munch on lemony cucumbers, zesty salsa, and tasty tortillas (tohr TEE yahz). A tortilla is a flat, round bread made of corn or flour. We can learn to sing in other languages. Christine says,

> **"I**t is very useful for me and other people living in Texas to know about Mexican culture and traditions. We are living so close to our Mexican neighbors. Not only that, but learning about other cultures can be fun, too.**"**

Look around you. Look around your neighborhood. What would you like to know about the folklife of your community? What traditions could you share?

Christine shares her culture with children who come to the library where she works.

Ask Yourself

A community's folklife is made up of its music, stories, food, and other traditions.

Name some traditions that are special in your community.

? ? ? ? ? ? ? ? ? ? ? ? ?

Lesson Review

1. **Key Vocabulary:** Use the following words to describe the work that Pat Jasper does: **folklife, folklorist, tradition.**

2. **Focus:** How does a folklorist learn about the customs of a community?

3. **Focus:** How do folklorists teach people about the folklife of a community?

4. **Critical Thinking: Interpret** What could you learn about a community by listening to the radio?

5. **Citizenship:** Why is it important to learn about the folklife of different cultures in your community?

6. **Geography/Arts Activity:** Find a map that shows the United States and Mexico. Trace the state of Texas. Then trace the country of Mexico. Why do you think Mexican folklife is important in Texas?

Government Close-Up

Main Idea People learn about communities by studying how their government works.

Key Vocabulary

government

elect

city council

mayor

petition

Don't run down the halls. *Raise your hand in class if you have a question. Wait until it's your turn.* Do we really need rules like these?

Yes, we do! Rules are important because they help keep things in order. Rules help keep people safe. Your school needs rules, and so does your community. Your community's rules are called laws.

Government makes these laws. **Government** is an organization that keeps a community, state, or country in order. It also provides services. Communities must have a government. Take a look at Austin's government. Find out about the type of government your community has.

Gus Garcia is a member of Austin's government. He reads a lot to get the information he needs to make good decisions. He also studies maps.

A Community Grows

Focus *What does the city council do?*

Some people who work in the government make decisions for the community. Often, these people are **elected**. They have their jobs because people have chosen them.

Do you ever work in the yard or in a garden? People in Austin work together in community gardens.

One part of Austin's government is the city council. The **city council** makes plans for the city. Gus Garcia is one of the council's six elected members. Austin's mayor works with the city council, too. A **mayor** is the chief government official in some communities.

The city council works to give the people of a community places to learn, work, and play. It works to help people live in clean, healthy places. Gus Garcia wanted people in Austin to eat healthy food. He helped start a community garden program. In this program, children and adults work together to grow vegetables on city land.

Gus Garcia listens carefully to others at a city council meeting.

Splash! Both adults and children enjoy jumping into the cool waters of Barton Springs. People in Austin worked to keep it safe to swim there.

Working Together

Focus **How do people make government work for them?**

People are an important part of government. They can make a difference in the way their government works.

People in Austin worked to make a difference. They believed that a natural area was being threatened by pollution. They worked together to save it. They formed a group called the "Save Our Springs Coalition."

Barton Springs is one of Austin's landmarks. Cool, clear water shoots up into the springs from large, deep caves. Barton Creek feeds the springs. To save Barton Springs from pollution, people wrote letters to the newspaper and to city officials. They went to city council meetings.

The people in Austin didn't stop there. A group went to houses and apartments, asking others to sign a petition. A **petition** is a written request. Their petition asked for a law to protect the springs. Almost 27,000 people signed it! Hard work helped save Barton Springs.

This girl was one of the many people who worked to save Barton Springs. **Citizenship:** *At what kind of community meeting might she be speaking?*

S.O.S.

SAVE OUR SPRINGS COALITION

Paid for by the S.O.S. Coalition, P.O. Box 2046, Austin, TX 78678

The Austin community showed that the government belongs to the people. The government works for the people in your community, too. People can affect the way their government works.

Most community governments meet to talk about what is going on in the community. In Austin, people can go to city council meetings. They can ask questions or just listen.

Find out what is happening in your own community's government. What decisions are being made? How do people affect those decisions?

Lesson Review

1. **Key Vocabulary:** Write sentences using **government**, **city council**, **mayor**, **elect**, **petition**.

2. **Focus:** What does the city council do?

3. **Focus:** How do people make government work for them?

4. **Critical Thinking: Interpret** What kinds of problems might people want city council members to solve for their community?

5. **Geography:** Remember that Lee Hoy is a transportation planner in Austin. He plans new roads. What laws might the city council pass about those roads so that they won't hurt the land?

6. **Citizenship/Writing Activity:** What are some of the rules in your classroom? Talk to your teacher and classmates. Write down five rules and explain why you think these rules are important.

★ CITIZENSHIP ★

Participating

What Do Flags Mean?

Did you ever make a fort in your yard? Maybe you made one in a box. Did you put up a flag? That flag stood for you and your friends in the fort. The flag meant: "We are here. We are together. We are proud."

You probably have an American flag in your classroom. Maybe there is one outside your school, too, or by your post office. Where else have you seen the American flag?

Case Study

The Making of the United States Flag

Every country has a flag. In the United States, the first flag was made about 200 years ago. It had a copy of the British flag in the corner. It also had 13 stripes — to represent the 13 colonies. When two new states joined the original 13, people added two stripes. In 1818, the United States government limited the number of stripes to 13.

Stars on the flags were sometimes in a circle, but not usually. Today, the 50 stars stand for the 50 states.

Until 1912, flag makers could make the flag however they wanted. They just needed to use red and white stripes and stars on blue. Now they all use one design.

| 1775 | 1777 | 1795 | 1818 | 1861 |

Take Action

Think about a flag that could stand for everyone in your classroom. Think of the students in your class. What is special about them? Design a flag for your class.

1 List your ideas for a class flag and give a reason for each idea.

2 Get a partner and share your lists and reasons.

3 Agree on what should be in the flag design.

4 Draw and color your idea for the flag.

5 Present your flag to the class. Explain why you made the flag the way you did.

Tips for Participating

- Listen carefully while someone is talking.
- Tell others what you like about their ideas.
- Try to find something you can all agree on.

Research Activity

Look up rules for displaying the American flag. Then make up three or four rules about when and where to hang your flag. Write your rules down so others can read them. Hang your rules up next to your flag.

A pledge is a way of promising to be loyal to a flag and the country or state it stands for. A national or state anthem is a song that expresses patriotic feelings for a country or state.

The Pledge of Allegiance

I pledge allegiance to the Flag
of the United States of America,
and to the Republic for which it stands,
one Nation under God, indivisible,
with liberty and justice for all.

The Star-Spangled Banner

Oh say, can you see, by the dawn's early light,
What so proudly we hailed at the twilight's last gleaming,
Whose broad stripes and bright stars,
through the perilous fight,
O'er the ramparts we watched
were so gallantly streaming?

And the rockets' red glare, the bombs bursting in air,
Gave proof through the night that our flag was still there.
Oh say, does that Star-Spangled Banner yet wave
O'er the land of the free and the home of the brave?

republic –
a form of government

twilight –
time of day when there's little light left in the sky

perilous –
dangerous

rampart –
a wall around a place used for protection

Pledge and Salute to the Texas Flag

Honor the Texas Flag.
I pledge allegiance to thee,
Texas, one and indivisible.

The Texas State Song
Texas, Our Texas

Texas, our Texas! All hail the
mighty State!
Texas, our Texas! So wonderful,
so great!
Boldest and grandest, withstanding
every test;
O empire wide and glorious, you
stand supremely blest.

God bless you, Texas! And keep you
brave and strong.
That you may grow in power and
worth, thoughout the ages long.

indivisible –
*not able to be separated
or divided*

emblem –
*something that stands
for something else*

Response Activities

1. **Predict** Are pledges and anthems likely to help people respect the laws and rules of their community? Explain.

2. **Expressive: Write an Anthem** Write an anthem for your community. Think about the land, past, work, culture, and government of your community. Include information about one or more of these features in your song.

3. **Citizenship: Make a Poster** Find and write out the words to your state anthem on a poster. Decorate it with pictures you make yourself or that you clip from magazines or booklets. Contact your state office of commerce or tourism for pictures of your state.

Chapter Review

Summarizing the Main Idea

1 Copy the chart. Fill in the ways that geography, history, economics, culture, and government affect a community.

Austin Close-Up	
Geography	
History	
Economics	
Culture	
Government	

Vocabulary

2 Use at least ten of the words below to write a paragraph. Describe the things that make up a community.

geography (p. 32)
geographer (p. 32)
pollution (p. 34)
habitat (p. 35)
car-pool (p. 35)
history (p. 39)
historian (p. 39)
research (p. 40)

landmark (p. 41)
architecture (p. 42)
economics (p. 48)
economist (p. 48)
manufacture (p. 50)
high tech (p. 50)
folklife (p. 53)
folklorist (p. 54)

tradition (p. 55)
government (p. 58)
elected (p. 59)
city council (p. 59)
mayor (p. 59)
petition (p. 60)

Reviewing the Facts

3 What does a transportation planner do to help the community?

4 How can people in a community use information about the community's past?

5 What are some ways that businesses depend on a community?

6 What is a community's folklife?

7 What does government do for the people in a community?

8 Suppose you were going to interview Sally Hunter, the historian from Lesson 2. What questions would you ask her about the changes she has found in Austin? List five questions you would ask.

9 Who could you ask about your community's folklife? Does he or she know about the music, arts, crafts, or dances that are special to your community? List five questions you would ask this person.

Geography Skills

Use the map on page 33.

10 Compare the different land features near the trails shown on the map. List some features you find.

11 Suppose you were giving a tour of a trail. Write what you would say during the tour. Describe what you would see and do on the walk. Would there be any uphill climbing or downhill steps?

Writing: Citizenship and Culture

12 **Citizenship** People in Austin wrote to city leaders to protect Barton Springs. Think of something in your community that you want to change. Write a letter to a city leader. Explain what you would like the government to do to help you.

13 **Culture** Tish Hinojosa writes music that describes her family and its traditions. Think of one of your favorite songs. Then, change the words to the song. Describe your family or a celebration or tradition that is special to you.

Activities

History/Research Activity
Read some old newspapers from your community. Find out what it was like to live in your community in the past. Write a paragraph that describes what you've learned from each story.

Economics/Art Activity
Draw a picture of an important business where you live. Use pictures from a magazine or book to show the kinds of things you can buy there and who might shop there.

Internet Option

Check the **Internet Social Studies Center** for ideas on how to extend your theme project beyond your classroom.

THEME PROJECT CHECK-IN

Look at the bulletin board of your community and answer these questions:
• Have you included a map that shows the geography of your community?
• Have you shown the people who live and work in your community? Who works with geography? Is there a historian or a folklorist? Who works in government?

American Communities in History

"Give me your tired, your poor, Your huddled masses yearning to breathe free,"

Emma Lazarus, these words appear on the Statue of Liberty

· T H E M E ·

Change

❝ *My community changed when businesses came in. Then some government offices moved in. Maybe some malls will move in, too.* **❞**

Thu Nguyen, Eatontown, New Jersey

Change is all around you. You can look at old pictures of yourself and see how you have changed. Your community changes too. There are many reasons why a community changes. When new people come to a community, they change it. New kinds of businesses bring change. Machines can change the way people live. Look around your community. Change is happening all the time. In this unit, you will read about some of the ways communities can change.

Theme Project

Design a Walking Tour

Learn about the ways your community has changed. Plan a walk that leads people to different buildings or places in your community. Tell them about the ways each building or place has changed. To collect information for your walking tour:

- Look for dates on buildings.
- Talk to people who remember or have heard stories about things that happened long ago in your community.
- Visit the library to look at old pictures, letters, and newspapers.

◀ Immigrants often build new communities.

69

2
WHEN & WHERE
ATLAS

In 1500, North America had many Native American communities. You can see two of these communities on the map. When European settlers arrived, they started their own communities. Over time, European and Native American communities changed.

In this unit, you will learn about early Native American communities. You will also read about communities the Europeans started. Finally, you will read how new machines and newly arrived people have changed American communities.

Unit 2 Chapters

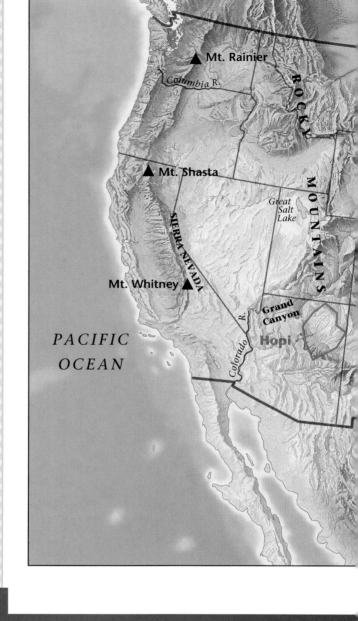

Mt. Rainier

Columbia R.

ROCKY

Mt. Shasta

Great Salt Lake

MOUNTAINS

SIERRA NEVADA

Mt. Whitney ▲

PACIFIC OCEAN

Colorado R.

Grand Canyon

Hopi

Unit Timeline

1500	1600	1700

Desert Living 1500s

Buildings like these may have been the first apartments. *Chapter 3, Lesson 1*

A Growing Place

Bite into a piece of the past! *Chapter 3, Lesson 2*

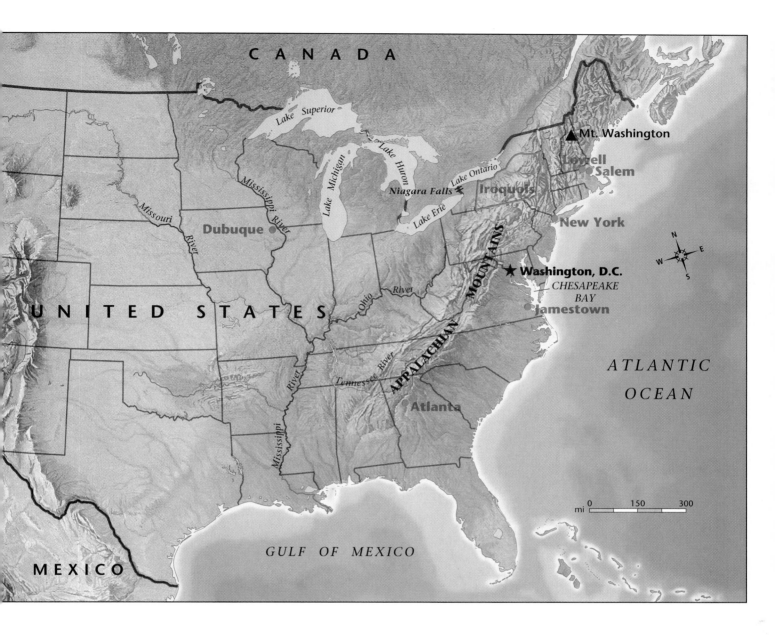

CANADA

Lake Superior

Lake Michigan

Lake Huron

Lake Ontario

Niagara Falls

Lake Erie

Iroquois

Mt. Washington

Lowell

Salem

New York

Missouri River

Mississippi River

Dubuque

UNITED STATES

Ohio River

Washington, D.C.

CHESAPEAKE BAY

Jamestown

ATLANTIC OCEAN

APPALACHIAN MOUNTAINS

Mississippi River

Tennessee River

Atlanta

N
E
W
S

mi 0   150   300

MEXICO

GULF OF MEXICO

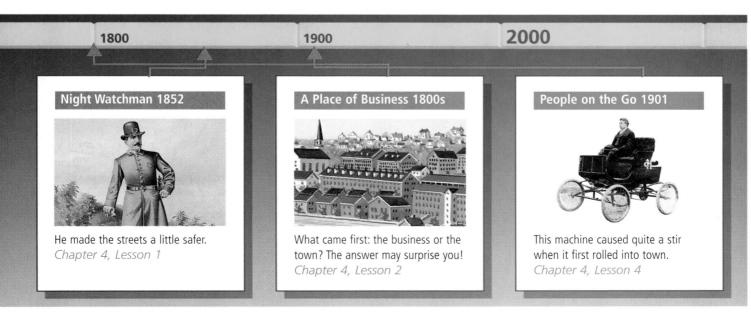

1800

1900

2000

Night Watchman 1852

He made the streets a little safer.
Chapter 4, Lesson 1

A Place of Business 1800s

What came first: the business or the town? The answer may surprise you!
Chapter 4, Lesson 2

People on the Go 1901

This machine caused quite a stir when it first rolled into town.
Chapter 4, Lesson 4

Early America

Chapter Preview: *People, Places, and Events*

1400	1480	1560

An Iroquois Village 1500s

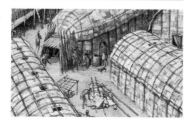

How many families lived here?
Lesson I, Page 74

Hopi Pottery

Potters created art out of clay and water. *Lesson 1, Page 78*

Jamestown, Virginia 1617

Have you seen this girl in a movie?
Lesson 2, Page 87

Native American Communities

Main Idea By forming communities, Native Americans adapted to different kinds of land.

The time is 400 years ago. An icy wind blows snow around a long, wooden house. Ten families live inside. One evening, the children gather by the fire. A grandmother shares stories of life long ago. Later parents, in each family's room, cover their sleepy children with fur blankets. Soon all is quiet.

These families were Iroquois (IHR uh kwoy). The Iroquois are one of hundreds of Native American groups that still live in North America. Living in communities helps people today, as it did in the past, use the land around them.

Iroquois people made pots like this of clay.

◄ These buildings in Colorado are from a community built about 800 years ago.

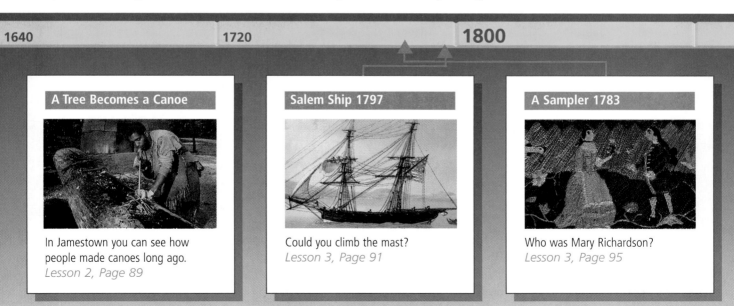

1640	1720	1800

A Tree Becomes a Canoe

In Jamestown you can see how people made canoes long ago.
Lesson 2, Page 89

Salem Ship 1797

Could you climb the mast?
Lesson 3, Page 91

A Sampler 1783

Who was Mary Richardson?
Lesson 3, Page 95

The Iroquois of the Woodlands

Focus *How did living in a community help the Iroquois adapt to the woodland?*

The map on the left shows where the Iroquois lived 400 years ago. This land was covered with thick forests. Birds, deer, and other animals lived in these forests. Rivers were filled with fish. These Native Americans adapted to their land. When people **adapt**, they learn to use their surroundings. They use the land to get what they need to live.

The Iroquois worked together. They made their houses from big trees. Logs formed the frame of the houses. The Iroquois used logs that were thick and strong. They also used thin branches that could be bent to form the frame of the house. They used bark peeled from logs to cover walls and roofs.

As many as ten families lived in one long building. That home was called a **long house**. Living together in one long house made it easier to keep warm in winter. Each

Long Houses

An Iroquois community, such as the one shown below, was made up of a group of long houses. **Geography:** *What materials did the Iroquois get from the land to build their houses?*

The entire village of Iroquois long houses was protected by a large fence. A fence kept out wolves, deer, and other animals.

The Iroquois built holes in the roofs of long houses to let out smoke from their fires.

family had its own space. In that space, they slept and stored their things. Some families had one glowing fire. Two families often shared the same fire.

A group of long houses made a village. A village was surrounded by a big wall. The Iroquois lived in a village to be safe from attack by other people.

Iroquois girls and boys had important jobs in the village. Men and boys cleared away the trees to make room for gardens. Girls worked with women to plant vegetables and gather berries. Sometimes men hunted in groups for deer. Women and girls made clothes from animal skins.

After about 10 or 20 years, the whole village moved. The soil in the gardens had worn out. Together the families looked for a new place to settle. Then they built a new village.

Peeled bark from trees covers the outside walls and roofs of long houses.

Frames hold up the buildings. They are made from the trunks and limbs of trees.

The Great Peace

Focus *Describe some ways in which the Iroquois used resources to bring peace to their communities.*

Long ago in the land of the Iroquois there were many wars. Native American groups living there fought with one another. The Iroquois tell the story of a great leader, Hiawatha, who was sick with sadness about the wars.

It is said that Hiawatha went off by himself. He stayed alone in the forest for many days and nights. He thought about how to bring peace to his people.

Near a lake, Hiawatha discovered tiny white and purple shells that he could use. He wove the shells onto long grasses. Hiawatha made a belt. These shell beads that were made into belts are called **wampum**. As Hiawatha wove the wampum, he dreamed of a lasting peace among all his people. Hiawatha's sadness began to leave him.

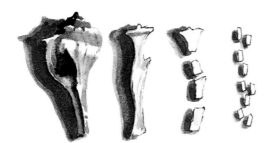

Wampum was carefully made from two kinds of shells — quahog and whelk. To begin, most of the whelk shell was knocked off. Only the long and thin "spine" of this shell was used. Next, the spine was cut into pieces to make small beads.

Purple beads were made from quahog shells. You can see this in the drawing below.

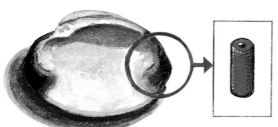

Quahogs are a kind of clam shell. Some snail shells are called whelks.

Hiawatha visited many villages to speak of peace. He said he knew how hard it was to not fight. He said that those who were able to keep the peace, rather than fight, were the truly great heroes. Hiawatha gave people wampum as a symbol of peace. All the Native American people who lived in that area came together to live in peace. They called themselves the Iroquois.

To this day, Hiawatha is remembered as an honored leader of the Iroquois. Who are the honored leaders in your community's history?

· Tell Me More ·

Iroquois and the Land Today

Steve Thome, an Iroquois, grew up in a community where his people have lived for 200 years. Today, this community is in New York State. He loved the great beauty of the land. When he grew up, Steve went away to college. Now he is back at home. Today Steve works for the Indian Health Services. He tests for clean air and water. Steve studies the health of his people. He looks for answers to health problems. Steve is proud of his Iroquois culture. He says, "A lot of Iroquois feel a closeness to the land. Iroquois culture teaches us this. We need to think how the land affects everyone. What we do now will affect the people seven generations from now."

Steve Thome receives a medal for his good work from two people in the United States Public Health Service.

The Hopi of the Desert

Focus *Describe some ways that Hopi communities used the resources of their land.*

The Hopi lived in what we now call Arizona. The land of the Hopi is desert land — hot and dry. There are few trees. It is hard to grow some plants in a desert.

The Hopi were not discouraged, however. Hopi people thought of other ways to make a community. They learned to grow food and build houses in a different way than the Iroquois.

These people of the desert built houses of stone and earth. Only the frame was made of wood. The Hopi houses looked like apartment houses. They were square and were from two to five floors high. Together, these houses were called a **pueblo** (PWEB low).

Today, Hopi women and girls continue to make clay pots. **Arts:** *What colors do Hopi artists use to decorate their pots?*

The Hopi used ladders to enter their homes through a hole in the ceiling.

Building a Village

When they needed more living space, the Hopi added a new home on top of the ones already there. The men and boys went far out into the desert to look for trees. It might take them many days to find enough wood for a frame.

Hopi women and girls used thin tree trunks to make a frame for the house. They stuffed branches and leaves in between the thin trunks. They piled up rocks to make the walls. They covered the rocks with mud for smooth walls. The hot sun baked the walls until they were hard.

Pueblo Villages

Today, the Hopi live in about 12 villages on top of mesas in Arizona. Mesas are the flat tops of mountains. One of these Hopi villages has been a home for about 800 years.

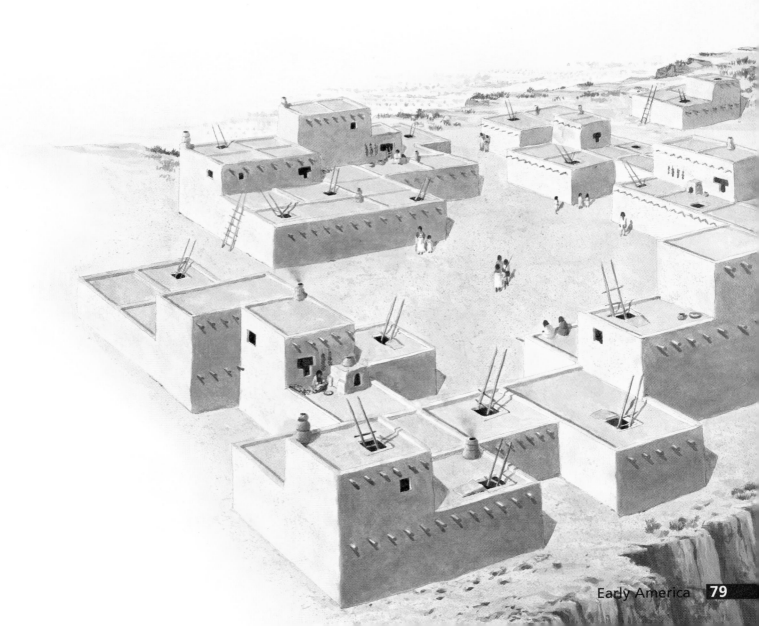

To grow the corn in this picture, farmers put a handful of kernels into holes. The holes are made a foot deep with digging sticks. **Science:** *How could long roots help plants grow in a dry climate?*

Before the Planting

Focus *How do the Hopi use resources as gifts?*

In the Iroquois woodlands, it rains from one to five inches every month. In the Arizona desert, it rains only about eight inches in the whole year! Without enough water, certain plants will not grow. Therefore, healthy plants are seen as a special gift from the land. In spring, before the Hopi begin their planting, they have special ceremonies. One of these — the Bean Ceremony — happens every February.

At sunrise on the day of the Bean Ceremony, Crow Mother comes into the village. The Hopi believe that Crow Mother is the mother of kachinas. The Bean Ceremony is the way the Hopi welcome the kachinas into the village after the winter. Crow Mother and other kachinas have come to lead prayers — for rain, a large harvest of crops, and good health for all people.

Inside each house, Hopi families get ready for the kachinas. Women cook food. Men weave cloth or watch out the window for the kachinas. Children are excited. They are waiting for the kachinas to come to their door. When they come, Hopi mothers go to the door to welcome the kachinas. The mothers thank the kachinas for coming with their prayers.

Rattles, dolls, and sticks are given to Hopi children in the Bean Ceremony.

The kachinas bring bean sprouts to the Hopi people. Girls receive kachina dolls as gifts. Boys get painted lightning sticks and rattles. Some gifts remind Hopi children of rain or snow. Rattles sound like thunder. Lightning streaks decorate sticks used in dances. Later, everyone enjoys a stew made from the bean sprouts.

The changing seasons are important in every community. How does your community celebrate seasons?

Lesson Review

1. **Key Vocabulary:** Write a paragraph about the ways the Iroquois and Hopi used the land. Use the terms *adapt, long house, wampum,* and *pueblo.*

2. **Focus:** How did living in a community help the Iroquois adapt to the woodland?

3. **Focus:** Describe some ways in which the Iroquois used resources to bring peace to their communities.

4. **Focus:** Describe some ways that Hopi communities used the resources of their land.

5. **Critical Thinking:Generalize** Why do people living in a community adapt better to their land? Could a single person do as well?

6. **Geography:Math** In the Arizona desert, it rains up to 8 inches a year. How much rain would Hopi crops get in a year if 8 inches of rain fell every month?

7. **Citizenship/Art Activity:** Draw a picture of a person in your community who cooperates with others.

Monte, Rex, and Oren Lyons are part of a long line of Onondaga lacrosse players.

Onondaga; Seneca –
The Onondaga and Seneca people are two of the six nations of the Iroquois Confederacy. The other four are Cayuga, Mohawk, Oneida, and Tuscarora.

Sticking to Tradition

by Marty Kaminsky

Iroquois kids grow up playing the fast-paced game of lacrosse.

Nine-year-old Onondaga Indian Tyler Bucktooth streaks across the field, cradling the ball snugly in the pocket of his lacrosse stick. Three Seneca defenders slash at Tyler's stick, kicking up a cloud of dust as they rumble after him. His teammates sprint toward the action calling, "Breakaway, Tyler, breakaway!"

Crouched before the goal like a knight guarding his castle, the Seneca goalie blocks Tyler's path. Tyler tilts his stick back and fakes with his head and shoulders. As the goalie lunges forward, Tyler fires a shot past him and into the goal. Score!

On the sidelines, Freeman Bucktooth, Tyler's father and coach, smiles proudly.

The Iroquois are often credited with inventing lacrosse. The Iroquois, however, believe lacrosse was not invented but was a gift from the Creator. Tewaarathon, as the game was called, served many purposes for the Iroquois people.

Freeman Bucktooth says, "We believe the Creator gave us the game to help keep our bodies and minds strong. It's a deep part of our culture and traditional way of life."

Centuries ago, lacrosse equipment consisted of a ball — a deer-hide cover sewn tightly around a ball of deer hair, a hickory lacrosse stick, moccasins, a breechcloth, body paint, and a charm known as a talisman. Sometimes teams of one hundred players would play for days at a time. To prepare for games players trained hard and asked the spirits of swift and powerful animals for help in special ceremonies.

Ceremonies are still held before important games. By comparison, however, today's players wear padding from head to toe, including helmets, shoulder pads, and thick gloves. Players also wear knee and elbow pads to soften the bumps and bruises from falling.

Today's players, like those on Tyler Bucktooth's team, enjoy the benefits of sturdy helmets and lightweight sticks, but they do not forget the ancient roots of lacrosse.

"The beginnings of the game are as old as our people," says former Onondaga Chief Oren Lyons. "Lacrosse is one of our gifts to the world. My father and grandfather stand behind me on the lacrosse field just as I stand behind my own son and grandson."

originated –
started

hickory –
a tall North American tree that has hard, tough wood

breechcloth –
a piece of clothing that covers the area between the waist and the hips

In the picture below, on the left, Butch Elm III and Teri Bucktooth chase the ball during practice.

 Response Activities

1. **Generalize** How did Iroquois lacrosse players of long ago use the animals and plants around them?

2. **Descriptive: Play-by-Play** You are a sportscaster standing on the sidelines at a lacrosse game. Describe what is happening on the field.

3. **History: Picture the Past** What games do you play on the playground? Where and how did these and other games begin? Choose a sport or game. Find out what people used to wear to play the game. Draw a picture of what a player looks like today and someone who played the game in the past.

Settlers in Jamestown

Main Idea Europeans and Africans had to adapt to a new land so that they could build successful communities.

Captain John Smith came with the first ship of English settlers to Jamestown.

At the right see a helmet that an English soldier wore nearly 400 years ago. Archaeologists discovered it buried in the ground at Jamestown. A part that protected the face is missing.

Sometimes dreams don't match the way things really are. Suppose you've always dreamed of moving to a land far away. That idea thrills you. You think your new life will have wonderful, exciting adventures. Maybe you'll even get rich. Suddenly you get the chance to do just what you dreamed about. You can't wait to go.

Then you get there. You find out that you haven't brought the things you need. You start to run short of food. You aren't prepared for the weather. Your new land isn't the way you thought it would be.

That is what happened to the first English settlers in Jamestown, Virginia. A settler is a person who goes to a new place to start a community. Jamestown's settlers were in for some surprises.

Jamestown

Focus *What did English settlers find along the James River?*

The first English settlers arrived at Jamestown in the spring of 1607. About 100 men and boys had come across the Atlantic Ocean from England.

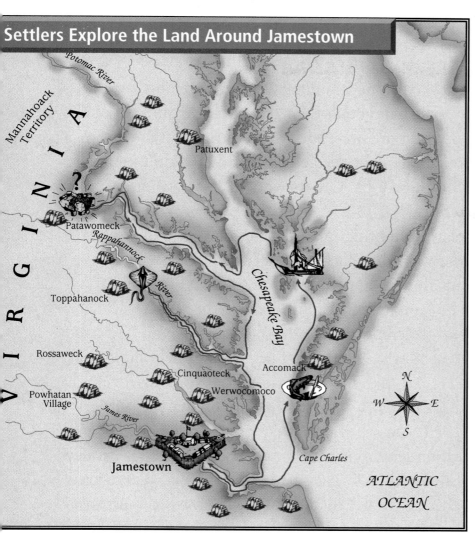

Settlers Explore the Land Around Jamestown

Mannahoack Territory

Potomac River

VIRGINIA

Patuxent

Patawomeck

Rappahannock River

Toppahanock

Rossaweck

Cinquaoteck

Powhatan Village

James River

Werwocomoco

Chesapeake Bay

Accomack

Cape Charles

Jamestown

ATLANTIC OCEAN

N W E S

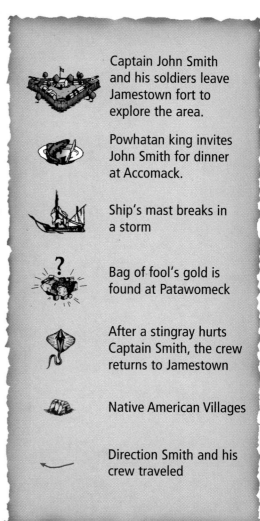

Captain John Smith and his soldiers leave Jamestown fort to explore the area.

Powhatan king invites John Smith for dinner at Accomack.

Ship's mast breaks in a storm

Bag of fool's gold is found at Patawomeck

After a stingray hurts Captain Smith, the crew returns to Jamestown

Native American Villages

Direction Smith and his crew traveled

Many of them were rich people. They had come to build a colony. A **colony** is a group of people who settle in another land. The men who started the Jamestown colony came to find riches.

No English person had ever lived in a place like Jamestown. This land was far away from England, the land the settlers knew. The plants in the new land were strange. The animals were strange too. The summer weather was hotter than it was in England. Winter weather was sometimes colder. How could they live in this new land?

The settlers built a fort. A **fort** is an area of buildings surrounded by walls for protection. People go to a fort to be safe from attack. Once the settlers had built the fort, they stopped working.

You can follow Captain John Smith as he left Jamestown in Virginia. **Map Skill:** *Where did Smith eat fish?*

James I was king of England when settlers came to Jamestown. The fort was named for him.

Providing for Basic Needs

Settlers needed to hunt animals and grow plants for food. To keep warm and cook their food, they should have gathered wood for fires. Many of the rich settlers had never done these things before. Some didn't know how to do these jobs. Others wanted someone else to do all the work.

Instead of hunting, planting, or gathering firewood, many men went bowling. They bowled in the streets. On days they didn't want to bowl, men looked for gold.

Then Captain John Smith became the settlers' leader. Smith had different ideas. He was a soldier who had lived all over the world. Smith used his skills to help build the colony. He did take men on expeditions looking for gold. While they stayed in Jamestown, though, he told settlers they needed to work if they were going to live.

Smith understood that the settlers needed to learn new ways of doing things. They had to learn what plants grew well in the area. They also had to learn how to hunt the animals in the forests and get fish from the waters. The Native Americans who lived all around the Jamestown fort knew those things. Smith believed that the Native Americans could teach the settlers their skills.

The Powhatan People

Focus *What did the Powhatan community teach the English settlers about living in a new land?*

The great Wahunsonacock (Wa hun SUN a cock) was the leader of the Native Americans in the area. He was called Chief Powhatan (POW hat an) by the settlers. His people, the Powhatan, lived along the seacoast. Native American people

Native Americans most often grew beans, corn, and squash in their fields.

had been there for thousands of years before English settlers arrived. Like the Iroquois and the Hopi, the Powhatan knew how to get food from the land. They did not have all of the metal tools that the settlers did. So they traded corn and other foods for the settlers' metal pots, axes, and knives. When people **trade**, they give something away to get something they want.

The Settlers Learn from the Powhatan

Captain John Smith learned to speak the Powhatan language. He wanted to know how Powhatan women grew vegetables so well. In the drawing on page 86, you can see their secret. Beans, corn, and squash grow close together. See how beans curl around the corn stalks? Powhatan men knew how to fish in the rivers using nets.

Without the Powhatan people, the settlers at Jamestown would never have lived. Captain John Smith admitted this. The land around Jamestown was filled with good things to eat. The settlers did not know how to grow, find, or catch them though. Captain Smith wrote down everything he learned from the Powhatan people about their area. He wanted the English settlers to build a successful community too.

Tobacco Brings Wealth

The Powhatan also taught the settlers about tobacco. Then settlers sold tobacco in Europe for a lot of money. Because of the tobacco, more settlers came to Jamestown after 1619.

The settlers did not ever discover the gold they hoped to find. Tobacco became their gold.

Pocahontas

Pocahontas was the daughter of Chief Wahunsonacock. She learned English after she became friends with the settlers. Captain John Smith said that she once saved his life. Pocahontas married a settler, John Rolfe. He took her to England for a visit. Pocahontas was welcomed by the Queen of England.

Pumpkins, persimmons, and wild grapes are foods Powhatan people ate.

Jamestown Today

Do you like a mystery? The people in these pictures are looking for clues about how people lived in Jamestown long ago. Not every clue is written down on paper in a letter or a diary. The people in these pictures are looking for clues in the ground! Buttons, coins, or broken pieces of pottery are clues about the way people used to live.

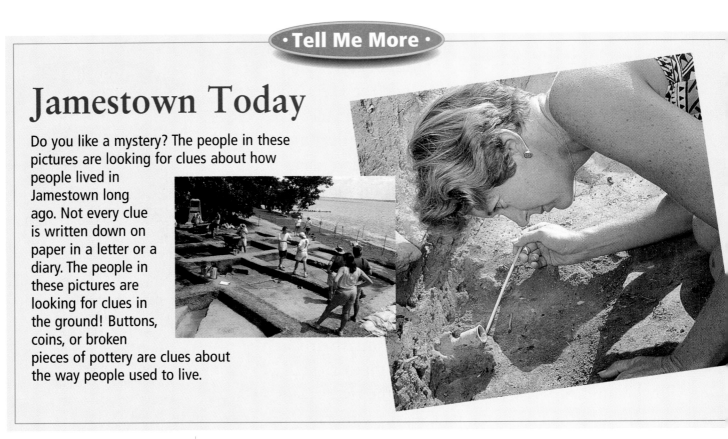

? Ask Yourself

One tailor, a barber, four carpenters, and a jewelry maker came to Jamestown. Few, if any farmers, made the trip.

If you were leader of a group going to a faraway place, what workers would you bring?

? ? ? ? ? ? ? ? ? ? ? ? ? ? ?

Africans Arrive

Focus *How did Africans adapt to this new land?*

In 1619, the first Africans came to Jamestown. They helped build the community almost from the beginning. The first African child born in Jamestown was William Tucker, son of Antony and Isabella. He was born in 1624. There were then 23 Africans and 1,200 English people in Jamestown. English settlers came to Jamestown of their own free will. Africans were forced to come.

Settlers planted more land with tobacco. As the tobacco business grew, more workers were needed. English settlers brought more Africans to Virginia.

The Africans found Jamestown strange at first, just as the English had. The weather was different from the weather in Africa. Africans had to adapt to a new land just as English settlers did. They learned to plant and grow corn the way the Powhatan people did. They grew new kinds of vegetables in gardens, too.

Henry Bond works at Jamestown today. Visitors to Jamestown today can learn about how people lived in Jamestown long ago.

Henry Bond is playing the role of a Jamestown settler who lived long ago. He is making a canoe out of a log the same way the Powhatan did. First he burns the log. Then he scrapes out the burned part with shells.

As more settlers arrived, new communities were built nearby. Some Africans started their own communities. They lived as free men and women. There were always free African American people in communities nearby, but most Africans around Jamestown were forced into slavery. In **slavery**, people are forced to work without pay. That was true for over 200 years until slavery in the United States ended after the Civil War.

Lesson Review

1. **Key Vocabulary:** Write a paragraph using **fort**, **colony**, **trade**, and **slavery** to describe Jamestown.

2. **Focus:** What did English settlers find along the James River?

3. **Focus:** What did the Powhatan community teach the English settlers about living in a new land?

4. **Focus:** How did Africans adapt to a new land?

5. **Critical Thinking:Generalize** Why is it so important for people of different backgrounds to work together in a community?

6. **Geography:** What body of water is between Africa and Jamestown?

7. **Citizenship/Writing Activity:** The Powhatan and English traded often. Write down three rules these people could have followed for trade.

Salem Takes to the Sea

Main Idea Salem became a wealthy community in the 1700s because of ships that traded around the world.

Key Vocabulary

cargo
merchant
wharf
import

If you grew up in Salem, Massachusetts, in the 1700s you had the sea in your bones. You smelled the salt air when you woke up. In winter, bitter ocean winds battered your home. In summer, you welcomed the soft sea breezes.

When you walked to the water, you saw the boats. Small boats brought fish for your supper. Great sailing ships carried fruits, spices, and cloth from distant parts of the world. Maybe, just maybe, you would one day be a sailor on a tall ship. Who knew how far you could travel?

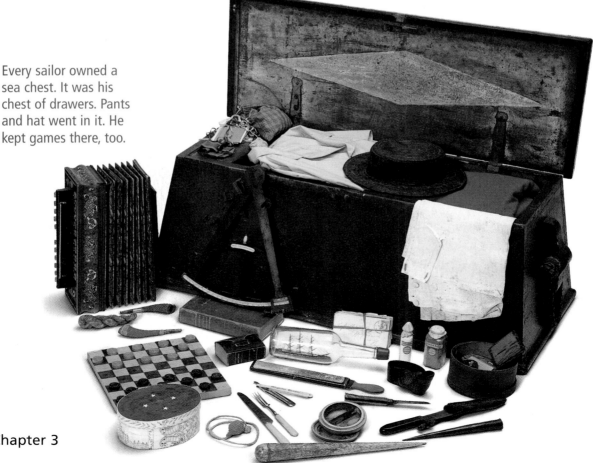

Every sailor owned a sea chest. It was his chest of drawers. Pants and hat went in it. He kept games there, too.

This ship is called the *Attatant*. It was built in Salem in 1797.

The Brigh Attatant of Boston Cap Taylor, coming in to Naples — anno 1800

Down to the Sea in Ships

Focus | *How was the location of Salem important?*

Salem was built on the ocean. Long ago, Native Americans called this spot Naumkeag (NAHM kehg) — "the fishing place." There was never enough farmland around Salem. Instead of becoming farmers, many people in Salem fished. Fishing boats brought cargoes of fish back to Salem. A ship's **cargo** is the things that it carries.

Fish were dried. Fish were salted. Fish were put into barrels. People in Salem couldn't eat all those fish. Then Salem merchants thought of something to do with the extra fish. A **merchant** is a person who buys and sells things to make money. Merchants used ships to carry fish and other things they had — like lumber — to other places.

A sailmaker's bag had tools for fixing ships' sails. Sailors needed needles to fix torn sails on ships.

This wharf was a place where ships unloaded cargoes. Dishes, items made of cloth, and silk thread were some of the things Salem imported from other countries. **Economics:** *Why is a wharf a good place to buy and sell things?*

Life in Salem

Many young boys from Salem longed for a life at sea. Some became sailors who worked for a sea captain. A ten-year-old boy might begin as a clerk. Clerks counted money for merchants. They lived and ate meals in the same place where they worked. For dinner, codfish stew often filled a boy's hunger.

With skill and hard work, a young clerk could become a sailor within two years. By the time he was twenty, he might have his own ship. Could he become rich? A lucky sea captain might end up with great wealth.

Suppose you could take a walk around Salem then. Follow the map on page 94. As you walk, listen. Everywhere people are at work. Carpenters hammer and pound, building new ships. Wagons loaded with vegetables and wheat rumble and creak. Pigs squeal on their way to market. Farmers who live inland are coming to Salem. Sailors shout to each other as they unload a ship's cargo on a wharf. A **wharf** is a landing place where ships tie up to load and unload their cargoes.

Salem's location on the sea created jobs. Some workers made ships. Others made things ships needed, such as ropes, sails, and tools. Merchants hired workers to build wharves for their ships. The picture at the top of this page shows what these wharves looked like. Some families with cargoes built their own wharves. Storehouses were built on each wharf where merchants kept goods. Clerks were also hired to count the money merchants made.

See how ships stopped along this wharf? Boats were tied up at posts. Cargoes were put into storehouses on the wharf.

Then & Now

In 1750, sailors could never be sure they would get their mail. Lucky men got letters if a ship carrying mail for them arrived at a port where they had stopped. Today, letters are flown by airplanes to meet ships around the world. Letters are given to sailors wherever they stop.

Teapots and Thread

Focus *How did the people of Salem trade and what did they get in return?*

Merchants traded ship cargoes for things people in Salem would buy. Sea captains from Salem sailed all around the world. When Salem merchants wanted tobacco, where did they find it? Jamestown, Virginia, had plenty! Trade with Europe was important. Ships carried cargoes to countries like England and Spain. Ships also sailed to Asia and Africa.

When ships returned to Salem, they carried cargoes from the places they had gone. Ships from Spain returned to Salem with raisins, silk handkerchiefs, and oranges.

Salem in 1760 was a busy town. People were everywhere. Follow the map.

Map Skill: *How many roads led to the South River in Salem?*

Map Key

1. School
2. Prison
3. St. Peter's Church
4. Common (Park)
5. Shipyard
6. Graveyard
7. First Meeting House
8. Courthouse

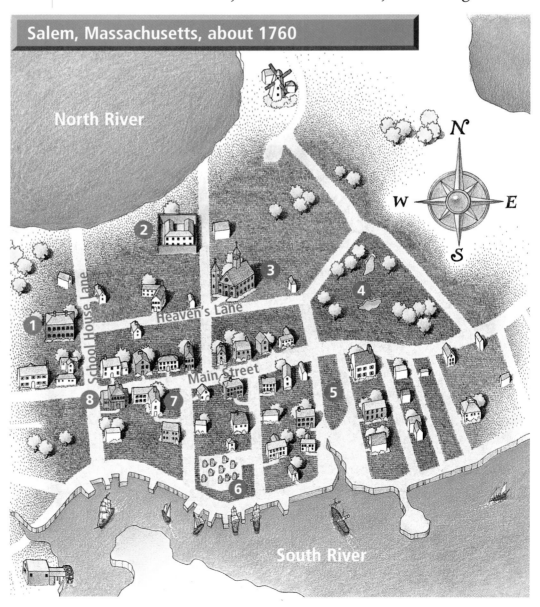

Salem, Massachusetts, about 1760

North River

Heaven's Lane

School House Lane

Main Street

South River

By the middle of the 1700s, Salem was no longer a fishing village. It was a busy place where almost 5,000 people lived.

Shipping and trading gave people more money. Some people sold fish and lumber to merchants for money. Other people made money by building ships or working for merchants or sea captains. People in Salem used their money to buy imported china teacups or thread. When you **import** something, you bring it in from another country. Salem stores sold fancy things that ships had brought from all around the world.

Fish, shipping, and trade made Salem one of the richest towns in what became the United States. Some merchants built bridges and roads that everyone in Salem could use. People in Salem used money to build schools and a library.

How do people in your community use money?

Mary Richardson was 12 years old when she made this sampler in 1783. She might have used imported thread.

People still shop in Salem today. At Derby Square they look for books.

Lesson Review:

1 **Vocabulary:** Write a paragraph using **cargo**, **merchant**, **wharf**, and **import** to describe Salem in 1760.

2 **Focus:** How was the location of Salem important?

3 **Focus:** How did the people of Salem trade and what did they get in return?

4 **Critical Thinking: Predict** If merchants had not traded fish, could Salem have become a wealthy community?

5 **Theme: Change** How could trading with people in other places change a community?

6 **Geography/Research Activity:** Look at a map of North America in 1760. Find three other communities along the seacoast besides Salem. Do research to discover whether they were also important trading places. How were they different from or similar to Salem?

Understanding Timelines

Get in Line

Where can Iroquois people, colonists from Jamestown, and colonists from Salem meet? On a timeline, of course! **Timelines** show events in history in the order in which they happened.

It's true that the Iroquois and those two groups of colonists settled in different places, at different times, and led different lives. However, if you use a timeline, you can see at a glance when each group did some things. By looking at the whole timeline at once, you can also learn how one event relates to another.

Timeline of Early American Communities

1500	1550	1600

1570
The Iroquois join in peace

1607
Jamestown is founded

1626
Salem is founded

This lead token was found in Jamestown.

This picture shows Salem townhouses.

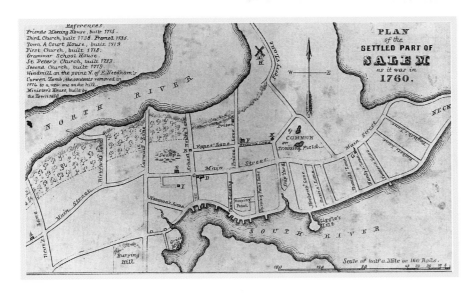

This map of Salem in 1760 shows when different buildings were built.

1 Here's How

Try reading this timeline.

- The title shows what the timeline covers. What is this timeline about?

- What are the first and last dates on this timeline? See how many years this timeline shows.

- Ten years make up a decade. How many decades does this timeline show?

- One hundred years make up a century. How many centuries does this timeline show?

2 Think It Through

Why is it important that the events on a timeline are in the correct order?

3 Use It

1. Copy the timeline on a sheet of paper.

2. Add the following events about communities in North America:

   1624 Birth of first African American in Jamestown

   1722 The Iroquois peace grows to include six nations

   1760 About 5,000 people live in Salem

3. Add other events from the chapter, or from other materials you have read. Color your timeline, or draw pictures of the people and events on your timeline.

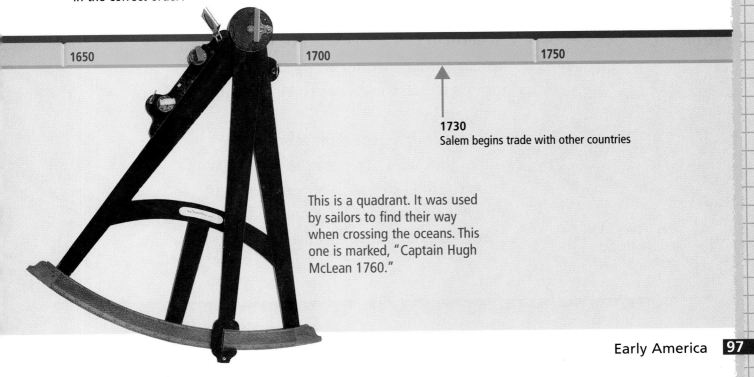

| 1650 | 1700 | 1750 |

1730
Salem begins trade with other countries

This is a quadrant. It was used by sailors to find their way when crossing the oceans. This one is marked, "Captain Hugh McLean 1760."

★ CITIZENSHIP ★

Making Decisions

What Do Schools Cost?

Have you ever wondered where the money to run your school comes from? How do people decide how much money to spend on books or supplies or teachers? This is how the people of early Salem paid for their school.

Case Study

Schools in Early Salem

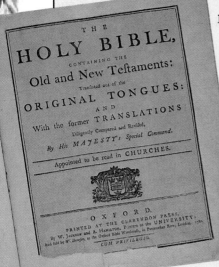

THE HOLY BIBLE, CONTAINING THE Old and New Testaments: Translated out of the ORIGINAL TONGUES: AND With the former TRANSLATIONS Diligently Compared and Revised, By His MAJESTY's Special Command. Appointed to be read in CHURCHES. OXFORD, PRINTED AT THE CLARENDON PRESS, By W. Jackson and A. Hamilton, Printers to the UNIVERSITY. And sold by Mr. Dawson, at the Oxford Bible Warehouse, in Paternoster Row, London, 1780. CUM PRIVILEGIO.

This Bible was used as a textbook in early Salem.

People in Salem in the 1600s had little money. They grew or traded for most of their food. They made or traded for their clothes and furniture, too. They didn't need money to get most of what they needed.

The people of Salem also wanted a school and a teacher. They paid the teacher with corn, wheat, peas, and beaver skins. When a teacher had too many skins or too much food, a student would sit by the window and try to sell the extras to rich people walking by.

In 1760, Salem built a brick schoolhouse. They paid the teacher with taxes. Taxes are money people pay to their government. That money is put toward community needs.

Take Action

What does your school need? It needs lots of things, like teachers, books, supplies, computers, heat, custodians, playgrounds, and so on. Everything costs money. So how do people decide what to spend money on? How do their choices affect your schooling? Try this, and see.

1 In small groups, list the things you think a school needs.

2 Decide the 10 most important. Number them in order of importance, #1 being the most important.

3 Imagine that you have a pie that represents all the money you have to spend on your school. How big a piece of pie will each of your 10 choices get? Decide and label your pie according to the size of each piece.

4 Explain your pie to the other groups. Do your pie charts all look alike? Why or why not?

Tips for Making Decisions

- List all the possible ways of doing something, and then think about which item is most important to you.
- Give reasons for what you decide.
- Think about the result of your decision, and ask yourself in advance if you will be happy with the result.

Research Activity

How have schools in your community changed? Ask adults to tell you about things they remember from their own school days. You can also look for information in books. Then write a paragraph that compares schools today with schools of long ago.

Chapter Review

Chapter Review Timeline

1400	**1500**	**1600**	**1700**	**1800**	

1607
English settlers arrive at Jamestown

1760
Salem has about 5000 residents

1570
Hiawatha brings peace to the Iroquois

1619
Africans arrive at Jamestown

Summarizing the Main Idea

1 Copy and fill in the chart below. Show how each group of people adapted to the land where they lived or settled.

How People Adapted to the Land on Which They Lived			
Iroquois	**Hopi**	**English Settlers in Jamestown**	**Settlers in Salem**
They built houses from logs and trees.			

Vocabulary

2 Choose six words. Describe early American communities.

long house (p. 74)	**fort (p. 85)**	**cargo (p. 91)**
wampum (p. 76)	**colony (p. 85)**	**merchant (p. 91)**
adapt (p. 74)	**trade (p. 87)**	**wharf (p. 93)**
pueblo (p. 78)	**slavery (p. 89)**	**import (p. 95)**

Reviewing the Facts

3 How did Hiawatha use resources from the land to bring peace to the tribes?

4 What resources from the land did the Hopi use to build their houses?

5 How did the Powhatan people help the English settlers of Jamestown?

6 What are some ways that people in Salem used the ocean?

7 What goods did Salem import?

Use the timeline on pages 96–97 for questions 8 and 9.

8 How many years did the settlers live in Jamestown before the first Africans arrived?

9 Study the timeline. Might there be one event that may have caused another event to happen? Write about what you think and why.

Critical Thinking

10 **Cause and Effect** There are few trees where the Hopi live. What is the effect on the land?

11 **Generalize** Why does the land affect people and the way people live?

12 **Compare** What was Jamestown like before Captain John Smith became the leader? Compare this with the way settlers lived in Jamestown after he became the leader.

Writing: Citizenship and Culture

13 **Citizenship** Suppose a newcomer came to live in your town. Suppose he or she did not know where to find food or where to live. Write about what you would do to help this newcomer live in your town.

14 **Culture** Take a trip back to Salem during the 1700s. Write a story about your life as a sailor. What is your ship's cargo? Where is it going? Is the sea calm, or is a bad storm headed your way?

Activities

Geography/Research Activity
Draw a map of the United States. Find out about three Native American groups. On the map, show where each lives and draw symbols to show the resources that are important to each.

Culture/Science Activity
Which is your favorite season: spring, summer, fall, or winter? Why? Find out what plants or vegetables grow during your season. Plan a festival that celebrates the season you chose.

Internet Option

Check the **Internet Social Studies Center** for ideas on how to extend your theme project beyond your classroom.

THEME PROJECT CHECK-IN

Look at your community history project and answer these questions:
• Have you included a description of the Native American people who lived in your area before new settlers came?
• Have you included a description of the special resources on the land in your community? How have the people in your community used these resources?

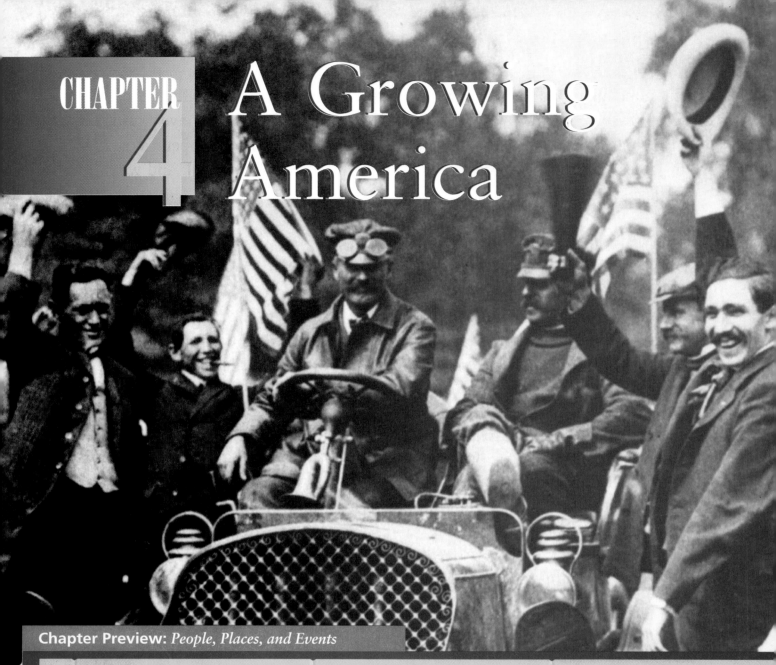

A Growing America

Chapter Preview: *People, Places, and Events*

1760	1810	1860

Below the Earth 1840s

What is this man doing far below the earth's surface? *Lesson 1, Page 104*

Working Hands

Find out what this woman is making. *Lesson 2, Page 111*

From Ship to Shore 1886

She has welcomed millions of people to the United States. *Lesson 3, Page 114*

Native Americans and Newcomers

Main Idea Settlers created new communities when they moved west.

Key Vocabulary
mine
mineral
territory

Chop! Chop! Crash! Another tree fell. Wagons lurched forward as settlers headed west. Settlers built new roads as they moved. Their roads were made of tree trunks. The logs made the ride bumpy, but it was easier to pull a wagon over bumpy logs than through mud.

Settlers moved west to find land. When they found a place they liked, they built a new community. One of those communities became Dubuque (duh BYOOK), Iowa.

Dubuque

◀ Communities changed as people began living and working differently.

1910   1960   2010

On the Move early 1900s

What do you think this little boy is carrying? *Lesson 3, Page 115*

Beep! Beep! 1904

A new type of transportation pushed horses and wagons off city streets. *Lesson 4, Page 120*

All Around the Town

You'll find a lot more than peaches on this important street in Atlanta, Georgia. *Lesson 4, Page 124*

John Casper Wild painted this picture of Dubuque in 1845. **Geography:** *Name some resources you see that Julien Dubuque and the Mesquakie may have used.*

Sharing the Land

Focus *Why did settlers build a community in Dubuque?*

Julien Dubuque was one of the new settlers in the west. He settled in an area that was the home of the Mesquakie (meh SKWAH kee) people.

Dubuque and the Mesquakie became friends. Have you ever shared something with a friend? The Mesquakie and Julien Dubuque did just that. The Mesquakie allowed Dubuque to **mine** lead, or dig it out of the earth. Lead is a **mineral** — a nonliving thing in the earth or water. Minerals are important resources. Dubuque and the Mesquakie sold the lead they mined.

Julien Dubuque died in 1810. After he died, new settlers came to work in the lead mines. Others came to farm the land around the mines. These settlers started a new community. They named their community Dubuque, after Julien Dubuque. Do you know how your community got its name?

At that time, this community in Iowa was not part of the United States. On July 4, 1838, that changed. Iowa became a **territory,** land that is an official part of the United States. The territory was not a real state yet. After Iowa became a territory Dubuque grew quickly.

A Heavy Metal

Lead is very heavy, yet very soft. Lead was used to make bullets and paint. It was also mixed with other metals. Lead and tin mixed together made pewter. Pewter was used in plates and candlesticks.

Working Underground

The miners went down about 80 feet into the ground through a long, narrow path they dug through the earth. Miners wore soft hats when they worked. They carried lanterns to light the darkness. Miners often worked on their hands and knees.

Working Tools

Miners used a pick like the one on the left to dig up small bits of lead from the earth. Miners hit a wedge, at right, with a hammer to break up big chunks of lead.

Dubuque Grows

Focus *What are some ways that Dubuque changed over the years?*

In 1838, a land office also opened in Dubuque. The land office sold land to settlers. Many people bought land because it didn't cost much then. They built farms in the countryside.

Not everyone lived on a farm. Suppose you were a man who came to Dubuque to work in the mines. You needed a place to stay. So, you moved into a hotel. There, hotel workers cooked your food and washed your clothes. Growing Dubuque had many hotels.

After dinner, you could stroll around town. By 1855, you wouldn't even have to carry your lantern! The city had put in gas lamps that glowed along Main Street. You would not be alone on your walk. By this time, Dubuque had hired men to watch the streets. They walked city streets from 10:00 at night to just after dawn.

By the 1850s, Dubuque also had a fire department. Fire was a real danger for many towns because they had no running water. A group formed in Dubuque to put out any fires that broke out in buildings or on land.

Dubuque formed its first police department in 1852. Six men were hired to watch city streets during the night. Later, police also worked during the day.

In 1857, each teacher had more than 88 students. **Math:** *Is this number greater or less than the number of students in your classroom?*

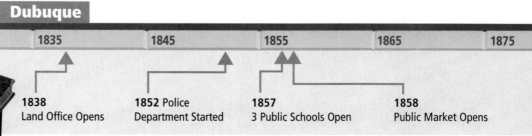

Dubuque				
1835	1845	1855	1865	1875

1838
Land Office Opens

1852 Police
Department Started

1857
3 Public Schools Open

1858
Public Market Opens

The Mesquakie Today

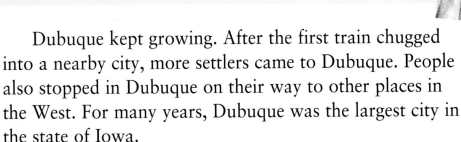

The Mesquakie were driven from their homeland in Iowa during the early 1800s. However, by the end of 1859, most Mesquakie people had returned to Iowa. There the Mesquakie started the town of Tama, Iowa.

On the right is Hallie Brown. She is one of the Mesquakie people who live in Tama. This third grader learns to speak the Mesquakie language at the Sax-Fox Settlement School.

Hallie also dances at Native American gatherings. She loves doing the Jingle Dance, a traditional Mesquakie dance. Hallie says, "My feet keep moving. This keeps the bells jingling."

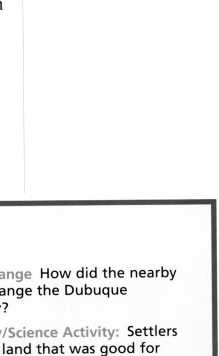

Dubuque kept growing. After the first train chugged into a nearby city, more settlers came to Dubuque. People also stopped in Dubuque on their way to other places in the West. For many years, Dubuque was the largest city in the state of Iowa.

Like any community, Dubuque changed as it grew. Three public schools opened in 1857. One year later, a public market opened. It even had a toilet that flushed! Today, more than 50,000 people live in Dubuque. How has your community changed since it began?

Lesson Review

1 **Key Vocabulary:** Use these words to write a paragraph about early Dubuque: mine, mineral, territory.

2 **Focus:** Why did settlers build a community in Dubuque?

3 **Focus:** What are some ways that Dubuque changed over the years?

4 **Critical Thinking: Interpret** Why do you think Julien Dubuque and the Mesquakie agreed to work together?

5 **Theme: Change** How did the nearby railroad change the Dubuque community?

6 **Geography/Science Activity:** Settlers looked for land that was good for growing crops. What type of land do you have in your area? Dig up some soil. Is it moist, sandy, rocky, dry?

THINK LIKE A
GEOGRAPHER

The Uses of Geography

How Did Settlers Use Rivers As Roads?

Many settlers who moved west in the early 1800s traveled on rivers for part of their trip. Roads hadn't been built to carry the settlers where they wanted to go. One of the most popular routes was along the Ohio River, which was the best way to get to Cincinnati. To make their river journeys the settlers used flatboats or keelboats. These boats had no engine, but floated along the river.

This painting, looking across the Ohio River from Kentucky to Ohio, shows the land the settlers passed on their journey.

You can trace the settlers' route on the map. Start at Pittsburgh where many settlers gathered for the trip. Many settlers left the Ohio River at Cincinnati; some others continued to the Mississippi and down to New Orleans.

Music Connection

Rivers are an important part of America's folklore. There are lots of songs about river life, like "Old Man River" and "Oh Shenandoah." Do you know any other river songs?

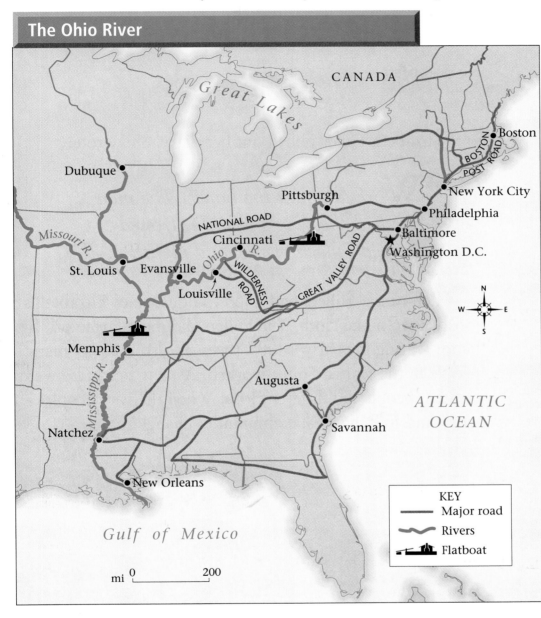

The Ohio River

Before many roads were developed, rivers and lakes were important for inland travel. The map shows roads and communities in 1820. Where are most of the cities located? How would you explain this?

Settlers loaded furniture, farm animals, tools, bags of food, and families onto flatboats for the trip downriver. At the end of the journey, the boats were taken apart and the wood used to build wagons or houses.

Research Activity

Traveling by river, instead of struggling over land without roads, was like taking a shortcut when walking or riding a bike.

1 Do you use shortcuts around your neighborhood? List when you use them.

2 Make a map of your neighborhood, showing any special routes you use.

From Farms to Factories

Main Idea Factories changed how people lived and worked.

Elizabeth Fuller pulled out her diary. She wrote:

> "**W**orked about the house. The men finished shearing sheep . . . Ironed . . . Helped milk morning and night . . . "

Each of the Fullers had a job to do. One of Elizabeth's jobs was to make cloth. The Fullers did most farmwork by hand. During the early 1800s, this was also the way many people in the United States worked. As new machines were created, people did different jobs. When the way people work and live changes, communities change too.

The town of Lowell is shown below. Workers visited churches and lived in boarding houses and hotels built near the mills.

Hotels   Boarding Houses   Churches

A New Place of Business

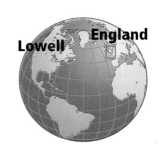

Focus *Where did the owners build their mill and why?*
One machine that changed the way people worked was the power loom. The power loom changed the way cloth was made. Before, girls like Elizabeth Fuller made cloth at home. They used hand looms. The new power looms could weave cloth much faster than hand looms.

People used power looms in factories. A **factory** is a building where people use machines to make things. A factory where people make cloth is called a **mill**. During the 1800s, mills used water power to run the looms. With water power, moving water in a river or a waterfall makes a big wheel turn. Then the turning wheel makes the machine parts move.

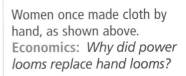

Women once made cloth by hand, as shown above.
Economics: *Why did power looms replace hand looms?*

A group of men decided to build a mill where they found strong water power. They built the mill at a place where the Concord and Merrimack rivers joined together. The river water flowed swiftly there — and that made strong water power. A town grew around the mill. This town was named Lowell, Massachusetts.

Lowell Mills

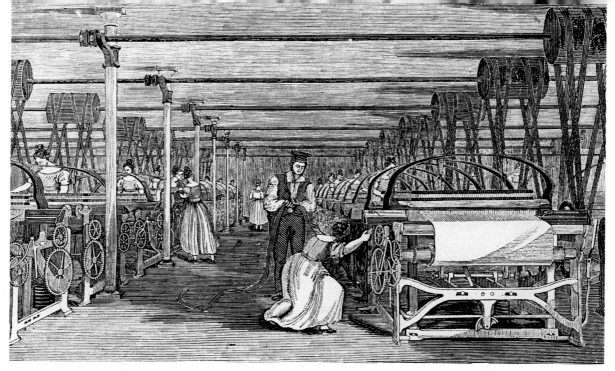

All the looms in the picture above were running at the same time. Just think of the noise!

A Different Way of Working

Focus *How did factories change the way people lived and worked?*

In the early 1800s, most people lived in **rural** areas — in the country, far from cities. They grew food on land near their homes. They made many of the things they needed.

When factories were built in a community, the community changed. Many communities became cities, or **urban** areas, as people moved to cities to work in the factories. Lowell, Massachusetts, was a factory community. It was built to house people who worked in the mill. At first, many of these mill workers were young women.

At one time, most young women worked only at their parents' farms, like Elizabeth Fuller. They cleaned, cooked, and did the laundry. They milked the cows. Often, the women helped other family members and neighbors.

The way young women worked changed. Many went to the city to find jobs in the mills. These Lowell "mill girls" lived in boarding houses with other girls and women. Boarding houses were like hotels.

Sometimes mill girls had to work more than one power loom like this one at a time.

The looms in the mills were very noisy. Dust filled the air. It would have made you cough and sneeze. All day, women worked and worked. By day's end, their hands and eyes were tired from all their hard work at the looms.

On the left are bobbins. They hold the thread or yarn while cloth is being woven or spun.

Life in the city could be fun and exciting too. By working in the mills, women earned their own money. They could talk about the latest books with their friends. By living in the city, they could go to concerts and hear speeches during their free time.

After a while, factory life changed. The people who ran the factories tried to make the women do more and more work. Many women quit their jobs. As women left the mills, other people stepped in to take their place. Many of these people had left their home countries in Europe to come to America. They found work in the factories.

Are there factories in your own community? What kinds of things are made there?

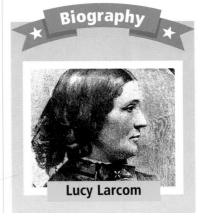
Lesson Review

1 **Key Vocabulary:** Write a paragraph about how communities like Lowell changed. Use **factory, mill, rural, urban.**

2 **Focus:** Where did the owners build their mill and why?

3 **Focus:** How did factories change the way people lived and worked?

4 **Critical Thinking: Compare** Compare a girl's life on a farm to her life as a mill worker in the early 1800s.

5 **Geography:** How did people who worked on farms use the land around them?

6 **Citizenship/Writing Activity:** Some of the "mill girls" wrote about their lives in *The Lowell Offering*, a magazine. Write a paragraph that explains why you think working is important to people in a community.

A Wave of Immigrants

Main Idea Immigrants often started new communities when they moved to the United States.

Key Vocabulary

immigrant
ethnic group

During the late 1800s and the early 1900s, the Statue of Liberty welcomed more than a million people to the shores of the United States.

The green fields of Ireland lay far across the sea. Elizabeth Phillips had left Ireland to start a new life. Now, at last, her ship was pulling into New York. Elizabeth stood shoulder to shoulder with other passengers on deck. Their eyes searched for the Statue of Liberty. Elizabeth remembered her first sight of the famous statue:

> **"A**ll *the people were rushing to the side of the boat . . . 'There she is, there she is,' like it was somebody who was greeting them.*"

Like Elizabeth, millions of people moved to the United States during the late 1800s and early 1900s. They were immigrants. An **immigrant** is a person who comes into a new country after leaving his or her home country.

Ships from around the world carried people to the United States. Many ships stopped in New York. After 1886, people who arrived there saw the Statue of Liberty. Her torch was a symbol of a new life in a new country.

One immigrant talks about his trip to the United States: "Time between meals was spent on the deck if the weather was good. Some immigrant would always come out with . . . some musical instrument and the dance would follow . . . "

From Shore to Shore

Focus *Why did so many people come to the United States in the late 1800s and early 1900s?*

Why do people move? People had many reasons for moving to the United States during the late 1800s and early 1900s. Some people had been farmers who couldn't grow enough food to feed their families. They came to the United States to get better farmland. Some wanted to be free to practice their own religion. Others wanted a better education for themselves and their children.

In the late 1800s and early 1900s, immigrants sailed to the United States on ships. These ships were packed with people. The trip often lasted many weeks. Some immigrants became sick on the way. Many had to leave family members behind. In spite of all this, immigrants kept coming. They wanted a new and better life.

Sometimes families got separated during the trip. Family members had to find one another after they arrived.

Immigrant children quickly learned to play games like baseball. **Culture:** *How might learning this new game have helped the children in their new country?*

New York City

Ask Yourself

Immigrants could not take many objects with them to their new home.

If you had to travel to a new country with only your clothes and two or three special objects, what would you take with you? Why?

? ? ? ? ? ? ? ? ? ? ? ? ? ?

New Ways of Living

Focus *How did early immigrants get used to life in the United States?*

After immigrants arrived in the United States, they made many changes in their way of life. Some learned to speak English. Immigrant children often learned English quickly and easily in school. Some immigrants learned new jobs. They had to make a living for themselves and their families. Many of them had only worked on farms before.

Immigrants often settled in cities. New York City, for example, became home to people from all over the world. Look at some neighborhoods in New York on the map on the next page.

For many immigrants, New York was very different from the communities they had left. People who had once lived in farmhouses lived in crowded apartment buildings. In their old communities, they might have heard a rooster crow every morning. Now they heard shouts, rumbling wheels, and other sounds of the busy city streets.

In New York and other cities, immigrants started new neighborhoods. Many wanted to keep their own customs and speak their own languages. They wanted to live near

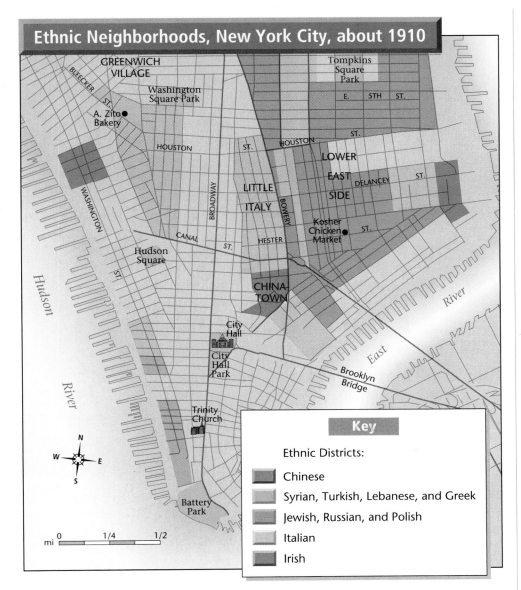

Ethnic Neighborhoods, New York City, about 1910

Key

Ethnic Districts:
- Chinese
- Syrian, Turkish, Lebanese, and Greek
- Jewish, Russian, and Polish
- Italian
- Irish

Map Skill: *In which direction would you travel to get from Trinity Church to Chinatown?*

At the top is an Italian store. The middle window is a store in a Jewish neighborhood. Look in the third window and see things people could find in China.

people in their own ethnic group. An **ethnic group** is made up of people who share the same culture.

Immigrant neighborhoods were a little like the country people had left. The stores sold the same kinds of foods and items that immigrants had bought in their home country. Signs were written in the language of the home country. When immigrants walked into shops like those in the pictures on this page, they felt a little less homesick.

Many immigrants only spoke English when they went to school or work. At the end of the day, they returned to their neighborhoods. There, they used the language and customs of their home country.

JEWISH ▪ SCOTCH ▪ ROUMANIAN ▪ ENGLISH ▪ AUSTRIAN ▪ SLAVIC ▪ ITALIAN ▪ POLISH ▪ RUSSIAN ▪ TURK ▪

This picture was taken in 1926. These schoolgirls may belong to different ethnic groups, but they are all Americans. **Citizenship:** *How did going to school help these students get used to their new life?*

These children live in the state of California. They are celebrating their Mexican heritage with a traditional dance.

Communities for Today and Tomorrow

Focus *How are today's immigrants similar to those who moved to the United States between 1890 and 1920?*

People still move to the United States from countries around the world. Between 1890 and 1920, most people who moved to the United States came from Europe. Since 1970, many people have come from Africa, Asia, Latin America, and from the islands in the Caribbean Sea.

Today, as in the past, many people come to find better jobs. Others want religious freedom. Some come to join family members who already live in the United States.

It can take time to get used to living in a different country. Ky Quan Ly (ky kwahn ly) left his home country of Vietnam and moved to the state of Massachusetts. He is in the third grade. Ky Quan remembers what it was like when he first moved to the United States:

"First it was weird, but now it's fun. I like it here because the students speak English and I can learn from them. I am always learning from the teacher."

Ky Quan Ly loves playing ball during recess.

Stephanie Desmornes (deh mohr NAY) is also from another country. She moved from Haiti two years ago. She is now a sixth grader in Florida. Stephanie has big plans for her future in the United States:

"I want to be a teacher and a doctor. A teacher so I can help people learn. A doctor so I can keep people healthy."

Stephanie Desmornes' favorite subjects are language arts and science.

Some immigrants still travel by boat to reach the United States. Most take planes. They settle all over the country. Like the immigrants of an earlier time, those of today hope to find a community where they will feel at home. Some new settlers move to neighborhoods started by immigrants many years ago. Do you know people from other countries who have moved to your community?

Lesson Review

1 **Key Vocabulary:** Describe New York City, using **immigrant** and **ethnic group**.

2 **Focus:** Why did so many people come to the United States in the late 1800s and early 1900s?

3 **Focus:** How did early immigrants get used to life in the United States?

4 **Focus:** How are today's immigrants similar to those who moved to the United States between 1890 and 1920?

5 **Critical Thinking: Generalize** If you moved to another country, what problems might you face?

6 **Theme: Change** How did newcomers bring change to communities in the United States?

7 **Geography/Research Activity:** Do any of your family members live in different parts of the United States? Trace a United States map. Mark the states in which they live.

The Age of the Automobile

Main Idea Communities change as transportation changes.

Below is a city street in Atlanta in the early 1900s. **Technology:** *What differences might you see if you visited the same Atlanta street today?*

In June of 1904, in Atlanta, Georgia, an automobile smashed into a horse-drawn carriage. Luckily, no one was badly hurt. The accident scared Mr. A. B. Steele, who was in the carriage. He said, "I am in favor of a law against this automobile business. Why, I consider it nothing short of a miracle that I escaped with my life."

Cars were a new technology in 1904. **Technology** (tehk NAHL uh jee) is the use of science to make something. Technology helps people, but it can create problems, too. Communities must solve such problems.

Mr. Steele just wanted cars to go away. But cars were there to stay. Atlanta grew because of them.

Cars Change a Community

Ding, ding goes the bell! Streetcars like the one in this picture rode on tracks down the middle of Atlanta's streets.

Focus *What was Atlanta like when the first cars arrived?*

Mr. Steele didn't get his wish, but his accident did make some things change. Right after the accident, Atlanta passed a new law about cars. The new law said that everyone driving a car had to have a license. A **license** is written permission to do something. To get a driver's license, you have to prove that you know how to drive.

Cars changed how people moved from place to place. Cars also changed the kind of work many people did. Fewer people worked making carriages. Look at the chart below, on the right. It shows how the number of blacksmiths, who made horseshoes, went down as the number of cars grew.

Atlanta Changes

When the first cars arrived, most streets in Atlanta were made of dirt. Few were paved. If you lived on an unpaved street, you squished through mud in winter. In summer, dust got in your eyes and made your clothes dirty.

Atlanta was a small city then. Nearly all its schools, churches, and stores were near the center of town. People could walk to shops and friends' houses. If they wanted to go farther, they could ride on streetcars. Streetcars ran on rails down the middle of the street. Streetcars are like buses: they can carry lots of people.

Cars could take people even farther than streetcars. So, many car owners moved to the suburbs around Atlanta. A **suburb** is a community just outside a city. People with cars could go wherever the road led. The only problem was finding a place to park!

The chart below shows the number of blacksmith shops found in Atlanta in 1899 and in 1935. **Chart Skill:** *How much did this number change by 1935?*

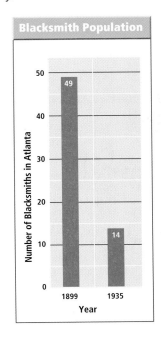

Blacksmith Population

Number of Blacksmiths in Atlanta

- 1899: 49
- 1935: 14

Year

Business owners built large office buildings in the city. There were fewer small shops and homes. In 1906, a 17-story office building went up. It even had elevators.

Cars really changed Atlanta. They made it easier for people to work in town and live in the suburbs. More and more people found jobs selling and fixing cars. The timeline below shows some of the other ways that cars changed Atlanta. Cars brought the same kinds of changes to communities all across the United States.

Moving Even Faster

Focus *How did Atlanta deal with the problems that cars created?*

Atlanta had narrow streets. As car traffic increased, the streets couldn't hold all the cars. The city built wider roads, but traffic just got worse.

City planners designed expressways in the 1950s. An **expressway** is a wide highway built to help traffic move quickly. The expressways ran north to south through Atlanta. They solved many traffic problems.

Expressways did not help everyone. The expressways cut through neighborhoods. People on one side of an

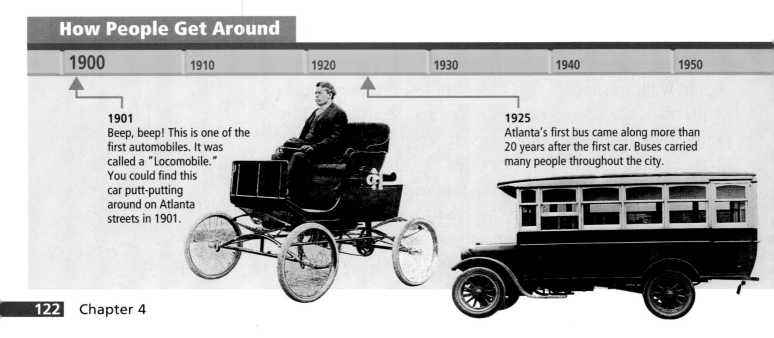

How People Get Around

| 1900 | 1910 | 1920 | 1930 | 1940 | 1950 |

1901
Beep, beep! This is one of the first automobiles. It was called a "Locomobile." You could find this car putt-putting around on Atlanta streets in 1901.

1925
Atlanta's first bus came along more than 20 years after the first car. Buses carried many people throughout the city.

expressway found it hard to visit friends and family on the other side. Expressways cut the suburbs off from the city.

The expressways made transportation easier, though. Good transportation brought new businesses to Atlanta. Those businesses brought jobs.

The shaded area in the large photograph shows the neighborhoods that were knocked down in 1954. They made way for the expressway in the smaller photograph.

| 1960 | 1970 | 1980 | 1990 | 2000 |

Present Day
Today, busy expressways and highways cut through Atlanta. More and more people drive cars. These people need roads that can get them to the places they want to go.

Peachtree Street has always been an important part of Atlanta. It is Atlanta's main street. Today, it is still a busy place. People go to Peachtree Street to shop, eat, or just to have fun!

Rapid Transit

Today, Atlanta has a modern system of **rapid transit**. This system is made up of high-speed trains, buses, and subways. Subways are trains that travel underground.

Atlanta also has a busy airport. The map on the next page shows the different airplane routes. Planes zoom into and out of Atlanta on these routes every day.

As the map shows, Atlanta is easy to reach from other cities. People from across the United States travel to Atlanta for meetings. Atlanta's transportation system is one reason the city was chosen to host the 1996 Summer Olympic

This subway takes travelers into Atlanta's busy airport.

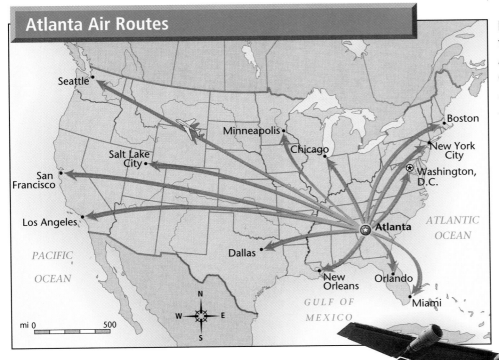

Atlanta Air Routes

Look at this map to see some of the airline routes that connect Atlanta to other major American cities. **Map Skill:** *Trace the route between Atlanta and San Francisco.*

games. Good transportation helped visitors travel around Atlanta during the games.

Transportation keeps changing. As more people use cars, people build new roads. New roads bring traffic, houses, businesses, and people. These things change communities.

What are some ways that transportation has changed the community where you live?

Lesson Review

1. **Key Vocabulary:** Write about your community's transportation, using these words: **technology, license, suburb, expressway, rapid transit.**

2. **Focus:** What was Atlanta like when the first cars arrived?

3. **Focus:** How did Atlanta deal with the problems that cars created?

4. **Critical Thinking: Cause and Effect** How did the automobile affect where people decided to live?

5. **Geography:** How did cars change the land around Atlanta?

6. **Citizenship/Writing Activity:** You must have a license to drive. Write a paragraph about why this is a good idea.

Biography

pioneer –
a person who does something first, leading the way for others

AMELIA EARHART

Pioneer of the Sky

by John Parlin
illustrated by Wayne Alfano

Airplanes changed the lives of many people, just as automobiles did. This story describes the effect that airplanes had on one person, Amelia Earhart. She wanted to be the first woman to fly across the Atlantic Ocean.

The writer used many facts to tell this true story. Did the writer actually hear everything that Amelia Earhart said? No, he didn't. That part of the story is not a fact, but is a nonfact. The writer had to make careful guesses to help tell the story in an interesting way.

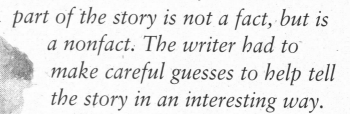

One day Amelia said to her husband, "I'd like to fly the Atlantic Ocean alone."

George knew the trip would be dangerous. But he had promised to help Amelia with her flying. "If you want to do it," he said, "I'll help you all I can."

Amelia bought a new Vega. When everything was ready she flew to Newfoundland. Just after 7 P.M. on May 20, 1932, she took off for Europe — alone.

While Amelia was over the Atlantic, Americans held their breath. Would she make it? Everywhere people prayed that she would.

Amelia did not have an easy flight. Ice formed on her plane's wings. She had to come down close to the sea where the air was warmer. When the ice melted she climbed again.

Suddenly she saw flames coming from the exhaust pipe. It could mean trouble. The plane might catch on fire.

Vega -
a type of airplane

Newfoundland
land off the eastern coast of Canada

exhaust pipe
a pipe that lets out gases

Then a gasoline tank started leaking. It would be terrible if the gasoline caught fire from the exhaust flames.

"I'd rather drown than burn up," Amelia said to herself. So she brought the plane down close to the waves again.

The flames did not seem to get any bigger. So Amelia felt safer. Her plane roared on and on through the night.

The sky slowly grew light. Amelia was hungry. She drank some hot chicken soup from a thermos bottle and ate two chocolate bars. Then she made a hole in a can of tomato juice and drank it.

Amelia had hoped to fly all the way to Paris. But she decided not to risk it. The flaming exhaust and the leaking tank made her change her plans.

She was certainly glad when she saw land ahead. She knew it was Ireland. At last she had flown the Atlantic alone. Solo!

Amelia brought her plane down in a field. It had taken her just 15 hours and 18 minutes to fly across the Atlantic. It was a new record.

Soon after she landed, Amelia went to London. A newspaper said, "Not America only, not women only, but the whole world is proud of her."

Meet the Author

John Parlin wrote more than 25 books, most of them biographies of famous Americans. Before writing this book about Amelia Earhart, he talked to many people who had actually known her. John Parlin's real name was Charles Parlin Graves. He died in 1972.

Additional Books to Read

Eureka! It's an Automobile!
by Jeanne Bendick
How automobiles were invented.

Will and Orv
by Walter A. Schulz
The day the Wright brothers flew.

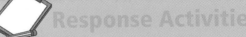

Response Activities

1. **Compare** Airplanes made traveling long distances easier. How did cars do the same for people in Atlanta, Georgia?

2. **Narrative: Be a Reporter** Write down some questions you would ask Amelia Earhart. Then write a newspaper article, describing her exciting trip across the ocean.

3. **Geography: Draw a Map** What if you could fly across the United States? Trace a map of the United States. Plan your trip. What stops will you make? In what state would you end your trip? Why?

Using a Road Map to Find Distance

Hit the Road

Your family is visiting Atlanta, Georgia. At Hartsfield International Airport, you pick up a rental car. Now you must drive to your hotel in downtown Atlanta. Which way do you go? How far away is the hotel? A road map is the perfect tool to help you.

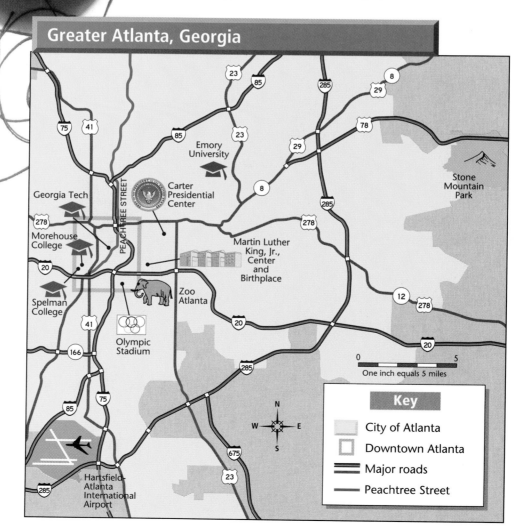

Greater Atlanta, Georgia

One inch equals 5 miles

Key

- City of Atlanta
- Downtown Atlanta
- Major roads
- Peachtree Street

① Here's How

- Study the map. Different symbols stand for different places of interest. What symbol shows the location of Spelman College? Locate other places of interest with that symbol.

- The map key has symbols for some roads. Find symbols for major roads in the key and on the map. Now find the symbol for Peachtree Street. Locate it on the map.

- How far is it from the airport to the Olympic Stadium? First, locate the airport and stadium on the map. Interstate 85 runs between them. Place one end of a piece of string at the airport. Lay the string along Interstate 85 to the stadium. Mark this point on the string.

- With a ruler, measure the distance between the marks on the string. Is it about two inches? Look at the scale of distance in the map key. Each inch stands for five miles. Multiply two inches by five miles. The distance from airport to stadium is about 10 miles.

② Think It Through

If a map has no scale for distance, can you measure distances between places? Why would a traveler want to know the distance between places?

③ Use It

During your trip to Atlanta, you will read the road map. Find a route and measure the distances between these places:

1. The airport and Spelman College

2. The airport and Stone Mountain Park

3. Spelman College to Emory University

4. Stone Mountain Park to Emory University

5. Zoo Atlanta to Georgia Tech

CHAPTER 4

Chapter Review

Chapter Review Timeline

1800 — 1900 — 2000

1810 Julien Dubuque dies

1822 First mill built in Lowell, Massachusetts

1886 Statue of Liberty installed in New York Harbor

1954 Expressway is built through downtown Atlanta

Summarizing the Main Idea

1 Copy and fill in the chart below. List ways that Dubuque, Lowell, and New York City changed during the 1800s.

Changes During the 1800s

Dubuque	Lowell	New York
	Women moved from farms to work in factories.	

Vocabulary

2 Create a crossword puzzle. Use ten words below as answers.

mine (p. 104)
mineral (p. 104)
territory (p. 104)
factory (p. 111)
mill (p. 111)
rural (p. 112)
urban (p. 112)
immigrant (p. 114)
ethnic group (p. 117)
technology (p. 120)
license (p. 121)
suburb (p. 121)
expressway (p. 122)
rapid transit (p. 124)

Reviewing the Facts

3 What made Dubuque grow?

4 How and why did rural communities change during the 1800s?

5 How did immigrants make their new homes like their home countries?

6 What was life in Atlanta like before cars arrived? How did cars change Atlanta in the years to come?

Skill Review: Calculating Distance on a Road Map

Use the map on page 130 to answer questions 7 and 8.

7 What road would you use to travel from Spelman College to the zoo?

8 How far is it from Georgia Tech to Stone Mountain?

Geography Skills

9 Look at the map on page 117. Suppose you were standing on the eastern shore of the Hudson River. What if you wanted to get to the Lower East Side? What route would you take to get there?

10 What immigrant neighborhoods are located near Chinatown? What effects do you think these two neighborhoods have on each other? Why do you think that?

Writing: Citizenship and Economics

11 Citizenship Suppose a child from another country became a new student at your school. Write a letter to the child that explains important classroom rules and laws in your community.

12 Economics Suppose you were an explorer, and you just settled in a small, rural town. One day, an oil well gushed on your land. Describe the ways that the small town might change or grow because of your discovery.

Activities

Geography/Science Activity
The mineral, lead, was an important resource to Dubuque settlers. Find out about other important minerals that we use. How are they used? Where can you find some of these minerals?

Culture/Language Arts Activity
Interview someone who has visited or is from another country. Find out how life in his or her home country is different from life in the United States. How are they alike?

Internet Option

Check the **Internet Social Studies Center** for ideas on how to extend your theme project beyond your classroom.

THEME PROJECT CHECK-IN

Have you used what you have learned about change in your project?
- What Native American people lived in your community? Do any still live there?
- What are some of the home countries of the people who live in your community?
- How did people travel in your community before cars arrived? What other types of transportation do people in your community use?

Communities and Their Geography

"What will you find at the edge of the world?
A footprint,
a feather,
desert sand swirled?"

Eve Merriam

· T H E M E ·

Environment

The things that I like about the environment of my community are playing in leaves, going to the park, and going to the circus.

Jessica Atkins, Wichita, Kansas

Your environment is where you live, work, play, and learn. Think about the environment in your community. Is it flat or hilly? Do you wear a coat in winter? Do you wear shorts all year long? A community's environment affects the work people do, the clothes they wear, the food they eat, and the houses they build. This unit will help you think about some of the ways the environment affects people in your community and in other places too.

Theme Project

Make a Model

Use paper, clay, sticks, stones, and other materials to make a model of the land around your community. While you are building your model:

- Locate rivers, lakes, or other bodies of water in or near your community.
- Label hills, mountains, and valleys.
- Estimate the size of forests, farms, and meadows.
- Include major roads and highways.

◄ These farmlands are one kind of environment.

3

WHEN & WHERE
ATLAS

Find the United States, China, and Mexico on this world map. Locate Portland, Oregon, and Greenville, Mississippi, in the United States. Then locate Xiashen in China and Mexico City in Mexico. These communities are very different from each other. Yet, like all communities, they are similar in one important way. The environment has influenced how each community has used its natural resources to grow and change.

In this unit, you will study the impact of the environment on four communities.

Unit 3 Chapters

Chapter 5   This Land of Ours
Chapter 6   World
            Environments

CANADA

NORTH AMERICA

Portland

Washington, D.C.

Los Angeles   UNITED STATES

Greenville

MEXICO

Mexico City

PACIFIC OCEAN

SOUTH AMERICA

Lima

N
W   E
S

Unit Timeline

1300	1440	1580

Many Resources

This woman is picking raspberries. Find out where they grow. *Chapter 5, Lesson 1*

Where Houses Come From

How did trees from Portland, Oregon, turn into this house? *Chapter 5, Lesson 1*

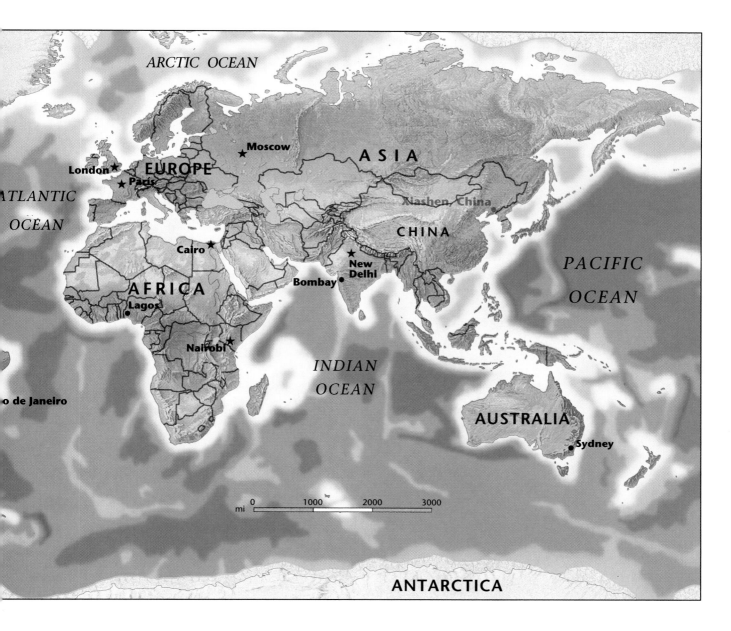

ARCTIC OCEAN

Moscow ★

ASIA

London ★
EUROPE

★ Paris

ATLANTIC
OCEAN

Xiashen, China

CHINA

Cairo ★

New
Delhi ★

AFRICA

Bombay ●

PACIFIC
OCEAN

Lagos ●

Nairobi ★

INDIAN
OCEAN

o de Janeiro

AUSTRALIA

● Sydney

```
mi  0    1000   2000   3000
```

ANTARCTICA

| 1720 | 1860 | 2000 |

The Mighty Mississippi

Come take a ride on the longest river in the United States! *Chapter 5, Lesson 2*

Using the Land

This crop feeds many people. What is it? Where does it grow? *Chapter 6, Lesson 1*

City Living

This park is in the middle of the largest city in the world. *Chapter 6, Lesson 2*

CHAPTER 5
This Land of Ours

Chapter Preview: *People, Places, and Events*

| 1760 | 1810 | 1860 |

A City's Resources

Portland, Oregon, is a big and busy city. *Lesson 1, Page 140*

Tall, Dark, and Green

Take a walk through one of Portland's rich pine forests. *Lesson 1, Page 141*

Saving the Trees

Because of this man, 13 national forests protect trees. *Lesson 1, Page 141*

A City and Its Forest

LESSON 1

Main Idea People in Portland, Oregon, use the natural resources of the area around them.

Suppose you were in an airplane flying toward Portland, Oregon. What would you see? You might see trees covering the land like a green blanket. You might also see orchards and farm fields. The Columbia and Willamette rivers wind through the land like silver threads.

Forests, farms, and rivers are all part of the environment around Portland. The **environment** is the natural world around us. Every community is located in an environment. That environment affects the way people in the community live.

Key Vocabulary

environment
natural resource
port
product

More than 600 airplanes fly in and out of Portland International Airport each day. **Economics:** *What resources bring people to Portland?*

◀ The forests around Portland are full of tall, straight trees like these.

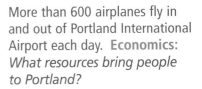

1910	1960	2010

A City on a River

Sailboat, tugboat, freighter and steamboat — which ships stop at Greenville? *Lesson 2, Page 151*

A Flood in Mississippi

Out for a boat ride — down a city street? *Lesson 2, Page 153*

When Disasters Happen

Kids near Des Moines, Iowa, help pack sandbags on levees. *Lesson 2, Page 154*

Greetings from

Portland

- Portland is located on the Willamette River.
- 495,000 people live in the city.
- Portland is a city of bridges. It has seventeen!
- Portland is the only U.S. city with an extinct volcano (Mount Tabor) within its city limits.

Farm stands sell vegetables grown around Portland.

Resources of Portland

Focus *What natural resources do the people of Portland use?*

The rich soil, rivers, and forests around Portland are all natural resources. A **natural resource** is anything found in the environment that people use. In Unit 2, you saw how the Hopi people used the natural resources of the desert to build their communities. Lead was an important natural resource for the people of Dubuque.

Some land near Portland is good for farming. Wheat, green peas, potatoes, and corn all grow in its rich soil. Mild temperatures and lots of rain help them grow. These vegetables end up on tables in Portland and other places.

Portland is on the Willamette River. The river is an important resource. People everywhere use water for drinking and washing. If you've taken a boat ride, you know that

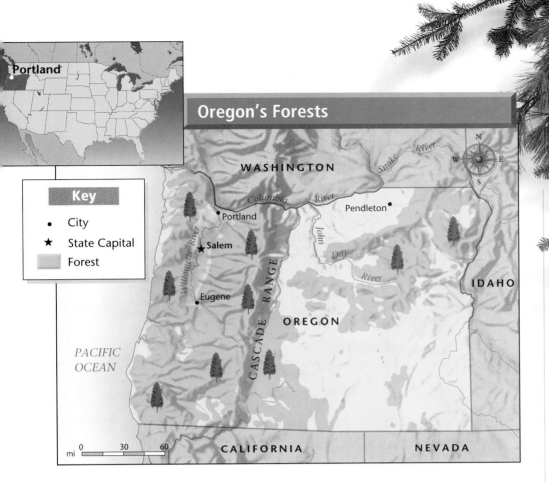

Oregon's Forests

Key

- • City
- ★ State Capital
- ▨ Forest

WASHINGTON

Snake River

Columbia River

Portland

Pendleton

John Day River

Willamette River

Salem

CASCADE RANGE

Eugene

OREGON

IDAHO

PACIFIC OCEAN

mi 0 30 60

CALIFORNIA   NEVADA

The little map shows where Portland is in the United States. The big map shows forests in the state of Oregon. **Map Skill:** *Are there more forests in the eastern or western part of Oregon?*

people also use water for transportation. Portland has an important port. A **port** is a place on a river, lake, or ocean where boats can dock. People load goods onto boats to be sent to other places.

Find Portland on the map above. The environment around Portland is ideal for growing trees. The weather is wet and not too hot or too cold. The big map shows that forest land covers almost half of Oregon, the state where the city of Portland is located. In the forests near Portland, most trees are Douglas firs. Douglas firs are evergreen trees. They have needles instead of leaves. These trees can grow to be towering giants. The largest Douglas fir is 329 feet tall. That's taller than a 25-story building!

Some trees in these forests are cut down and then sawed into boards, called lumber. Lots of lumber comes from the forests around Portland.

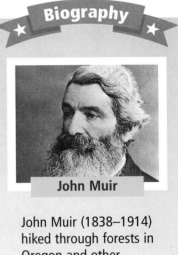

How a Tree Becomes a House

Houses can be made from many natural resources: earth, rocks, and trees. What kind of house do you live in? The drawings below show how a tree becomes part of a wooden house.

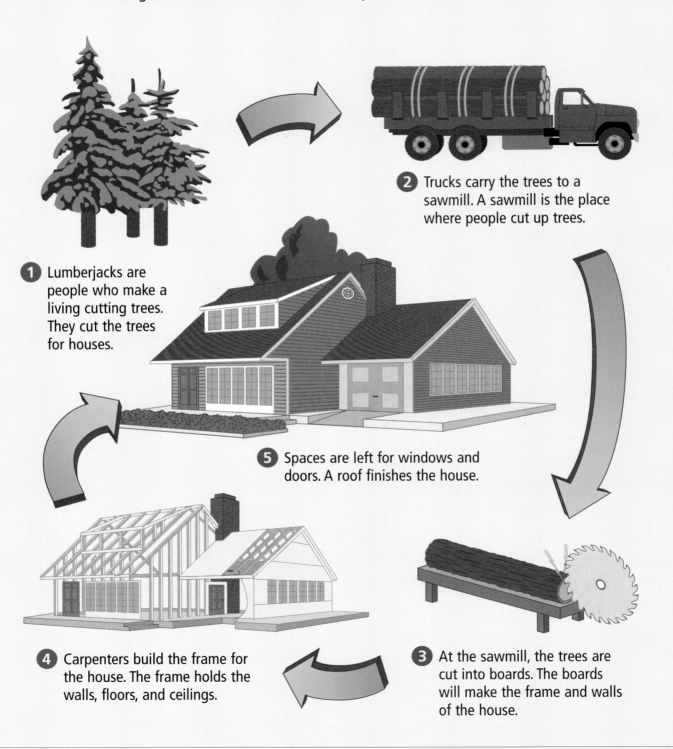

2 Trucks carry the trees to a sawmill. A sawmill is the place where people cut up trees.

1 Lumberjacks are people who make a living cutting trees. They cut the trees for houses.

5 Spaces are left for windows and doors. A roof finishes the house.

4 Carpenters build the frame for the house. The frame holds the walls, floors, and ceilings.

3 At the sawmill, the trees are cut into boards. The boards will make the frame and walls of the house.

A Center for Lumber

Focus *What are some ways people use trees?*

Something that people make is called a **product**. Many products come from trees. The paper in this book was made from wood chips. Pencils also have wood in them. Do you like juicy hamburgers cooked over charcoal? Well, charcoal comes from wood, too.

Boards are a very important forest product. Boards from Douglas firs are especially strong and lightweight. These boards are used to frame many buildings. The frame is the part that holds the building up. Read more about how a tree becomes a house on the opposite page.

Many people in Portland have jobs connected to the nearby forests. Forest rangers help decide which trees will be cut. Lumberjacks cut down the trees. Truckers move logs out of the forests. Carpenters build furniture and parts of houses from wood.

Wood products are sent from Portland to all parts of the country. Have you visited a store that sells wood cabinets or doors? These products may well have come from forests near Portland. What products are made from natural resources in your community's environment?

Curious Facts

People in the United States use lots of wood. Every year, each person uses about as much wood as you get from a 100-foot tree. Cardboard, paper grocery bags, and wooden baseball bats are made from wood.

Lesson Review

1. **Key Vocabulary:** Use these words in sentences: **environment**, **natural resource**, **port**, and **product**.

2. **Focus:** What natural resources do the people of Portland use?

3. **Focus:** What are some ways people use trees?

4. **Critical Thinking: Predict** When trees are cut, new trees are planted to take their place. What would happen if new trees weren't planted?

5. **Citizenship:** Is it important to protect natural resources such as forests and rivers? Why or why not?

6. **Geography/Arts Activity:** Portland, Oregon, is named for Portland, Maine. Find a map that shows both cities. Draw a map with both cities on it. What do they have in common? How are they different?

ANNO'S FIND-IT GAME

by Mitsumasa Anno

Like Kriss and Kross, mapmakers also put lines and numbers on maps. These help people find their way from one place to another. Every place on the earth has its own special address.

Our friends, Kriss and Kross, took one square of paper.

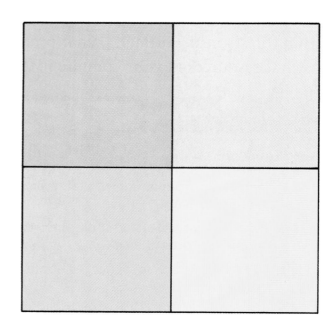

They divided it into four and painted each section a different color.

Then they took each colored square, divided it into four again, and added the spade, club, heart, and diamond symbols.

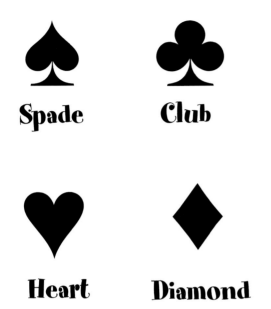

Spade   Club

Heart   Diamond

Finally they divided each of these squares into four again and numbered them from 1 to 4.

Now then —

Where is the blue diamond 3?

Where is the yellow club 2?

Where is the green heart 4?

And how about the pink spade 1?

Look at the houses on the next pages.

See if you can make up addresses for these houses, using the same colors, symbols, and numbers that you used on the other pages.

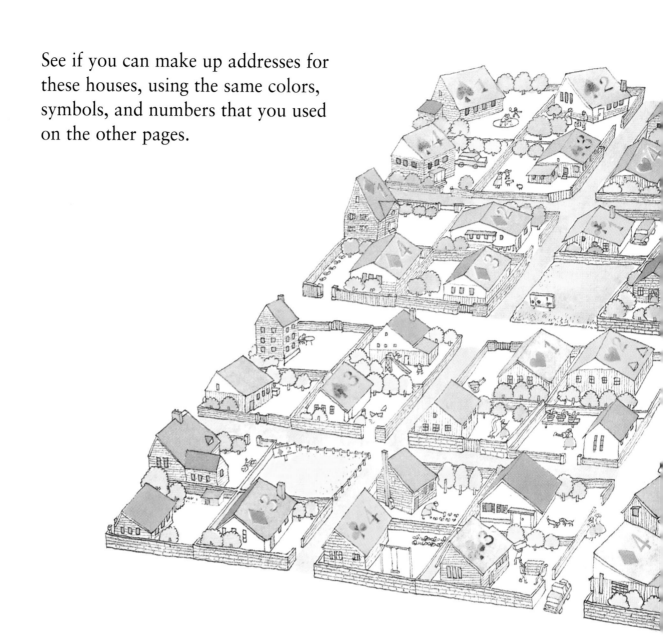

Response Activities

1. Critical Thinking: Compare
How is the map of houses on this page like the map of Oregon on page 141? How is it different? What could you use each map to do?

2. Descriptive: Write a Travel Guide
Write directions for someone coming to visit the neighborhood whose map is on this page. Make sure you use the addresses for buildings.

3. Geography: Play a Guessing Game
Choose a square on the map. Have a friend try to guess which square you chose. Give clues that will help your friend figure out the address.

Places and Regions

What's Life Like in a Different Place?

People who live in different regions use the resources around them. The forests near Portland, Oregon, provide wood. Other environments do not have forests, but they provide other resources.

Many Yup'ik people in Alaska live along the lower Yukon River. Their environment is very different from the one around Portland. The climate is colder. There are fewer trees. However, there are many kinds of fish, game, and wild plants. The Yup'ik trade and sell some of the fish and game they catch for other goods and money.

People get fish, such as salmon, from the river. These pieces of salmon will be dried and smoked. That will keep them from spoiling. How else do people preserve food?

Health Connection

The Yup'ik eat a lot of fish. Find out why fish is good for you to eat. A nutrient (NOO-tree-uhnt) is something your body gets from food. What are some nutrients that are found in fish? Where does fish belong in the Food Guide Pyramid?

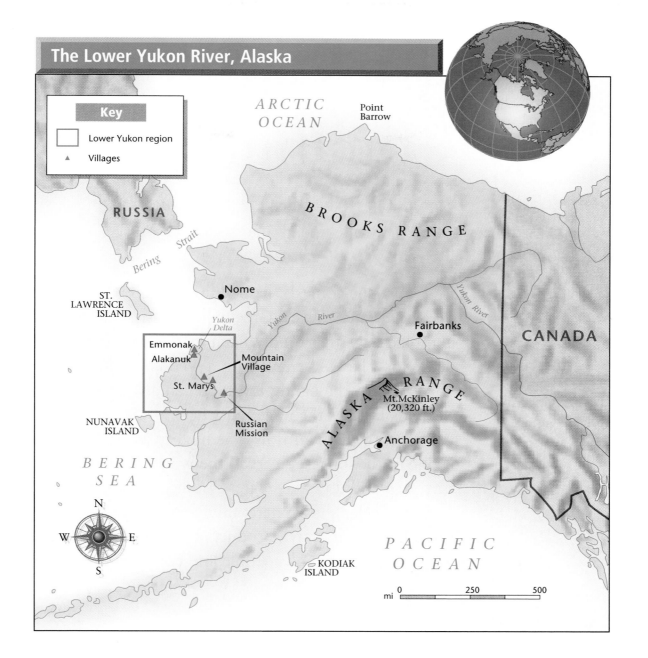

The Lower Yukon River, Alaska

Key
- Lower Yukon region
- ▲ Villages

ARCTIC OCEAN

Point Barrow

RUSSIA

BROOKS RANGE

Bering Strait

Nome

ST. LAWRENCE ISLAND

Yukon Delta

Yukon River

Yukon River

Fairbanks

CANADA

Emmonak
Alakanuk
Mountain Village
St. Marys

ALASKA RANGE
Mt.McKinley (20,320 ft.)

NUNAVAK ISLAND

Russian Mission

Anchorage

BERING SEA

N
W E
S

PACIFIC OCEAN

KODIAK ISLAND

mi 0   250   500

Research Activity

1 Pick another environment, like the rain forest or a desert.

2 Find out what resources people use to make their lives there.

The area around the river is flat enough that in this photograph you can see for miles. What would the land where you live look like from above? How is it different from that in the Lower Yukon?

A River Community

Main Idea The Mississippi River affects the lives of people who live in and around Greenville.

The paddle wheel on this boat weighs about 44 tons!

Here she comes! The paddle-wheel boat steams across the wide water toward Greenville, Mississippi. Red, white, and blue flags fly proudly from its top deck. The white decks look lacy, like layers on a wedding cake. Listen — you can hear the band play! You can also hear the engine throb as it turns the huge red wheel.

Beneath the boat flows the mighty Mississippi River. It is one of the longest rivers in the world. Boats of all sizes travel up and down its waters. Some, like the paddlewheeler shown here, take people on trips that are fun. Other boats carry products from sellers to buyers. The Mississippi River links people and communities together.

Greetings from
Greenville

- The average rainfall is more than 50 inches a year.

- About 45,000 people live in Greenville.

- Each September, the Mississippi Delta Blues Festival is held in Greenville. This music festival brings 30,000 visitors from all over the world.

A City That Depends on a River

Focus *How do people who live in communities along the Mississippi use the river?*

For thousands of years, people have lived by the Mississippi. They have caught fish from the river. They have traveled on the river. People have farmed the soil beside the river. They have built communities by the river. Greenville, Mississippi, is one of these communities. Find it on the map on the right. The river is one of Greenville's natural resources.

Agriculture, or farming, is important to Greenville. The soil is fertile, which means it's good for plants. This is partly because the Mississippi has flooded in the past. Floodwater carries fine dirt particles called **silt**. When the floodwaters dry, the silt stays. The silt makes the soil fertile. Fertile soil is a natural resource.

Summer temperatures in Greenville are warm, and the growing season is long. Cotton, rice, and soybeans are three of Greenville's important crops. A **crop** is a plant that is grown to be used, eaten, or sold.

Soybeans, cotton, and rice, shown below, do well in the soil near Greenville.

By the mid-1800s, steamboats carried furs, grain, cotton and sugar along the Mississippi River. Soon thousands of paddle-wheelers moved up and down between Minnesota and Louisiana. When railroads came, steamboats lost popularity. Today, six steamboats carry only tourists along the Mississippi River.

People try to control floods by building levees. Here waters of the Mississippi break a levee.

From Greenville, farmers can ship their crops up and down the river. Like Portland, Greenville is a port. Because of its port, businesses have located in and around the community. Rugs, clothing, and cardboard boxes are made in Greenville. Some products from Greenville may travel to as far away as South America or Asia.

Raging River

Focus *How did the flood of 1927 affect Greenville?*
Mark Twain wrote *The Adventures of Tom Sawyer* and other books about life on the Mississippi River. He wrote that no one could tell the river:

"Go *here, or Go there, and make it obey.* **"**

Rivers bring many good things to communities near them. But people in river communities also live with the danger of floods.

Every year, melting snow and rain run off the land into the Mississippi. Sometimes the snow melts fast or the rains are heavy. That can bring floods.

The Big Flood

In the spring of 1927, heavy rain fell for weeks. People in Greenville and other communities along the lower Mississippi didn't worry at first. The land was protected by levees. A **levee** (LEHV ee) is a bank of dirt that has been raised to prevent a river from overflowing. Many communities along the Mississippi have levees.

The rain kept falling, though. The water rose higher and higher. Early in the morning on April 21, a levee broke. At that moment, General Alexander G. Paxton was in Greenville. He was talking on the phone to the people who were trying to save the levee. "We can't hold it much longer," a worker told him. As the general said, "Then followed three words that I shall remember as long as I live — 'There she goes.'" Water rushed through the break and flooded the countryside.

Water destroyed homes, businesses, and farms. About 750 stores were damaged. Farmers could not plant crops in fields covered with water. There was no cotton crop that year. Thousands of Greenville homes were ruined. It took a long time for the city to recover from the damage.

People set up shelters for those who lost houses in the flood. **Citizenship:** *What are some things you could do to help during a flood?*

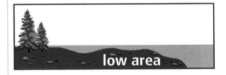

The levees along the Mississippi River are 20 to 35 feet high. They are 25 feet wide at the top. Some are more than 300 feet wide at the bottom!

How do you travel when your town is under water? By boat, like this man and his goat!

The Flood of '93

People all along the Mississippi have to help each other deal with the danger of floods.

Floods affect many river communities. In the spring of 1993, heavy rains fell on part of the United States. Floods swept down the northern Mississippi River and other rivers. These floods were far from Greenville, but they caused the same kinds of damage as the 1927 flood.

Des Moines, Iowa, was one community affected by the flood of '93. On Saturday, July 10, a huge crest of water poured through the city. The flood covered parks and cut off city streets.

As in Greenville, people in Des Moines helped each other. Workers piled sandbags to try to stop the water. Shelters were set up for those who had to leave their homes. Volunteers cooked meals. A woman in Des Moines said, "It's made the city into one big family."

People worked hard to protect their homes. The water covered streets and houses.

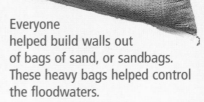

Everyone helped build walls out of bags of sand, or sandbags. These heavy bags helped control the floodwaters.

Geography and the Community

Focus *How does the environment affect communities in different ways?*

The flood of 1927 was terrible, but people in Greenville helped each other. First, volunteers rescued people who had been stranded by the flood. Then, volunteers found food and shelter for people made homeless by the flood. Today, Greenville is a thriving, busy city.

People help each other live in their environment, in good times and bad times. Farmers in Greenville use the rich soil left by Mississippi River floods. They also help each other recover from flood damage. Forest rangers watch for fires in forests near Portland. They also decide which trees are ready to be cut for lumber.

Different environments affect people in different ways. Natural resources are part of a community's environment. But the people who live in the community decide which resources are important and how to use them. Large bodies of water are important natural resources in Greenville, Mississippi. Forests are more important to people in Portland, Oregon. How does the environment affect your community?

Ask Yourself

People in Greenville helped one another during the flood of 1927. How do people in your community help each other?

? ? ? ? ? ? ? ? ? ? ? ? ? ?

Lesson Review

1 **Key Vocabulary:** Write a paragraph about life on the Mississippi River. Use **levee, agriculture, crop,** and **silt.**

2 **Focus:** How do people who live in communities along the Mississippi use the river?

3 **Focus:** How did the flood of 1927 affect Greenville?

4 **Focus:** How does the environment affect communities in different ways?

5 **Critical Thinking: Conclude** Why won't the problem of flooding along the Mississippi ever be totally solved?

6 **Theme: Environment** Would you move to an environment like Greenville's? Why or why not?

7 **Citizenship/Writing Activity:** During floods, people help one another. Write a story about what might happen if a disaster struck your community.

Using Diagrams

The Power of Water

Flooding can change the path a river takes. You can see how this happens by looking at the pictures in the diagram. They show you how a river forms an oxbow lake. The arrows in the diagram help you understand the order of events. People use diagrams every day. Diagrams can show you how to open a sardine can or make a telephone call.

This photograph, of part of the Alatna River in Alaska, shows both oxbow lakes and curves that might become oxbow lakes. How many oxbow lakes can you find? Which curves might become lakes next?

Formation of an Oxbow Lake

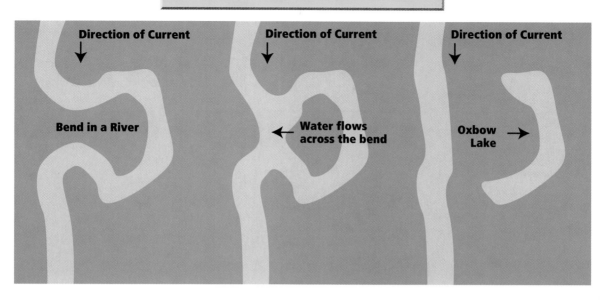

Direction of Current

Direction of Current

Direction of Current

Bend in a River

Water flows across the bend

Oxbow Lake

1 Here's How

- Read the title of the diagram. What do you think the diagram is trying to show about rivers?

- Look at the pictures. Where does the water flow? Read the words in each part of the diagram. What does each part show?

- Find the arrows. Use them to decide which way to read. Which step in making the oxbow came first? What happened next? Which was the last step?

- Cover the middle part of the diagram. Look at the parts before and after. What do you think was happening on the river in the covered step? Try to describe that step.

2 Think It Through

Think of something that happens in your life that you could explain in a diagram with arrows.

3 Use It

Look at the changes that the diagram shows in the river and land. Write about what each picture shows. Number the steps 1, 2, and 3.

Realistic Fiction

THREE DAYS ON A RIVER IN A RED CANOE

by Vera B. Williams

A river can go through mountains, farmlands, forests, and cities. A canoe trip down a river is a fun way to learn about the surrounding environment.

As soon as we got home with the canoe, Aunt Rosie and Mom took out their maps. The canoe trips they had taken before Sam or I was even born were marked in colors. They found a three-day trip that could be just right for us.

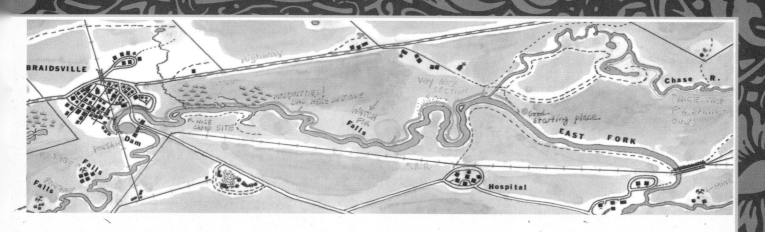

WE DROVE AND DROVE

AND DROVE AND DROVE

AND DROVE AND DROVE

We drove all day. Now we are at the place Aunt Rosie and Mom had chosen for our first camp. We start on the river in the morning. Sam and I unloaded the car. Mom and Aunt Rosie put up the tent. We hurried to get inside before it got too dark and the mosquitoes took too many bites out of us. We lay in our tent listening to the river.

When I poked my head out in the morning, everything was wet. Yet it wasn't even raining. We couldn't see our car. We could hardly see the river. We carried our canoe down to the water anyway.

Here are Mom and Aunt Rosie paddling into a part of the river like a hot green tunnel. I fell asleep. I think Sam did too. It's good Mom and Rosie didn't. Right here is where they heard the roaring of the waterfall.

Sam isn't much of a weather predictor. In the morning we sat in our sleeping bags and ate crackers and raisins. Aunt Rosie made cocoa on the little camping stove.

We set out on the river with all our things even though it was pouring rain. I am shaking my paddle at the sky and yelling.

Suddenly as we came around this bend in the river the sun came out through a hole in the clouds. A big rainbow spread across the sky.

Meet the Author

Of the 14 books Vera B. Williams has illustrated, she also wrote 11 of them, so she's mostly an author/illustrator. She wrote another book about boats and water, *Stringbean's Trip to the Shining Sea*, and her daughter Jennifer helped her illustrate it.

Additional Books to Read

Maps and Globes
by Jack Knowlton
Learning about making and using maps.

A Prairie Alphabet
by Jo Bannatyne-Cugnet
A book about living on the land.

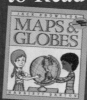

Chapter Review

Summarizing the Main Idea

1 Copy and fill in the table below. Show how the geography of the two places affects the way people live.

Communities and Their Geography		
	Portland, Oregon	Greenville, Mississippi
Geographical Feature		Mississippi River
How People Live with Their Geography		

Vocabulary

2 Use the words below to write a paragraph about how the geography of a community affects the way people live.

environment (p. 139)   **port (p. 141)**   **silt (p. 151)**
natural resource (p. 140)   **product (p. 143)**   **crop (p. 151)**
   agriculture (p. 151)   **levee (p. 153)**

Reviewing the Facts

3 How do people in Portland use the fertile soil there?

4 How is the port in Portland important to people there?

5 How are the forests in Portland used as a natural resource?

6 What jobs do people do involving lumber in Portland?

7 What landform in Greenville is important to how people live there?

8 What are some ways that Greenville depends on the Mississippi River?

9 What are some crops that are grown in Greenville?

10 What causes flooding in communities near the Mississippi River?

11 How did the people of Greenville help one another during the flood of 1927?

12 Look at the diagram on page 142 about building a house. Choose an idea that is described but not shown on the diagram. Draw the picture. Where would you put the picture? Where would you place an arrow?

13 Choose an activity to show in a diagram. Draw the diagram. Show the order of events with arrows.

Geography Skills

Use the maps on page 141 for questions 14 and 15.

14 Find the Willamette River on the map. What other cities are near this river? Are they near forests?

15 Where would be another good place for a port in Oregon? Trace the map of Oregon. Use a symbol to show your new port. Write a paragraph about why you chose that place.

Writing: Citizenship and History

16 Citizenship Suppose you are a carpenter who builds houses. Write a letter to a lumberjack telling how you use lumber. How are the two of you working together? Who else works with you?

17 History Look at the picture on page 152 of the waters of the Mississippi River breaking a levee. Write a story about what it would be like to live on that street during a flood.

Activities

Economics/Arts Activity
Make a collage or poster showing products made from trees. How many can you find? What jobs do you think people did to make these products?

Geography/Math Activity
Use the postcards on pages 140 and 151 to make a chart comparing the number of people who live in Portland and Greenville. Which has more people? Why do you think it does?

Internet Option

Check the **Internet Social Studies Center** for ideas on how to extend your theme project beyond your classroom.

THEME PROJECT CHECK-IN

Look at the model of your area and answer these questions:
- Have you included any natural resources in your area?
- Have you included any landforms which are important to people's lives?

Chapter Preview: *People, Places, and Events*

1500 — 1600 — 1700

The Village of Xiashen

Say hello to students in Xiashen. *Lesson 1, Page 166*

Feeding Many People

What crop is this? Find out. *Lesson 1, Page 166*

Life in a Village

Take a shopping trip with people in China. *Lesson 1, Page 168*

A Farming Village

Main Idea Farmers in a Chinese village use the natural resources of their region to farm successfully.

Geographer Elizabeth Leppman went to China to learn about the people and their land. She wrote this about China:

A perfect day for a bike ride! I rode to the village of Xiashen (shyah shuhn). The Yangs live there. Yang Xu (yahng shue), their son, is 12 years old.

The land is so flat that riding a bike is easy. Soon I came to the rice paddies of Xiashen. A rice paddy is a special field for growing rice. Yang Xu and his father were busy cutting rice with long knives. After they greeted me, I asked, "Was the rice crop good this year?" Mr. Yang answered, "Yes. We will have plenty to eat this winter."

Elizabeth Leppman with two young friends in China.

◀ Most people in China are farmers, like this woman.

1800	1900	2000

In the City

Mexico City has been a center of activity for hundreds of years. *Lesson 2, Page 171*

Big, Bigger, Biggest!

There are more people here than in any other city in the world. *Lesson 2, Page 174*

Make Them Laugh

This is one of the most beloved faces in Mexico City. *Lesson 2, Page 175*

Greetings from
Xiashen

- Children your age attend this elementary school in Xiashen. Here, the students stand in front of the school.

- Xiashen means "lower depths" in Chinese. The name probably came from the village's location near a river.

- The population is about 2,000.

The Land of Rice

Focus *Why is the environment of Xiashen good for growing rice?*

Xiashen is a village that Elizabeth Leppman studied in China. Find it on the map of China on the left. When you study the geography of a community, you learn a lot about it. You find out what kinds of work the people do and what they eat. You also learn what their land is like.

Most people in Xiashen are farmers. China needs a lot of farmers to grow food for its huge population. The **population** is the number of people who live in a place. One out of every five people on earth lives in China!

To feed all those people, every little bit of farmland has to be used well. In Xiashen, rice is the main crop. By growing rice, farmers can produce a lot of food on a small piece of land.

The soil of Xiashen is an important natural resource. The soil is good for growing crops like rice. For hundreds of years, farmers have added fertilizer to the soil.

Xiashen is in the northern part of China.

Rice fields near Xiashen. The land is very flat. That's good for farming. **Geography:** *What does the land around your community look like?*

Fertilizer makes the soil even better for crops.

Climate is the kind of weather a place has over a long time. Climate is another natural resource. The climate in Xiashen is good for growing rice. Winters are very cold, but summers are warm. Most of the rain comes in summer. That's when plants need water most. Farmers add to the water from rain by using irrigation. **Irrigation** is bringing water to fields. Most irrigation water in Xiashen comes from rivers. Some comes from wells. Water is a natural resource, too.

Rice isn't the only crop grown in Xiashen. Farmers also raise tomatoes, cabbage, and other vegetables. The Yang family has a small vegetable garden.

The rice grains on the right come from stalks like those on the left. The grains are the part of the plant that people eat.

· Tell Me More ·

How is rice grown?

The Chinese have been growing rice for thousands of years. Rice growing takes place in steps. The drawings below show some of the steps. Just about everyone in the village helps out — even children your age. Children help out after school and on weekends.

1 Farmers give their rice plants a head start. Around March, they plant the seeds under plastic sheets. The sheets keep the ground warm. The seeds sprout and grow.

2 In May, farmers flood the rice paddies with water. They move the rice plants from under the plastic sheets and plant them in the paddies. It's hard work, but everyone helps.

3 The rice grows all summer and is ready to be cut in October. The workers cut the plants with knives. Then they bundle the cut stalks together. They have to hurry — winter is coming!

People shop for foods such as tomatoes, carrots, and string beans in Chinese markets. **Economics:** *Why would people who live in a farming village go to a market to buy vegetables?*

Village Life

Focus *How does farming affect life in Xiashen?*

In the United States, farm families usually live on the land they farm, next to their fields. This is not true in China. The Yang family and other Xiashen farm families live in the village, next to each other. Each morning the farmers walk or ride bikes to their fields.

Farmers in Xiashen grow rice and other food. People eat rice at almost every meal. With the rice they eat vegetables. Sometimes they add a little meat or fish. Now and then, they'll have a special treat, like an ice pop.

Farmers owe part of their rice crop to the government of China. They can sell any extra crops. People from Xiashen and other nearby villages sell their crops in the market in the larger town of Baita (by tah). A **market** is a place where people buy and sell things they need.

One shop in Baita sells snacks and newspapers. At the village clinic, sick people can see a doctor. Bicycles are the

most important way to get around, so the person who fixes bikes is always busy.

Xiashen has an elementary school. Yang Xu's mother, Zhao Yazhen (jow yah jun), is a teacher at the school. Yang Xu's parents want him to be a good student.

Yang Xu may not be a farmer when he grows up. But if he still lives in Xiashen, farming will affect his life. His breakfast, lunch, and dinner will come from the fields.

Elizabeth Leppman says, "I enjoyed the time I spent in China. It's fun to learn how geography affects communities around the world."

If you lived in China, you might buy toys and word cards in a market.

同學

老師 teacher

Lesson Review

1 **Vocabulary:** Write about Xiashen using the words **population**, **climate**, **irrigation**, and **market**.

2 **Focus:** Why is the environment of Xiashen good for growing rice?

3 **Focus:** How does farming affect life in Xiashen?

4 **Critical Thinking: Cause and Effect:** Houses in Xiashen are close together and neighbors live nearby. Suppose farm families in Xiashen lived on their own land instead of in the village. How might their lives be different?

5 **Citizenship:** How does China's huge population affect the way that farmers use the land?

6 **Geography/Science Activity:** The seeds of plants must germinate, or sprout. Learn what makes seeds germinate. Then explain how farmers in Xiashen help rice seeds germinate.

The World's Largest City

Main Idea Geographic location affects the way of life in Mexico City.

Long ago, an old story says, the Aztec people looked for a home. They were told, "Look for an eagle on a cactus with a snake in its beak. Build your city there."

After many years, they came to a lake. On an island, they saw an eagle on a cactus. A snake was in its beak.

There the Aztecs built the city of Tenochtitlán (teh nawch tee TLAHN). Many years later, Mexico City was built in the same place.

The Aztecs built this pyramid. It was discovered when a subway station was built in Mexico City. Mexican coins, like those above, have the Aztec eagle on them.

- The country of Mexico and Mexico City get their names from Mexica, an early name for the Aztecs.
- Mexico City's high location keeps it cool, even though it is in a part of the world that is usually hot.
- Over 20 million people live in the city.

A Central Location

Focus *What was the environment of Tenochtitlán like?*

The land the Aztecs settled lies in what is central Mexico today. The land was wet and soft. The Aztecs drove long wooden poles into the swampy ground. These poles made a strong foundation for buildings. They scooped up mud from the bottom of the lake. The Aztecs added the mud to the island to make it bigger and drier.

To make land, the Aztecs built rafts in the lake and piled dirt on them. They grew **maize** (mayz), or corn. The roots of larger plants, like the willow trees in the picture, held the rafts to the bottom of the lake. The picture shows how this happened.

The place where Tenochtitlán was located has a pleasant climate. It doesn't get too cold in the winter or too warm in the summer. The main difference between summer and winter is the amount of rain. Most of the rain comes in the summer. Winter is the dry season.

The Aztecs built Tenochtitlán in the middle of the land where they lived. People from all over their land could get to Tenochtitlán. Its central location made it a good place for a

To grow crops, the Aztecs built rafts piled with dirt. Plant roots held the rafts in place. **Science:** *What kind of roots would be needed for holding the rafts in place?*

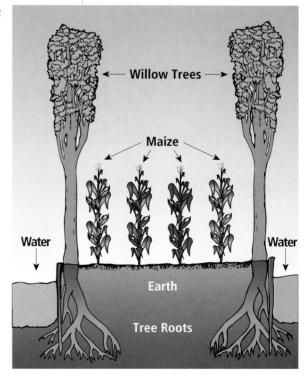

Willow Trees

Maize

Water

Water

Earth

Tree Roots

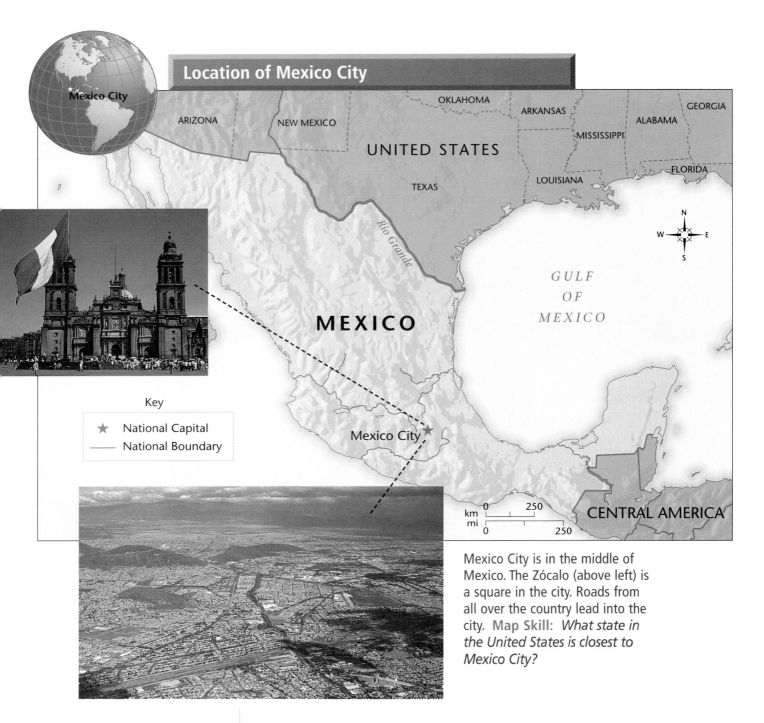

Location of Mexico City

Mexico City

OKLAHOMA
ARIZONA
NEW MEXICO
ARKANSAS
GEORGIA
ALABAMA
MISSISSIPPI
UNITED STATES
FLORIDA
TEXAS
LOUISIANA
Rio Grande

GULF
OF
MEXICO

MEXICO

Key

★ National Capital
— National Boundary

Mexico City

km   0   250
mi   0   250

CENTRAL AMERICA

Mexico City is in the middle of Mexico. The Zócalo (above left) is a square in the city. Roads from all over the country lead into the city. **Map Skill:** *What state in the United States is closest to Mexico City?*

capital. A **capital** is the center of an area's government.

Almost 500 years ago, explorers from Spain conquered the Aztecs. They tore down Tenochtitlán and built Mexico City in the same place. Today, Mexico City is the capital of the country of Mexico. The map above shows that Mexico City is in the middle of Mexico. Many capital cities have a central location.

Solving a Problem

Focus *How has population growth affected the air in Mexico City?*

Mexico City has the largest population of any city in the world. The graph shows you that it is much bigger than New York City, the biggest city in the United States. All these people use a lot of cars and trucks. Cars and trucks can cause **air pollution**, which is dirt and chemicals in the air that can harm people. Factories can also cause air pollution. So can gas used for cooking and heating.

Many cities in the world have air pollution. But Mexico City's location makes the problem worse. The city is surrounded by mountains. These mountains cut off the wind. Therefore, the pollution cannot blow away.

In winter, when there is no rain to wash the dirt out of the air, the pollution gets worse. Factories must slow down their work. Sometimes schools close and children cannot go outdoors to play.

Over the years, air pollution has become worse in Mexico City. That happened because the city's population has grown very fast. People from other parts of Mexico have moved to the capital.

Two Big Cities

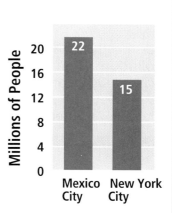

Mexico City has a lot of people! It has many more people than New York City, the largest U.S. city. **Chart Skill:** *How many people live in Mexico City?*

Tall mountains can trap the air over a city. Pollution cannot be blown away. Many cities surrounded by mountains have problems with pollution. **Science:** *What role does wind play in cleaning the air?*

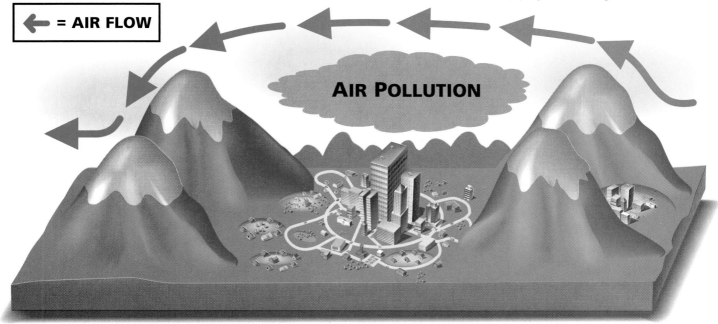

← = **AIR FLOW**

AIR POLLUTION

Ask Yourself

Cars produce air pollution. What other ways could people use to get from one place to another?

? ? ? ? ? ? ? ? ? ? ? ? ? ?

Mexico City's public parks are lively spots. People gather in the parks to relax and enjoy themselves.

An Exciting Community

In many countries, people move from small towns and rural areas to cities. Urban areas have more kinds of businesses than rural areas. People move there to look for jobs. Many people who live in rural Mexico cannot find work. They hear from friends, relatives, radio, and television that there are jobs in Mexico City. At one time during the 1980s, about 1,000 people arrived in the city each day!

Whether they have arrived recently or have lived there all their lives, people in Mexico City need clean air to breathe. When people drive less, air pollution decreases. People who drive in Mexico City have been told to leave their cars at home on certain days.

To help them, the government is building more subway lines. That way, people can ride subways instead of cars. The government is also buying new buses. These buses will give off less pollution.

Boat rides in the park are one way people enjoy Mexico City's environment.

Mario Moreno

A comedian makes people laugh. Mario Moreno was a great comedian. Under the name Cantinflas (kahn TEEN flahs), he made 49 movies. Born in Mexico City in 1911, he was beloved in Mexico and other Spanish-speaking countries when he died in 1993. His picture is in the center of a giant Mexico City mural.

Mexico City is an exciting community. People love to live there. Mexico City is the country's center for business. It is home to Mexico's oldest college and biggest banks. Artists come to paint pictures. You can hear music in the streets. Mexico City has a pleasant climate, a long history, and a central location. No wonder so many people have decided to move there!

Geography affects every community. Natural resources and location are important parts of geography. Geography affects what people eat, where they live, and the work they do. How does geography affect your community?

Lesson Review

1 **Vocabulary:** Write a paragraph about Mexico City using the words capital, air pollution and maize.

2 **Focus:** What was the environment of Tenochtitlán like?

3 **Focus:** How has population growth affected the air in Mexico City?

4 **Critical Thinking: Cause and Effect** In 1985 Mexico City had a very bad earthquake. Many people's everyday activities were stopped. The air was clearer than usual then. Why?

5 **Theme: Environment** In what ways is Mexico City's location a good thing?

6 **Citizenship/Writing Activity:** People in Mexico City are trying to solve the problem of air pollution. Learn about a problem that your community is trying to solve. Make a list of ways you or other people might help.

Skills Workshop

Using Climate and Resource Maps

What Grows Where?

Maps can show where all kinds of things are located. One kind of map shows the climate in different places. Another kind of map shows where resources are, like bodies of water or growing areas for crops. You can learn a lot from the information on different maps.

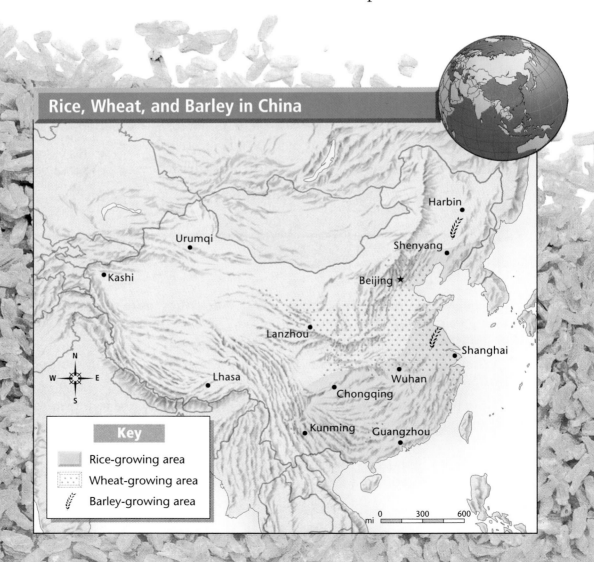

Rice, Wheat, and Barley in China

Harbin

Urumqi

Shenyang

Kashi

Beijing ★

Lanzhou

Shanghai

Lhasa

Wuhan

Chongqing

Kunming   Guangzhou

N
W   E
S

Key

Rice-growing area

Wheat-growing area

Barley-growing area

mi   0   300   600

1 Here's How

These two maps tell about the climate and crops in China.

- Study the temperature map and its map key. What does each color stand for? Find each color on the map. Where is China's climate coldest? Warmest?

- Study the map that shows where barley, rice, and wheat grow. What symbol stands for each crop?

- Find each crop symbol on the map. Which crop grows in the fewest places in China?

2 Think It Through

Why might it be useful to compare the information on different maps?

3 Use It

Use the maps to find the average temperatures and the crops that grow around the following cities:

1. Beijing   3. Shanghai

2. Guangzhou   4. Chongqing

Average Temperatures in China in July

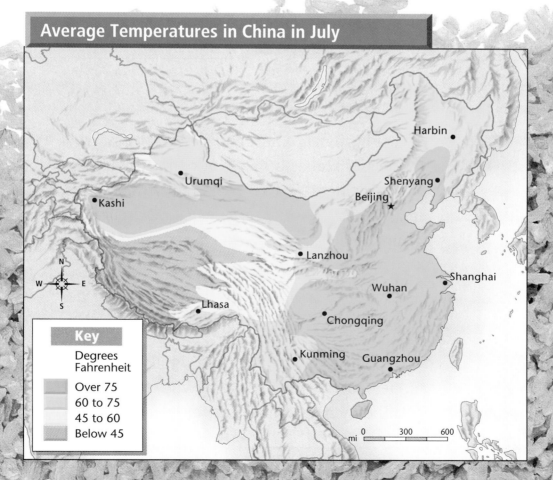

Key

Degrees Fahrenheit

Over 75
60 to 75
45 to 60
Below 45

0   300   600
mi

★ CITIZENSHIP ★

Participating

What Can You Do to Help the Environment?

What will the earth be like when you grow up? That depends on what everyone does now. You and your community can recycle things. You can turn off lights when you aren't using them. You can walk, bike, or ride public transportation, if possible. In Illinois, some people found ways to do less driving. They wanted to help keep the air cleaner. You can read about them below!

Case Study

Car-pooling for Clean Air

In a suburb near Chicago, Illinois, five nearby businesses realized that a lot of their workers were driving to work in cars all by themselves. Imagine 10 people driving in 10 different cars. Think of the dirty air and wasted space! These companies set up a booth where workers could sign up to drive together, or car-pool. The companies rewarded the car-poolers by giving them good parking.

People liked the change a lot. They saved money on gas. They made new friends. Most of all, they helped make the air cleaner.

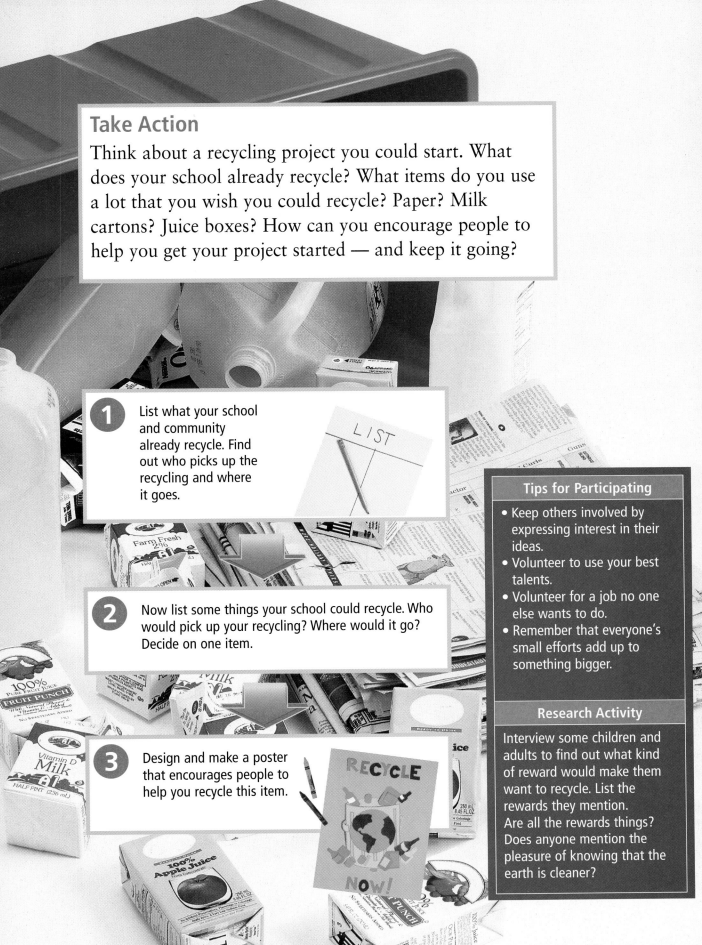

Take Action

Think about a recycling project you could start. What does your school already recycle? What items do you use a lot that you wish you could recycle? Paper? Milk cartons? Juice boxes? How can you encourage people to help you get your project started — and keep it going?

1 List what your school and community already recycle. Find out who picks up the recycling and where it goes.

LIST

2 Now list some things your school could recycle. Who would pick up your recycling? Where would it go? Decide on one item.

3 Design and make a poster that encourages people to help you recycle this item.

RECYCLE NOW!

Tips for Participating

- Keep others involved by expressing interest in their ideas.
- Volunteer to use your best talents.
- Volunteer for a job no one else wants to do.
- Remember that everyone's small efforts add up to something bigger.

Research Activity

Interview some children and adults to find out what kind of reward would make them want to recycle. List the rewards they mention. Are all the rewards things? Does anyone mention the pleasure of knowing that the earth is cleaner?

Chapter Review

Summarizing the Main Idea

1 Copy the table below. Fill in the table. Show how the geography of each place affects the way people live there.

How Geography Affects Life in a Place		
	Xiashen, China	**Mexico City, Mexico**
The Land		
The Climate	*Summer rain helps rice grow. Rice is the main crop.*	

Vocabulary

2 Make a word web for each word below.

population (p. 166)   **irrigation (p. 167)**   **maize (p. 171)**

climate (p. 167)   **market (p. 168)**   **capital (p. 172)**

air pollution (p. 173)

Reviewing the Facts

3 What is the land like in Xiashen, China?

4 What is the climate like in Xiashen?

5 Why did the people in Xiashen choose to grow rice there?

6 How do people in Xiashen work and live together?

7 Why does Mexico City's geography make it a good place to be the capital of Mexico?

8 How do the land and climate in Mexico City affect the air?

9 How have people had to change their lives in Mexico City because of the land and climate?

10 Why is Mexico City a popular place to live?

Use the maps on pages 176 and 177 to answer questions 11 and 12.

11 What is the average daily temperature in Shenyang? What crop is grown there?

12 What temperature do you think is good for growing rice? Why do you think this?

Critical Thinking

13 **Sequence** Make a timeline to show what happens in each month when rice is grown.

14 **Comparing Then and Now** How was Tenochtitlán different from and similar to Mexico City?

15 **Predict** What do you think life will be like in Mexico City as it continues to grow?

Writing: Citizenship and Culture

16 **Citizenship** In Mexico City, people are told not to drive their cars some days of the week. Write a letter to convince a friend of what you both might do to reduce air pollution in your community.

17 **Culture** Suppose you were going to live and work with a family in Xiashen. Write a journal about what you do during one day. Which season is it? What do you do in the rice fields? Are you going to the market?

Activities

Geography/Research Activity
Which communities in the United States grow rice as the main crop? Do research to find out. Compare the land and climate with that of Xiashen.

Cultures/Music Activity
Find a recording of Mexican music and listen to it. How are the songs like songs you listen to? How are they different?

Internet Option

Check the **Internet Social Studies Center** for ideas on how to extend your theme project beyond your classroom.

THEME PROJECT CHECK-IN

Look at your model. Have you used what you have learned about environments?
- What is the land like where you live?
- What is the climate like where you live?
- Are there crops grown where you live? What are they?
- Are problems caused by the land or the climate? How do people solve them?

Earning a Living

"*This bread I break was once the oat, . . .*"

Dylan Thomas

· T H E M E ·

Depending on One Another

❝ *We depend on one another to meet our basic needs. Firefighters, police, and letter carriers are people we depend on in our community.* **❞**

Ulice Jefferson, Gary, Indiana

Think about all the ways you depend on other people. Do you go to a store to buy food? Think of the people who worked to get the food to you. Think of the people who built the roads and sidewalks you traveled on to get to the store! All of us depend on other people. People build the houses and buildings we live in. People who build houses depend on others to make boards, nails, and tools. This unit shows lots of ways people depend on each other.

 Theme Project

Start a Business

Think about a business you could start in your school. It might be a business in which you make something — like muffins. It might be a business in which you do something for others — like wash cars. Decide:

- What would you sell, or what would you do for others?
- Where would you sell your product or provide your service?
- Who would want what you offer?
- How much would you charge?

◄ Americans depend on one another to get things done.

UNIT 4

WHEN & WHERE ATLAS

Long ago, families and communities took care of their own needs. Today, people in communities around the world depend on each other more and more. Some of the communities on this map depend on each other, too. People in Casper, Wyoming, may eat grapes that come from Chile. People in Chile may use oil that comes from Wyoming.

In this unit, you will study four communities. You will see how people in these communities depend on each other and on the people in other communities.

Unit 4 Chapters

Chapter 7   Americans Working Together

Chapter 8   Goods and Services Around the World

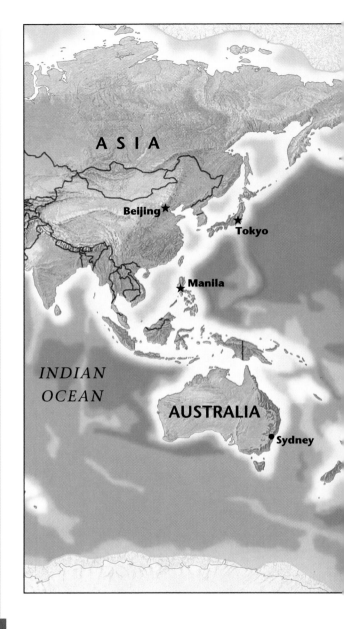

ASIA

Beijing★

★ Tokyo

■ Manila

INDIAN OCEAN

AUSTRALIA

● Sydney

Unit Timeline

1600	1680	1760

Casper's Braille Trail

Touch, smell, and listen to nature on the Braille Trail! *Chapter 7, Lesson 1*

Wyoming's Merchants

What do people in Casper, Wyoming, do for a living? *Chapter 7, Lesson 1*

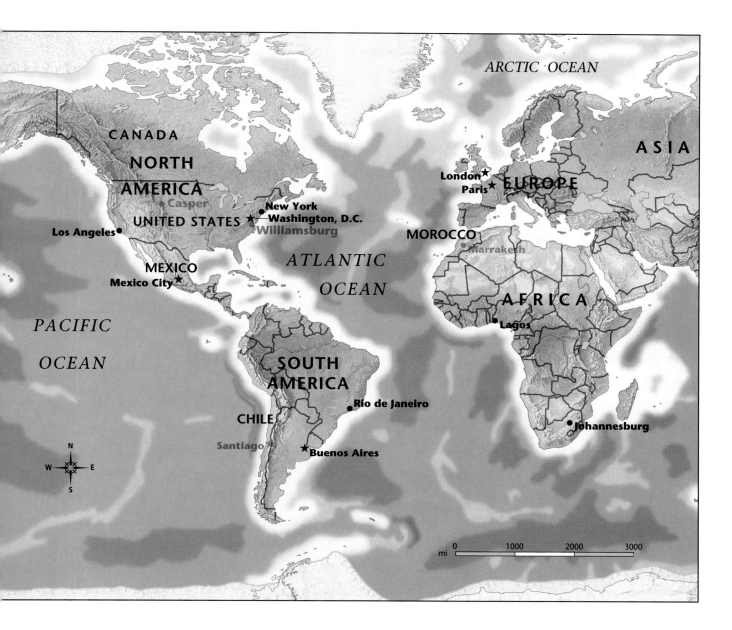

ARCTIC OCEAN

ASIA

CANADA

NORTH
AMERICA

London ★
Paris ★ EUROPE

MOROCCO

• Casper

New York
Washington, D.C.
Williamsburg

UNITED STATES ★

Los Angeles ●

• Marrakesh

ATLANTIC

OCEAN

MEXICO

Mexico City ★

PACIFIC

OCEAN

AFRICA

SOUTH
AMERICA

• Lagos

CHILE

• Río de Janeiro

Santiago

• Johannesburg

★ Buenos Aires

N
W ✦ E
S

0   1000   2000   3000
mi

| 1840 | 1920 | **2000** |

Children as Teachers?

What do visitors to Colonial Williamsburg learn and from whom?
Chapter 7, Lesson 2

Fruit from Chile

PRODUCE OF CHILE

Why is Chile's fruit special?
Chapter 8, Lesson 1

Yarn from Marrakesh

Where do people in Marrakesh, Morocco, buy the things they need?
Chapter 8, Lesson 2

CHAPTER 7 Americans Working Together

Chapter Preview: *People, Places, and Events*

1600	1700	1800

Welcome to Casper

CASPER
POP 46742
ELEV 5123

What do more than 46,000 people do in Casper, Wyoming? *Lesson 1, Page 190*

Casper, Wyoming

Why is this tower important to the people of Casper? *Lesson 1, Page 188*

North Platte River

Ferries once carried loaded wagons across this river. *Lesson 1, Page 187*

Oil Makes Jobs

Main Idea Some people earn money by making or selling goods. They use their money to buy goods for themselves.

Over 100 years ago, families piled their clothes, chairs, and other belongings into wagons. The wagons creaked and rolled on the trail. They were heading west. At one place, a ferry took them across the North Platte River. That river crossing would one day grow into the city of Casper, Wyoming.

In 1888, the railroad came. The hiss and screech of the train replaced the creak and groan of wagons. Now people began to settle there rather than just pass through.

In 1889 oil was discovered near Casper. Oil was something that people could sell. Some people began to use it to earn a living.

Key Vocabulary
goods
demand
employment

Casper, Wyoming

◀ Americans have always worked together to make the things they need.

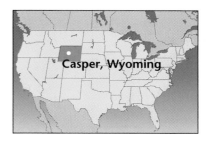

1900	2000	2100

Williamsburg, Virginia 1693

This woman's name traveled across an ocean. *Lesson 2, Page 195*

Colonial Williamsburg

Why does this town look so old? *Lesson 2, Page 195*

Williamsburg Hospital

What services do people in Williamsburg need? *Lesson 2, Page 199*

Oil must be refined before it can be used. Refining cleans oil and separates it into parts. Those parts can be made into useful goods. Gasoline, jet fuel, heating oil, plastics, and fabrics like polyester and nylon all come from oil. **Economics:** *Look around your classroom. How many things made of plastic can you find?*

fabrics

gasoline

plastics

A Town Grows on Oil

Focus *Why is oil important to Casper's economy?*

Selling, buying, and earning a living are all important to a community's economy. Every city and town has an economy. Think about the economy of your community as you read about Casper.

Oil is an important natural resource in Casper. It helps Casper's economy. Many people there make their living from oil.

Oil companies in Casper pump oil out of the ground so that they can sell it. But the oil is not yet ready to use. It must be cleaned and processed in a refinery. Refined oil can be used to make useful goods. **Goods** are things that are made or grown that can be sold. On the left you can see goods that are made from oil or that use oil.

Once oil was discovered near Casper, pumping and refining it made new jobs there. The demand for Casper's oil grew when people started driving cars in the early 1900s. **Demand** is the wish to buy or use something. Now that people owned cars, they needed gasoline to fuel them. Gasoline was in demand. Casper's refinery began turning oil into gasoline. It could be sold to meet the demand.

Casper's refinery still sells oil and gasoline. It sends these goods to other states to meet their demand. The map on the next page shows where Casper's oil goes.

Casper changes as the demand for oil changes. When the demand for oil is high, oil companies hire more workers. Those workers spend their money in Casper. They use it to buy the things they need. That means stores and businesses make money too.

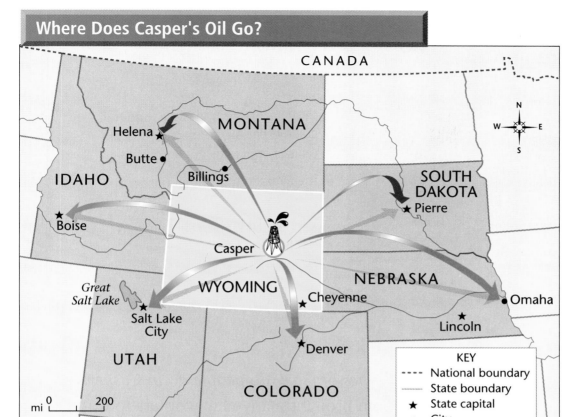

This map shows where oil and oil products go when they leave Casper's refinery.
Map Skill: *What do the symbols and the arrows on the map tell you about Casper's trade in oil?*

In the late 1970s, Casper had an oil boom. In a boom, the demand for oil is high. There are lots of jobs. Cities grow very quickly. During the boom, many people moved to Casper. They worked for the oil companies. Others came to sell goods that the oil workers needed, like groceries and furniture.

In 1983, the demand for Casper's oil dropped. Oil companies in Casper sold less oil. There were fewer jobs in Casper. People left and businesses closed.

Oil derricks like this one were once used to drill oil wells. This wooden oil derrick reminds people in Casper of oil's importance to their community.

Greetings from Casper

- Casper's Braille Trail is a nature trail made especially for people who are visually impaired.

- The average snowfall in Casper is 77 inches a year. That's over 6 feet!

- Deer, prairie dogs, mountain lions, and bears live in and around Casper.

This chart shows the population in Casper and the area around Casper from 1970 to 1995. It also predicts the population in the future. **Chart Skill:** *When was Casper's population the highest?*

Working in Casper

Focus *What types of work do people do in Casper?*

The last oil boom brought many new workers to Casper. They moved to Casper for employment. **Employment** is work people do for a living. When the oil boom ended, lots of people lost their jobs. Many oil workers found employment in other cities. They moved away from Casper. Look at Casper's population chart below. It shows how the oil boom changed the population of the city.

Some people liked Casper so much, they didn't want to move. Third graders in Casper today say one of the best things about Casper is the outdoors. Near Casper they can go "sledding, hiking, skiing, and camping." They also like Casper because it's not crowded with vehicles or people.

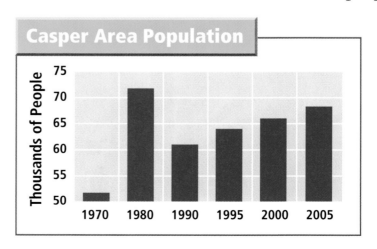

Casper Area Population

Thousands of People

Year	1970	1980	1990	1995	2000	2005

Louis Taubert, Jr., sells clothing and boots, like the ones you see here, to people in Casper, Wyoming.

For these reasons and others, workers chose to stay in Casper after the oil boom ended. They found new employment there. A few still work for the oil companies. Others work for banks or museums. Some sell goods like shoes or groceries. Some raise cattle, sheep, or horses.

Louis Taubert, Jr., works in Casper. His store sells Western-style clothing, cowboy hats, and saddles for horseback riding. Taubert says he likes living in Casper because of its "outdoors, clean air, and few people."

Many people are employed making or selling goods. Employment affects people who live in every community. How are people in your community employed?

Lesson Review

1 **Key Vocabulary:** Write a paragraph about your community's economy, using **goods**, **demand**, and **employment**.

2 **Focus:** Why is oil important to Casper's economy?

3 **Focus:** What types of work do people do in Casper?

4 **Critical Thinking: Predict** How would Casper be different today if the demand for oil had stayed high?

5 **Citizenship:** What kinds of goods do people in your community sell? Who buys them?

6 **Geography/Writing Activity:** Oil is an important resource because of the many things that are made from it. But what if there was no oil? Write a paragraph describing how your life would be different without oil.

★ CITIZENSHIP ★

Participating

How Does Cooperating Make Work Easier?

Have you ever had to move lots of books from one room to another all by yourself? Or rake a big yard all by yourself? Working by yourself can be really hard. Sharing the work can make it easier. A long time ago, some farmers learned that working together could make their jobs easier. You can read about them in the case study.

Case Study

An Orange Grove Co-op

An orange grove has hundreds of orange trees. It requires lots of work. Farmers need to care for the trees. They need to pick, sort, box, and ship the oranges all over the country. They need to advertise, decide prices, and collect money. Long ago, many farmers worked alone.

Then farmers started to work together. They chose leaders to help make decisions, but everyone voted on decisions. They shared shippers and warehouses. Working together, they made more money and made their lives a little easier.

Take Action

How could sharing work make your life easier? To find out, try this. Suppose there is a "Best School" contest in your state. To enter your school in the contest, you need to make a booklet describing your school.

1 Working in small groups, list the best things about your school.

2 Decide which things you want to show in a booklet. How will you show them?

3 List the different jobs needed to make a booklet. Let each person choose one job. Make a booklet!

4 Present your finished booklet to the class. Discuss these questions: How did you cooperate? How would the project have been different if you had worked alone?

Why our School is the best

Tips for Participating

- Listen to other people's ideas as carefully as you want them to listen to yours.
- List lots of ideas so you have more to choose from in the end.
- Pick a job that makes good use of your talents.
- Do the job you say you will do.

Research Activity

Interview someone in your community or school who works with other people. What does that person do if two people want to do the same job? What does he or she do if two or three people plan to work together, but then one of them doesn't do his or her share of the work?

History Makes Jobs

Main Idea Services, as well as goods, bring money into a community.

P HONE FOOD MOTEL On a long car or bus trip, drivers look for those signs. Travelers need services like pay phones, restaurants, and motels. A **service** is work that someone does for other people, like cook their lunch.

Suppose you drove from Casper, Wyoming, to Williamsburg, Virginia. The trip would take about five days. You would need to find places to get gas for your car. You would also need food to eat and a bed to sleep in. When you go on vacation, what services do you need?

History as a Resource

Focus *What is Williamsburg's resource?*

People travel to visit Williamsburg because Williamsburg has a special resource — its history. Visitors want to see what a colonial city was like. **Colonial** means from the time

These signs help travelers find services. **Economics:** *What service does each sign stand for?*

In 1693 a college was started in Williamsburg. It was named the College of William and Mary after King William and Queen Mary of England who are shown here. The college brought people to Williamsburg. A few years later, Williamsburg became the capital of Virginia. Then the city grew even more. The picture below shows Williamsburg as it is today.

when Williamsburg was part of a colony. Williamsburg was an important community when Virginia was a colony of England. That was over 200 years ago.

In colonial times, Williamsburg was a busy place. But by the early 1920s, many old buildings were falling down. Reverend William Goodwin, a minister in Williamsburg, wanted to see the city as it had been in colonial times. He shared his dream with John D. Rockefeller, Jr., a wealthy American. Rockefeller gave the money to rebuild and save the old part of the city.

Many people go to Williamsburg, Virginia, to learn about life in a colonial city.

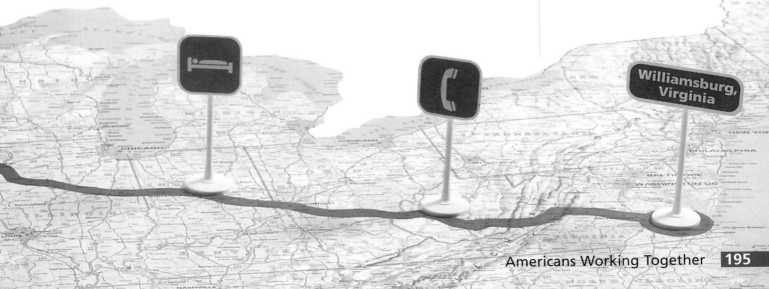

Williamsburg, Virginia

Learning to Teach

Focus *What service do people who work at Colonial Williamsburg provide to visitors?*

Today, part of Williamsburg is a modern, up-to-date community. The other part of it, Colonial Williamsburg, is the old city that has been saved. Let's walk through Colonial Williamsburg together.

Along the unpaved streets, you see old-fashioned houses and shops. People in colonial-style clothing talk with one another. Women carry baskets and wear hats and long skirts. Some men wear wigs. Their knee-length pants and long stockings remind you of a time long ago.

Inside one building, you see men fitting pieces of wood together. These men are coopers. Coopers make barrels and buckets. As they work, coopers in Williamsburg talk to visitors. They tell visitors about the wood and tools they use. They also talk about how people lived in colonial times.

Coopers are a few of the people

This museum worker shows visitors the work of a cooper. He makes barrels and buckets from wood. Coopers train for six years to learn how to shave, shape, and bind wood into containers.

who work at Colonial Williamsburg. There, a cooper's job has two parts. One part is making barrels and buckets. The other part of the job is teaching visitors about the city's past. The teaching is a service. Coopers must learn their trade and the history of Williamsburg.

As we come out of the coopers' shop, we see a woman leading visitors into a building. Like the coopers, she works at Colonial Williamsburg. She learned about the history of Williamsburg so that she could teach it to visitors. Down the street, children in costumes are playing games in a garden. Read below to learn more about children who volunteer at Colonial Williamsburg.

• Tell Me More •

Children Teach at Colonial Williamsburg

Ashley Bristow is 11 years old. She is a volunteer at Colonial Williamsburg. Ashley went to a week of training to learn to teach visitors about the past. She says "They gave us a huge book to study. We spent a day on each subject and one day at the house learning what to say to visitors."

Now Ashley wears a costume. She works in different areas of a colonial house. She tells visitors about the area she's in. Then she answers their questions. She says, "Sometimes we play cricket for the visitors to watch. They always say, 'Shouldn't the girls be inside washing dishes?' But girls really played back then."

Greetings from

Williamsburg

- Many people visit Colonial Williamsburg to learn about the city's history.

- Williamsburg was first settled in 1633.

- Williamsburg was named after King William the Third of England.

You can use the chart below to compare the number of people who live in Williamsburg to the number who visit each year. **Chart Skill:** *How would you describe the difference in numbers of the two groups of people shown in this chart?*

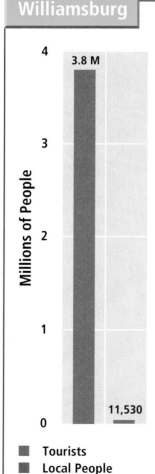

Tourism and Population: Williamsburg

Millions of People

- 4 — 3.8 M
- 3
- 2
- 1
- 0 — 11,530

■ Tourists
■ Local People

Services in Williamsburg

Focus *What services do people who live in Williamsburg need?*

Millions of people visit Colonial Williamsburg each year. That's a lot of people in one small city! Look at the graph on this page. Compare the number of tourists to the number of people who actually live in Williamsburg.

Every morning men and women go to work in Williamsburg. Many provide services to the visitors. Some, like coopers, teach the tourists. Others sell tickets or work in hotels or restaurants. This is their employment.

As the number of visitors to Williamsburg grows, more people are needed to provide services to them. This means there are more jobs in Williamsburg. People go there to find employment. Then they become part of the community.

The people who live in Willamsburg need services too. Think of a family that has just moved to Williamsburg. First, they need a place to live. A realtor helps them find just the right house. Then movers haul their beds, tables, and chairs into that house. Teachers will welcome the

When someone needs a doctor or a nurse in Williamsburg, they can go to the hospital. People working at the hospital provide them with the services they need. In 1991, 180 babies were born in Williamsburg, Virginia.

family's children to their schools. Banks hold the family's money safely. Realtors, movers, teachers, and bankers all make money by providing services to people. They help people who live in their community.

People in a community need goods and services. The resources there, like history or oil, make new jobs. Jobs give people the money to buy the goods and services they need. When communities grow, more people are needed to sell goods and services to the people who live in them.

Think about your own community. What goods and services do people in your community provide?

Ask Yourself

Some people work selling goods or services to others.

When you are grown up, what kind of work would you like to do?

? ? ? ? ? ? ? ? ? ? ? ? ?

Lesson Review

1 Key Vocabulary: Define the words service and colonial.

2 Focus: What is Williamsburg's resource?

3 Focus: What service do people who work at Colonial Williamsburg provide to visitors?

4 Focus: What services do people who live in Williamsburg need?

5 Critical Thinking: Compare and Contrast Would you rather live in Casper or Williamsburg? Explain your choice.

6 Theme: Depending on One Another The people who live in Williamsburg and the visitors to that city depend on one another. What do visitors get from the people who live there? What do people who live there get from the visitors?

7 Citizenship/Research Activity: Williamsburg is an important city because of its history. Find out something interesting or important about the history of your community. Present what you find to your class.

Using Reference Books

Track It Down

After reading about oil in Casper, you may want to learn more about it. One good place to look is in **reference books**. Reference books give you information on many subjects. Dictionaries and encyclopedias are two kinds of reference books.

A **dictionary** is a reference book that tells you what words mean and how to say them. An **encyclopedia** has short articles about many subjects. Dictionaries and encyclopedias list subjects and words in alphabetical order.

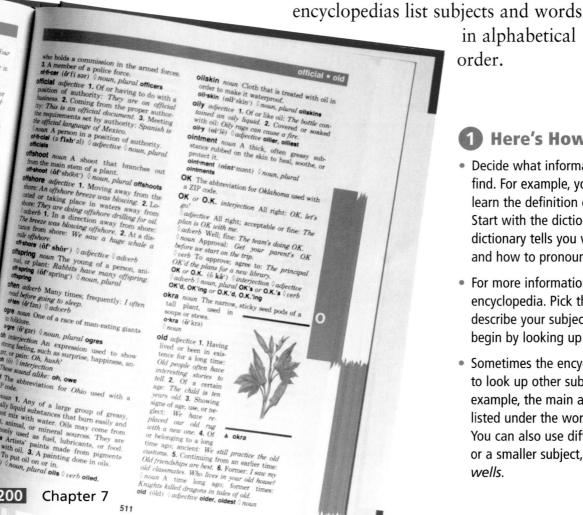

▲ okra

① Here's How

- Decide what information you want to find. For example, you might want to learn the definition of the word *oil*. Start with the dictionary. The dictionary tells you what *oil* means and how to pronounce it.

- For more information, look in the encyclopedia. Pick the best word to describe your subject. You might begin by looking up oil.

- Sometimes the encyclopedia tells you to look up other subjects. For example, the main article on oil is listed under the word *petroleum*. You can also use different key words, or a smaller subject, such as *oil wells*.

② Think It Through

What can you learn about oil from a dictionary? From an encyclopedia? How are the two books the same? How are they different?

③ Use It

On a piece of paper, list the subject words you would use to look for information about each question below. Then write down which book you would use to find that information.

1. How many oil wells are there in Wyoming?

2. What does the word *petroleum* mean? How do you pronounce it?

3. Where in the world is oil found?

Look at the dictionary page to the left, and the encyclopedia page to the right. What is different about the pages and the listings? What is the same?

Encyclopedia page (within image)

330 Petroleum

Crude oil from Saudi Arabia

Crude oil from Australia

Crude oil from Venezuela

Tar sands from Canada

Oil shale from the United States

Top three photos, Standard Oil Company of California, bottom two WORLD BOOK

Most petroleum comes from the earth as a liquid called *crude oil* Different types of crude oil vary in color and thickness, ranging from a clear, thin fluid to a dark, tarlike substance. In some parts of the world, petroleum also occurs as a solid in certain sands and rocks.

Petroleum

Petroleum is one of the most valuable natural resources in the world. Some people call petroleum *black gold,* but it may be better described as the lifeblood of industrialized countries. Fuels made from petroleum provide power for automobiles, airplanes, factories, farm equipment, trucks, trains, and ships. Petroleum fuels also generate heat and electricity for many houses and business places. Altogether, petroleum provides nearly half the energy used in the world.

In addition to fuels, thousands of other products are made from petroleum. These products range from paving materials to drip-dry fabrics and from engine grease to cosmetics. Petroleum is used to make such items in the home as aspirins, carpets, curtains, detergents, phonograph records, plastic toys, and toothpaste.

Although we use a huge variety of products made from petroleum, few people ever see the substance itself. Most of it comes from deep within the earth as a liquid called *crude oil.* Different types of crude oil vary in thickness and color, ranging from a thin, clear oil to a thick, tarlike substance. Petroleum is also found in solid form in certain rocks and sands.

The word petroleum comes from two Latin words

meaning *rock* and *oil.* People gave it this name they first found it seeping up from the earth th cracks in surface rocks. Today, petroleum is re ferred to simply as *oil,* and most of it is found beneath the earth's surface.

People have used petroleum for thousan But few people recognized its full value ur when the kerosene lamp and the automob vented. These inventions created an enor for two petroleum fuels, kerosene and g about 1900, scientists have steadily incre and improved the quality of petroleum

Petroleum, like other minerals, cann after it has been used. People are usin petroleum each year, and the world's running out. If present rates of consu petroleum may become scarce som 2000s.

Most industrialized nations depe ported petroleum to meet their en sult of this dependence, oil-expor been able to use petroleum as a weapon by restricting exports to Oil exporters have also strained large number of countries, part by drastically increasing the pri

To prevent a full-scale energ experimenting with artificial fo sources of fuel. But even if ne quickly, people will have to re years. Conservation of oil has

Robert C. Laudon, the contributor of this article, is Associate Professor of Geology and Geophysics at the University of Mis-souri at Rolla.

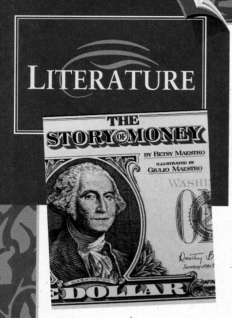
THE STORY OF MONEY

by Betsy Maestro, illustrated by Giulio Maestro

If you've ever bought an apple, a pen, or a doughnut, you know how money works. You give the seller the right amount of bills or coins, and you walk away with the thing you want. It wasn't always that way. On an ordinary market day five or six thousand years ago, there was plenty of buying and selling — but no money. Why? Because money hadn't been invented yet.

No money changed hands in the marketplace. All the buying and selling was in the form of barter. By trading, people were able to get the things they wanted and needed. Goods and supplies not available locally were often brought from far away. Merchants traveled long distances by boat or on pack animals to bring back items made or grown in other places.

    Most of the time this system of trade worked well. But sometimes, there were problems. Barter could work only when each trader wanted what the other had, and when

barter
to trade goods for other goods

both could agree on what made a fair trade. It could be difficult to work out an equal exchange when the items to be traded were very different from each other. The traders had to come to an agreement as to how many rugs might equal one cow or how many eggs would be exchanged for a loaf of bread.

To make trading easier, people began to use certain objects as money. Anything could be used as money if people agreed on its value and accepted it in trade for goods or labor. In many parts of the world, salt was used as money. Salt was valuable to people because they needed it to preserve and flavor food. It was also valuable because it was hard to find. Because it had great worth, people would accept salt as money.

Many other objects were also used as money. Tea leaves, shells, feathers, animal teeth, tobacco, and blankets were some of the items used at times around the world. In ancient Sumer, a civilization that flourished about five thousand years ago in what is now the Middle East, barley was used as money. Workers received barley in payment for their labor. The barley could then be used to buy goods.

Although barley and salt and other objects were valuable, they were not always convenient to use. Salt could melt in the rain. Blankets were hard to carry. Feathers could blow away in the wind. Little metal balls used in some places often rolled away as they were counted.

Sumerian merchants sometimes traveled great distances to trade. Barley was hard to handle in large amounts and it sometimes spoiled on the journey. The merchants looked

preserve
to keep from spoiling.

civilization
the culture of a group of people in one place and at one time in history.

flourish
to grow and be successful

barley
a grain that can be used for making food or drinks

labor
the work that people do

convenient
easy to use or to do

for a new medium of exchange. They needed something that was easy to handle and carry, something that wouldn't spoil or be damaged easily, and something that people everywhere would accept in trade. They began to use silver as money. Silver was a precious metal that was hard to find and so was very valuable. Everybody wanted it.

The Sumerians melted the silver and formed it into small bars. Each was stamped with its exact weight, which let people know how much silver they were getting or giving in return for goods or labor. The Sumerians had invented the world's first metal money.

medium of exchange
something of value that can be used for trading, buying, and selling

Coins like this one were made in Greece about 2,400 years ago.

Meet the Author

Betsy Maestro has written more than 40 children's books which have all been illustrated by her husband Giulio Maestro. If you enjoy nonfiction, look for their book called *The Story of the Statue of Liberty*.

Additional Books to Read

Family Farm
by Thomas Locker
A family must earn money to keep their farm.

Our Money
by Karen Bornemann Spies
A closer look at coins and dollar bills.

Response Activities

1. Compare Then and Now
What did people thousands of years ago use to pay for things? How did they get it? How does that compare to the people in Chapter 7?

2. Descriptive: Write a Story
Write a story that describes a market. What do people buy there? How do they pay for the goods they buy?

3. Economics: Make a Chart
Draw pictures of some of the items mentioned in the story. Which would be most valuable to you? Put your pictures in the order of their value to you. Write a paragraph that explains your order.

Chapter Review

Summarizing the Main Idea

1 Copy and fill in the table below. Show the resource, goods, services, and jobs in each community.

How People Live and Work in Two Towns		
	Casper, Wyoming	Williamsburg, Virginia
Resource		
Goods and Services		*real estate, schools, doctors, banks*
Jobs		

Vocabulary

2 Write a statement using each word below.

goods (p. 188) **employment (p. 190)** **colonial (p. 194)**
demand (p. 188) **service (p. 194)**

Reviewing the Facts

3 How does oil help people in Casper, Wyoming?

4 What kinds of goods are made from oil?

5 What happened in Casper when the demand for oil increased?

6 How do the people in Casper get the goods they need?

7 How does Williamsburg's resource provide work for the people who live there?

8 What do child volunteers do in Colonial Williamsburg?

List the words that you would use to look for information about each of the questions that follow. Which type of book would you use, a dictionary or an encyclopedia?

9 What are some states that have oil as a resource?

10 What is a colony?

11 What is a natural resource in Pittsburgh, Pennsylvania? What goods are made from it?

Critical Thinking

12 **Generalize** How do resources help people?

13 **Comparing Then and Now** How has the town of Casper changed from the time of high oil demand to the time of low oil demand?

14 **Cause and Effect** Sometimes many new people move to a town. What effect does that have on the people in the town?

Writing: Citizenship and History

15 **Citizenship** Why do you think some children volunteer to teach at Colonial Williamsburg? Write a paragraph that says what you'd like about volunteering there.

16 **History** Write a list of the chores, games, and activities that might be used to teach a child in the future about life today.

Activities

Economics/Language Arts Activity
Make a list of questions that will help you learn about selling particular kinds of goods. Then interview someone in your community who makes a living selling them.

History/Art Activity
Draw pictures that show important events in Casper. In your pictures, show how the city has changed over time.

Internet Option

Check the **Internet Social Studies Center** for ideas on how to extend your theme project beyond your classroom.

THEME PROJECT CHECK-IN

Look back at your theme project to see if you have used what you have learned about goods, demand, services, and jobs.
- What goods or service are you selling?
- What happens when many people are buying your goods or service? What happens when only a few people are buying your goods or service?

CHAPTER 8 Goods and Services Around the World

Chapter Preview: *People, Places, and Events*

1010	1210	1410

Fruit in Chile

Why can we eat grapes, plums, and berries in winter? *Lesson 1, Page 210*

Transporting Goods

Find out how fruit from Chile gets to you. *Lesson 1, Page 210*

Santiago, Chile

Where do people work in Santiago? *Lesson 1, Page 212*

A Global Market

Main Idea People in Chile work to make money to buy the goods and services they need.

"It's January. Let's go to the beach!" Believe it or not, in Chile (CHEEL eh), a country in South America, January is the time to get out your swimsuit. January may be winter in the United States, but in Chile it is warm. When snowballs fly through the air in the northern United States, beach balls are flying in Chile.

Part of Chile's economy depends on this difference in weather. Warm weather goods from Chile go to winter buyers in the United States.

Many things affect a community's economy. You've learned that a community's resources provide employment. Weather also affects a community's economy.

Key Vocabulary

export
global market

January is the time to go to the beach in Chile.

◀ People throughout the world buy and sell things in markets.

1610	1810	2010

Marrakesh, Morocco

Many traditions are alive in the city of Marrakesh. *Lesson 2, Page 217*

Goods in Morocco

What do people sell in the markets in Marrakesh? *Lesson 2, Page 218*

Services in Morocco

The brass cups of the water sellers shine in the markets of Marrakesh. *Lesson 2, Page 220*

This man is picking grapes. Between 1993 and 1994, Chile exported nearly 33 million boxes of grapes to the United States. That's about one box for every ten people in the United States.

Biography

Gabriela Mistral

Lucila Godoy Alcayaga was born in 1889 in Chile. She was the principal of a school in Santiago when she won a poetry award. When she wrote, she used the name Gabriela Mistral. In 1945, Mistral won the Nobel Prize for literature. The Nobel Prize is one of the world's most famous prizes for literature.

Growing Fruit in Chile

Focus *What do farmers in Chile sell on the global market?*

The economy of a community is based on the goods and services it makes and sells. Many farmers in Chile earn money by growing fruit. They **export** a lot of this fruit — that is, they send it to other countries. When it's winter in the United States, fruits like plums and grapes don't grow here. People have to get those fruits from someplace else. When you bite into a sweet, juicy plum in winter, you may have a farmer in faraway Chile to thank.

Find Chile on the climate map on the next page. You can see that the climate in central Chile is best for growing fruit. That is where most fruit is grown in Chile. Farmers plant fruit. Later, fruit is harvested, sorted, and packed.

Fruit from Chile has taken a long trip. It started out in Chile. Then a boat or plane carried it to the United States. On boats, fruit is chilled so it doesn't spoil.

Farmers in Chile sell fruit on the global market. A **global market** means that goods from one part of the globe can be sold in another part. In a global market, farmers from Chile make money growing fruit for the world.

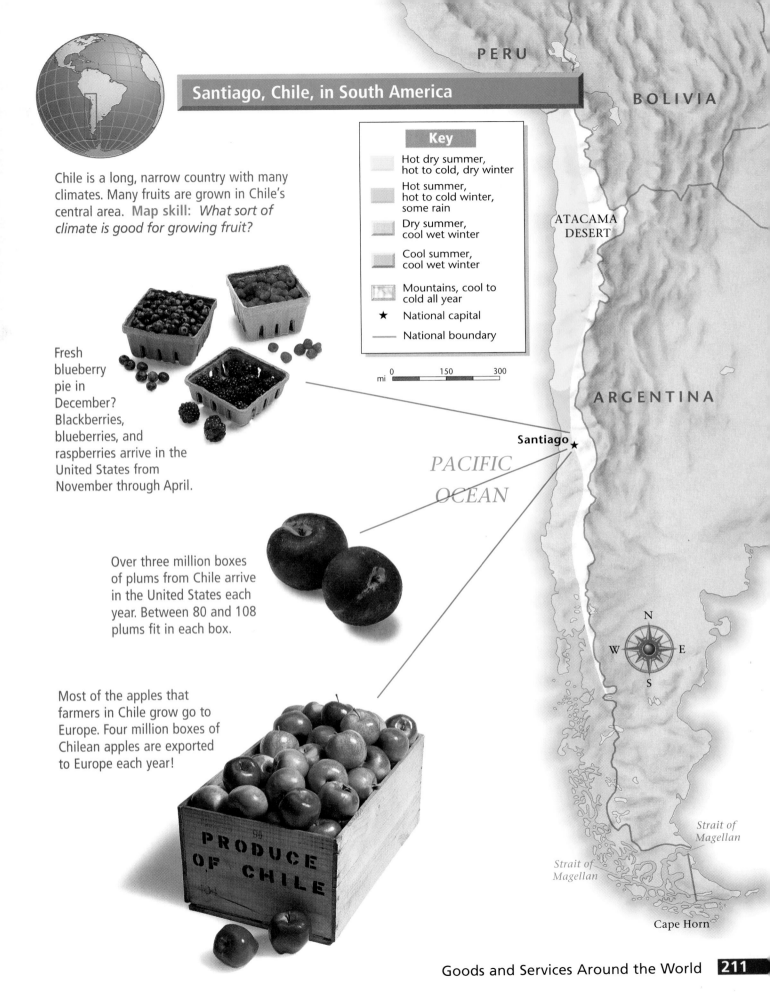

Santiago, Chile, in South America

Chile is a long, narrow country with many climates. Many fruits are grown in Chile's central area. **Map skill:** *What sort of climate is good for growing fruit?*

Key

Hot dry summer, hot to cold, dry winter

Hot summer, hot to cold winter, some rain

Dry summer, cool wet winter

Cool summer, cool wet winter

Mountains, cool to cold all year

★ National capital

— National boundary

mi 0 150 300

PERU

BOLIVIA

ATACAMA DESERT

ARGENTINA

Santiago ★

PACIFIC OCEAN

N
W E
S

Strait of Magellan

Strait of Magellan

Cape Horn

Fresh blueberry pie in December? Blackberries, blueberries, and raspberries arrive in the United States from November through April.

Over three million boxes of plums from Chile arrive in the United States each year. Between 80 and 108 plums fit in each box.

Most of the apples that farmers in Chile grow go to Europe. Four million boxes of Chilean apples are exported to Europe each year!

PRODUCE OF CHILE

Greetings from Santiago, Chile

- Children in Chile must go to school from the time they are five years old until they are 17.

- Santiago was founded in 1541. It is older than any city in the United States.

This girl is having her shoes shined in Santiago's *Plaza de Armas.* Many goods and services are sold there.
Economics: *Is shining shoes a good or a service?*

Working in Santiago

Focus *What types of work do people do in Santiago?*

Many fruit farms in Chile are near the city of Santiago (san tee AH goh). However, fewer than one in five workers in Chile are farmers. Most people in Chile live in cities, because that's where most jobs are. Jobs in factories or jobs selling goods or services bring people to the city.

Santiago is the capital of Chile. It is also the largest city in the country. Large cities everywhere offer many different kinds of goods and services. The farmers who live outside of Santiago go to the city for the goods and the services it offers. Others go to Santiago to work, shop, or visit. That makes Santiago important to Chile's economy.

The *Plaza de Armas* is a square in Santiago. It's a busy place — full of people. Some people go to the plaza just to sit and rest for a while. Other people work there. They sell goods and services. People visiting the plaza buy goods and services. For example, they might have their shoes shined. Artists in the plaza draw people's pictures. The shoeshiner and the artist both earn money for their work.

Many people in Chile enjoy playing and watching soccer. Santiago's stadium is very big. It can hold about 70,000 people. The stadium provides employment too.

In Chile, soccer is called *fútbol* (FOOT bohl). Many people go to Santiago to watch soccer matches.

The soccer players are employed playing soccer. Other people help the fans who come to the games. They take tickets, sell food, or clean the stands.

People in Chile can travel to Santiago on a bus. In Santiago, they can take the subway to get around the city. Buses and subway systems provide transportation. Transportation is a way of getting from one place to another. Bus and subway drivers are employed driving people from one place to the next. They provide a service for people who need transportation.

There are many kinds of employment. Some people grow food for export. Many other people find work in cities. Some sell goods and others provide services. What kinds of employment are there in your community?

Curious Facts

Flamingos and penguins in one place? Flamingos usually live in warm places. Penguins like the cold! Both kinds of birds live in southern Chile. It's not too cold for flamingos and close enough to the South Pole for penguins.

Lesson Review

1. **Key Vocabulary:** Use each word in a sentence: **export**, **global market**.

2. **Focus:** What do farmers in Chile sell on the global market?

3. **Focus:** What types of work do people do in Santiago?

4. **Critical Thinking: Sequence** What steps must a farmer take to grow fruit that can be shipped and sold?

5. **Theme: Depending on One Another** Name some goods that are made or grown in one part of the United States and sold in another.

6. **Geography/Science Activity:** Use the map of Chile to compare and contrast the different climates it shows. Write a paragraph that shows what you learned about Chile's climates from the map.

Human Systems

How Do Goods Travel Around the World?

A huge ship leaves San Antonio, Chile, and heads north along the coast of South America, bound for Philadelphia, Pennsylvania. This ship is carrying fruit to Philadelphia. Ships carrying goods from all over the world dock in Philadelphia. People in the United States also make and grow goods to sell to people in other parts of the world. People all over the world depend upon each other for the goods they need.

Math Connection

Goods can travel long distances. Use the scale on the map to measure the distance grapes travel from San Antonio, Chile, to Philadelphia, U.S.A.

Container ships like this one carry goods from one part of the world to another. They can carry almost anything, from rubber ducks to tennis shoes to car parts.

Research Activity

Signs and labels, in stores or on goods, can tell you where foods and goods are grown or made. Go on a goods search.

1 Make a list of goods at school, at home, or in a store.

2 After the name of each item, tell where it was made.

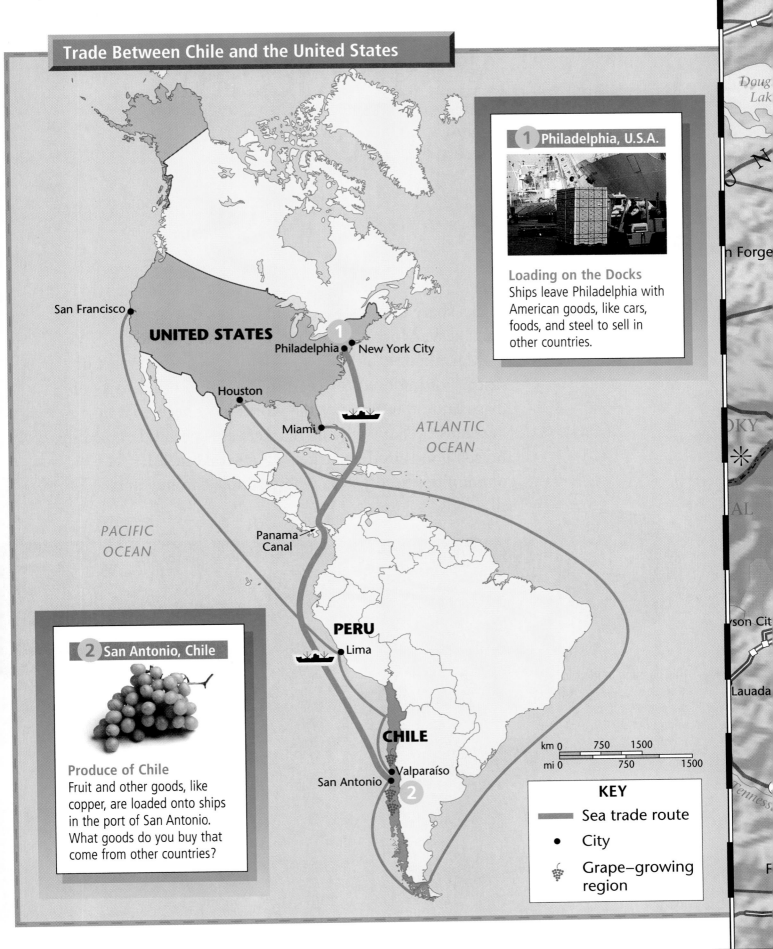

Trade Between Chile and the United States

San Francisco

UNITED STATES

Philadelphia • New York City

Houston

Miami

ATLANTIC OCEAN

PACIFIC OCEAN

Panama Canal

PERU
• Lima

CHILE

Valparaíso
San Antonio

1 Philadelphia, U.S.A.

Loading on the Docks
Ships leave Philadelphia with American goods, like cars, foods, and steel to sell in other countries.

2 San Antonio, Chile

Produce of Chile
Fruit and other goods, like copper, are loaded onto ships in the port of San Antonio. What goods do you buy that come from other countries?

km 0   750   1500
mi 0   750   1500

KEY
— Sea trade route
• City
🍇 Grape-growing region

A Moroccan Market

Main Idea People in Marrakesh buy and sell some goods and services in markets.

"Balek, balek!" calls the driver. "Make way, make way!" Trucks share the road with mules pulling wagons. In Marrakesh, Morocco, old and new meet every day.

Marrakesh is an old, old city in the northern part of Africa. For hundreds of years, goods from other parts of Africa and other parts of the world have been sold in Marrakesh. That's why its markets are special. People buy and sell goods in the markets of Marrakesh. All communities need places where people can buy and sell goods.

This bustling market in Marrakesh is filled with people buying and selling goods.

There are both large and small *souks* in Marrakesh. In this one, brightly colored yarn is sold.

Souks *in Marrakesh*

Focus *What is a* souk?

A *souk* (sook), or market, is one place where people in Morocco can shop. Some *souks* in Marrakesh are very large. At the *souks*, people from many towns come together. Farmers, craftspeople, and other merchants all sell goods. A merchant is a person who sells things. People who live in Marrakesh come to buy these goods. Tourists from all across the world buy goods too.

If you look for a price tag on goods in the *souks*, you may not find one. Instead, buyers ask the merchant what the price is. Then, buyer and seller start to bargain. When people **bargain**, there are no set prices for an item. The buyer and seller **negotiate**. They discuss the price in order to reach an agreement. Sometimes buyers pay with goods rather than with money. For example, to pay for a piece of cloth, a farmer might trade some vegetables. When buyer and seller agree, the bargaining stops.

•Tell Me More•

How Bargaining Works

Merchants (sellers) and customers (buyers) bargain for goods in Marrakesh. You can try it. Here's how it goes.

Customer: How much is this ball?
Merchant: I'll sell it to you for $5.

Customer: Ooh, that's too much. I'll give you $4.
Merchant: I can't sell it for $4, but I'll take $4.50.

Customer: I only have $4.25. I'll give you $4.25 and some lemonade.
Merchant: O.K., I'm thirsty.

Greetings from
Marrakesh

- This walled city was first built over 900 years ago. The Atlas Mountains separate the city from the Sahara.

- At school, children in Morocco learn in two languages, French and Arabic.

Goods in Marrakesh

Focus *What sorts of goods are for sale in Marrakesh?*

If you went to Marrakesh, you might see one of the largest *souks* in Morocco spread out before your eyes. Merchants and goods are all around you. Most people don't just look at those goods. They need to buy things for their families.

Merchants who sell the same types of goods have shops or stands near one another. A buyer moves about

Buyers and sellers from many places go to the largest *souk* in Marrakesh. **Economics:** *Have you ever been to an open-air market?*

the market. She buys some spices from a spice merchant. Then she buys fresh fruits and vegetables further on. Once she has paid for the goods, the buyer talks with the merchant. They tell each other their news. The *souk* is a good place for people to visit with one another.

Soon the buyer moves on. She looks at the baskets, but decides not to buy one. Now her shopping is done.

Some of the merchants make their goods right in the *souk*. Young boys carve wood that will be shaped into a table. Old men weave pieces of string into sturdy rope. Boys sit and knit caps in colorful patterns. Buyers can watch goods being made. Then they decide if they want to buy them. Many different goods are sold in the *souks*. Where do you shop for goods in your community?

Moroccan food is very spicy. Spices such as pepper, ginger, and mustard seed are ground fresh and sold in the *souk*.
Culture: *Does your family use spices to flavor food? Which spices are your favorites?*

Services in Marrakesh

This water seller keeps a goatskin full of water on his back. He sells a cup of water for five *centimes* (SAHN teem), or about a penny.

Focus *What are some of the services available in Marrakesh?*

Goods are not the only items for sale at the *souk*. Services are also sold there. Dentists pull teeth right in the *souk*. Water carriers sell sips of water in shiny brass cups. They also charge money to pose for pictures in their bright clothing.

People shopping in the *souk* may become hungry. Food sellers offer prepared food. For example, people can buy *shish kebab*. That is seasoned meat and vegetables roasted on sticks. Then they can go on shopping.

There is a large public square in Marrakesh. During the day, it too becomes a *souk*. Merchants sell goods there. In the afternoon, entertainers parade along the street. Acrobats leap, twirl, and tumble. Dancers thrill people with their graceful movements. Storytellers tell their tales. Some of those stories are sad. Some make you laugh. Others are scary. When the show is over, many people give money to the performers.

The *souk* is one center of commerce in Moroccan communities. **Commerce** is the buying and selling of goods. Like all

In Marrakesh, people use services like satellite dishes *(left)* and cellular telephones *(above)*. **Economics:** *How does technology help people in the world to communicate?*

Moroccan cities, Marrakesh also has the services of a modern community. It has a modern part with stores and doctors' offices. The airport, the police, and the hospitals are up-to-date. So are the telephones. Marrakesh is a modern city with many traditions.

Commerce is an important part of every community. Compare and contrast commerce in your community with commerce in Marrakesh.

Lesson Review

1 **Key Vocabulary:** Write a paragraph about a market using **bargain**, **negotiate**, and **commerce**.

2 **Focus:** What is a *souk*?

3 **Focus:** What sorts of goods are for sale in Marrakesh?

4 **Focus:** What are some of the services available in Marrakesh?

5 **Critical Thinking: Generalize** Why is it important that markets have both buyers and sellers?

6 **Citizenship:** In Marrakesh, people can exchange news in the marketplace. Where do people meet and exchange news in your community?

7 **Geography/Art Activity:** Where can people buy goods and services in your area? Draw a map that would help newcomers find goods and services.

Understanding Hemispheres

Half a World Away

North Pole

Equator

South Pole

The Earth has the shape of a sphere, or ball. We can't see a whole ball at once, but we can look at half a ball. The same is true of the Earth. Half the Earth is called a hemisphere. The word **hemisphere** comes from two Greek words: hemi=half, sphere=ball. If we slice the Earth through the Equator, we get the Northern Hemisphere and the Southern Hemisphere. We could slice the Earth in the other direction, from the North Pole to the South Pole. Then we get the Western Hemisphere and the Eastern Hemisphere.

Northern

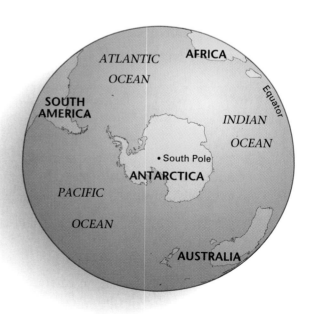

Southern

① Here's How

- Study the map of the Northern Hemisphere. The North Pole is in the center of this map. Which continents are in this hemisphere?

- Study the map of the Southern Hemisphere. What is at the center of this map? Which continents are in the Southern Hemisphere?

- Compare the maps of the Northern and Southern hemispheres. Which hemisphere has more land? Which has more water? Where do you live?

- Now study the maps of the Eastern and Western Hemispheres. Which continents appear in each hemisphere? Where do you live?

- The continent of North America is located in both the Northern and Western hemispheres. Find a continent located in the Southern and Eastern hemispheres.

② Think It Through

Why is it useful for geography to show the world in hemispheres?

③ Use It

Number and write the names of the seven continents. Look for the continents in each hemisphere. After each continent's name, list the hemispheres in which it can be found.

1. Africa   **5.** Europe

2. Antarctica   **6.** North America

3. Asia   **7.** South America

4. Australia

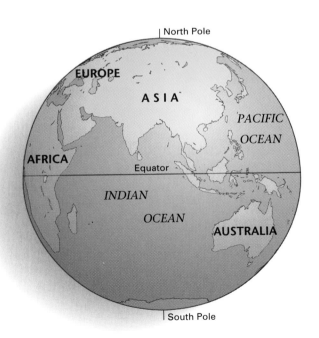

Eastern

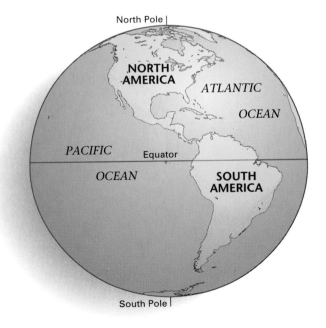

Western

Counting in Swahili

All around the world, counting is a part of exchanging goods and services, whether you are counting out pennies to buy bubble gum, or counting out eggs to trade for potatoes.

Swahili is widely spoken south of the Sahara Desert in Africa. It's the official language of Kenya and Tanzania. Swahili uses the same alphabet as English.

On Kenyan and Tanzanian farms, chickens run freely about the yard during the day, eating whatever they can find. Hunting for their eggs can take a while!

1 moja (MO-jah)
2 mbili (mm-BEE-lee)
3 tatu (TAH-too)
4 nne (NN-nay)
5 tano (TAH-no)
6 sita (SEE-tah)
7 saba (SAH-bah)
8 nane (NAH-nay)
9 tisa (TEE-sah)
10 kumi (KOO-mee)

The potter puts her own special designs on the pots she will take to market.

It's the job of the younger boys to take care of the family's goats and sheep.

 Response Activities

1. Classify
The people in the pictures on these pages are working. Which of them are making or getting goods. Which of them are providing services?

2. Descriptive: Write a Paragraph
In your paragraph, describe the people and animals in the illustrations. Tell what they are doing. Give the Swahili number for the people or animals in each illustration.

3. Geography: Find Them on a Map
Look at a map of Africa to find the countries in which Swahili is spoken. Locate the Sahara Desert, Kenya, and Tanzania.

Chapter Review

Summarizing the Main Idea

1 Copy and fill in the table below. Show how the communities of Chile and Marrakesh provide goods for others.

Goods and Services in the World		
	Santiago, Chile	Marrakesh, Morocco
Types of Goods		*spices, baskets, yarn*
Who Buys the Goods		
How the Goods Are Sold		

Vocabulary

2 Use all of the words below to write a paragraph about how a community might provide goods and services for others.

export (p. 210)   **bargain (p. 217)**   **commerce (p. 220)**

global market (p. 210)   **negotiate (p. 217)**

Reviewing the Facts

3 How does Chile's weather affect its economy?

4 What are some places to which Chile exports its goods?

5 How do Chile's goods get to the United States?

6 Why are *souks* important to people who live in Marrakesh?

7 Who are the people whom you might find in a *souk*?

8 What goods and services can people buy in Marrakesh?

Use the hemisphere maps on pages 222-223 to help you answer these questions.

9 What is a hemisphere?

10 What is the name of the hemisphere that is north of the equator?

11 Chile is in South America. What hemispheres is that in? Compare Chile to the United States, in North America. What hemisphere are they both in? What different hemispheres are they in?

Geography Skills

Use the map on page 211 for questions 12 and 13.

12 Compare the climates on the map. How are they the same? How are they different? How do you think the people in the different climates dress in the winter?

13 On the map, which climate seems to get the most rainfall? Which seems to get the least? Make a map that shows differences in rainfall. Use colors or symbols to show the difference in the amount of rainfall in different parts of Chile.

Writing: Citizenship and Culture

14 **Citizenship** Many people feel proud of their countries. Write a paragraph that shows how you think people in Chile felt when Gabriela Mistral won the Nobel Prize.

15 **Culture** Write a list of questions that you would like to ask the people in Marrakesh about their culture. Then write about how you could find the answers to your questions.

Activities

Economics/Research Activity
Use an encyclopedia to learn about a country that exports goods to sell on the global market. What types of goods does it sell? Write a short report about the information you found.

Economics/Math Activity
Set up a souk with your classmates. Decide what will be sold. Act out some bargaining situations. Make a chart that shows what was purchased and the price that it was sold for.

Internet Option

Check the
Internet Social Studies Center
for ideas on how to extend your theme project beyond your classroom.

THEME PROJECT CHECK-IN

Look at the business that you have decided on and answer these questions:
- Are you offering goods or a service that is different from others that are available?
- Is the price that you have set the best price? Might you bargain with a buyer to sell your goods or service? What would you accept besides money?

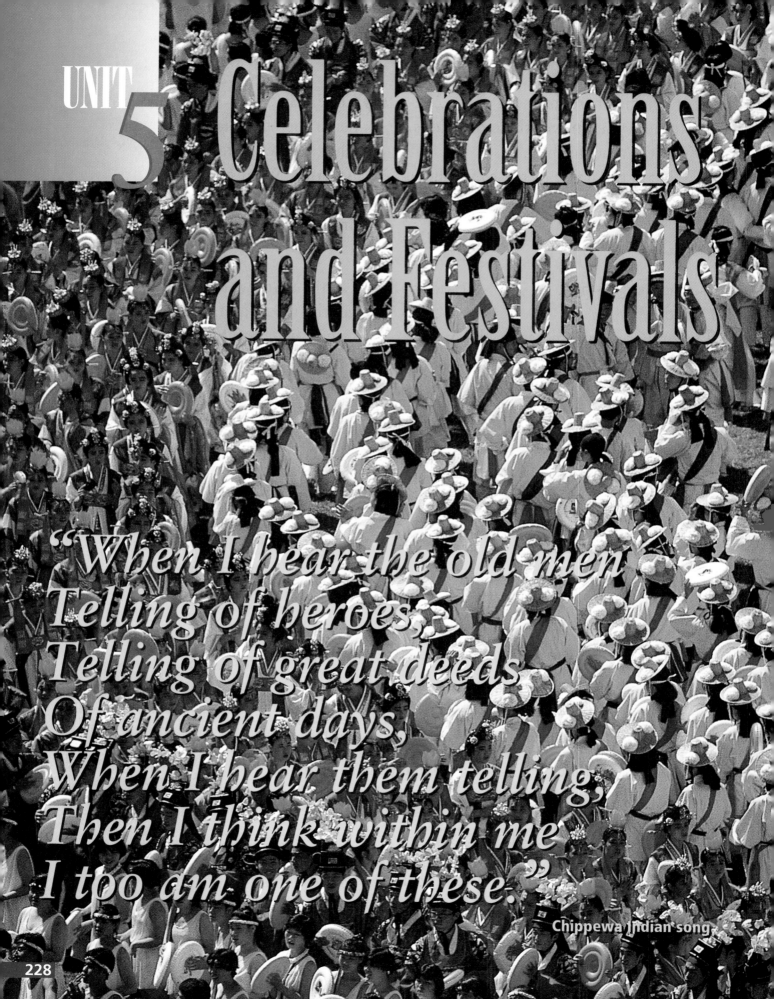

UNIT **5** Celebrations and Festivals

"When I hear the old men
Telling of heroes,
Telling of great deeds
Of ancient days,
When I hear them telling,
Then I think within me
I too am one of these."

Chippewa Indian song

228

· T H E M E ·

Traditions

" I like the Rice Festival because of the Cajun music and the food. Traditions are important because they express who you are. Holidays bring communities and families together. "

Brittney Mills, Crowley, Louisiana

Parades! Holidays! Festivals! These are things that happen on special days. They mean special music, special clothes, and special food. You can also learn a lot from these special events. Celebrations tell you what people in a community care about. They reflect the customs and traditions of the people who live there. By understanding why people celebrate the way they do, you can learn more about yourself and your own community. This unit invites you to do that!

 Theme Project

Perform a Play

Does your community have a festival to celebrate its beginning? Find out how your community was started. Then work with other students to write and perform a play about the beginning of your community. Find out:

- When your community was started.
- Who started your community.
- Why people started your community when they did and where they did.

◀ People everywhere come together to celebrate their cultures.

WHEN & WHERE
ATLAS

 The communities on this world map have different histories and cultures. Yet they are like everyone in the world in one important way. They celebrate the important events in their history.

In this unit, you will learn about the customs of people in the United States and other countries. You will read about some of the many ways communities celebrate events that are important to them. Learning about the special customs of different communities will help you better understand the people who practice them.

Unit 5 Chapters

Chapter 9 Our Country Celebrates

Chapter 10 A World of Celebrations

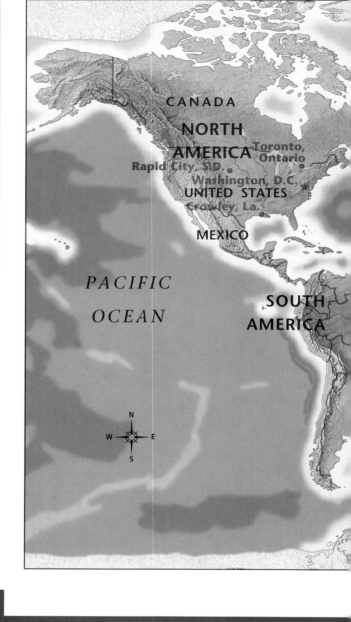

CANADA

NORTH

AMERICA   Toronto, Ontario

Rapid City, S.D.

Washington, D.C.

UNITED STATES

Crowley, La.

MEXICO

PACIFIC

OCEAN

SOUTH

AMERICA

N

W   E

S

Unit Timeline

1750	1800	1850

Clowning Around

Come celebrate the Fourth of July in Rapid City, South Dakota! *Chapter 9, Lesson 1*

Another U.S.

Is this your uncle? It's Uncle Sam, a symbol of the United States. *Chapter 9, Lesson 1*

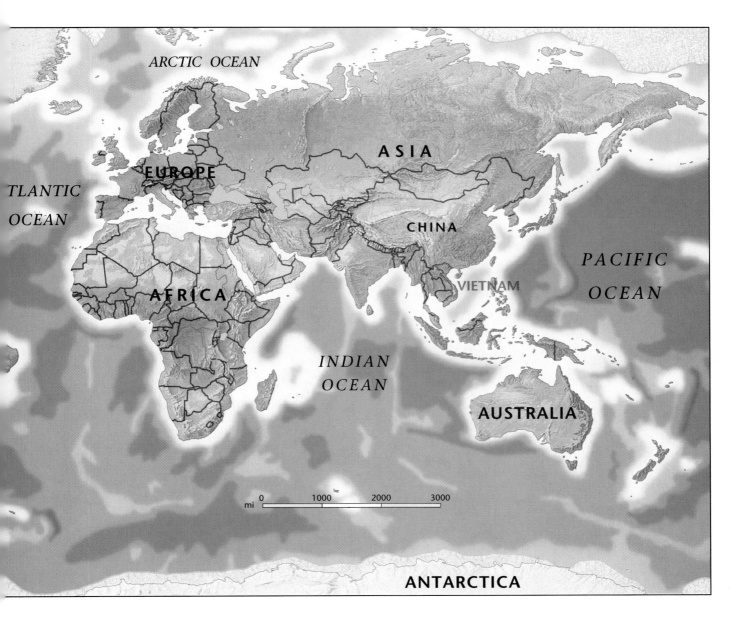

ARCTIC OCEAN

EUROPE

ASIA

ATLANTIC OCEAN

AFRICA

CHINA

VIETNAM

PACIFIC OCEAN

INDIAN OCEAN

AUSTRALIA

0   1000   2000   3000
mi

ANTARCTICA

1900   1950   2000

How Far Can She Jump?

Join in the fun at festivals in Louisiana! *Chapter 9, Lesson 2*

Celebrating Cultures

People share their cultures at Festival Caravan in Toronto. *Chapter 10, Lesson 1*

Put On a Happy Face

People in Vietnam celebrate the New Year with masks like these. *Chapter 10, Lesson 2*

Our Country Celebrates

Chapter Preview: *People, Places, and Events*

Dinosaurs!

You can see these giant dinosaur statues in Rapid City, South Dakota. *Lesson 1, Page 234*

Remembering Our Past 1776

Who made the earliest American flag? *Lesson 1, Page 236*

Happy Birthday, U.S.A.!

Find out how people in Washington, D.C., celebrate the Fourth of July. *Lesson 1, Page 237*

The Fourth of July

Main Idea The Fourth of July is a day of celebrating the United States and its communities.

Key Vocabulary
independent
Independence Day
heritage
fossil

Clang! Clang! Wildly and joyously, the bells rang out in July of 1776 from steeples in Philadelphia, Pennsylvania. One was the Liberty Bell. People rang bells to celebrate the Declaration of Independence. America's leaders approved the Declaration on July 4, 1776. It said that the colonies would form their own **independent** country. They would rule themselves. They would no longer be part of Great Britain.

Now July 4 is known as **Independence Day.** All over the United States on July 4, Americans celebrate their freedom. The Liberty Bell has become a symbol of independence.

This locator map shows you where Rapid City is. **Map Skill:** *Is Rapid City closer to Canada or to Mexico?*

◀ Fireworks explode as people in Washington, D.C., celebrate Independence Day.

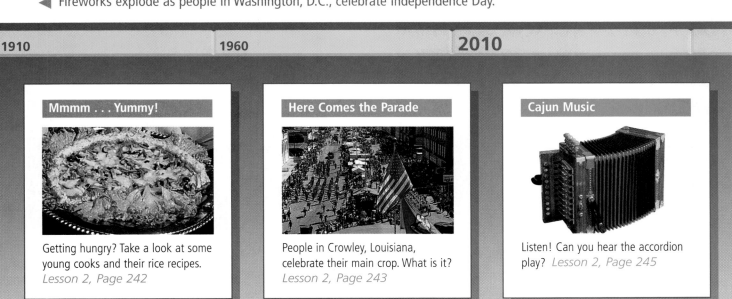

1910   1960   2010

Mmmm . . . Yummy!

Getting hungry? Take a look at some young cooks and their rice recipes. *Lesson 2, Page 242*

Here Comes the Parade

People in Crowley, Louisiana, celebrate their main crop. What is it? *Lesson 2, Page 243*

Cajun Music

Listen! Can you hear the accordion play? *Lesson 2, Page 245*

- The population is 54,523. Rapid City is the second largest city in South Dakota. (The largest city is Sioux Falls.)

- The Sioux Indian Museum has a beautiful collection of Sioux art.

- Life-size dinosaur models can be seen in Dinosaur Park.

Independence Day in Rapid City

Focus *How do people celebrate the Fourth of July in Rapid City, South Dakota?*

You probably have a favorite holiday. Some holidays honor people, like Martin Luther King, Jr. Others, like Independence Day, help people remember historic events. Still others are religious holidays. Many holidays bring people in a community together.

On the Fourth of July, communities all across the United States celebrate Independence Day. Often the celebration shows something special about a community.

This clown is just one of many people performing for kids in Rapid City. Red, white, and blue ribbons look like our flag!

Rapid City, South Dakota, has an interesting way to celebrate Independence Day. That community is located in the Black Hills. Rapid City celebrates the holiday with the Black Hills Heritage Festival. The **heritage** of a place or a group is people's language, customs, and beliefs. These have been passed down from parents to children.

Fossils and Fun

During the festival, cowboy poets read their poems. The cattle industry is very important in South Dakota. So people there are interested in cowhands' experiences.

People in Rapid City are also interested in what South Dakota was like long ago. In the Archaeology Fair, children learn about fossils that have been found in the area. A **fossil** is the remains of a living thing that died long ago. Many fossils have been found in South Dakota.

Native Americans like the Sioux (soo) teach people about their culture. Many Sioux live in the Black Hills area near Rapid City.

Children are a big part of any community. In the Black Hills Heritage Festival, children take part in art contests and talent shows. Both children and adults love to watch the fireworks.

Then & Now

The Declaration of Independence was approved on July 4, 1776. One year later, many cities held celebrations on the Fourth of July. People rang bells and held parades. Ever since then, the Fourth of July has been celebrated as the nation's birthday.

The people on the left are learning about fossils. The artist on the right is painting a tipi.

Declaration of Independence

The Declaration of Independence played a big part in the history of the United States. Before there was a country called the United States, there were 13 colonies in America. Great Britain and its king, George III, ruled the colonies. But many colonists began to think that Great Britain was not treating them fairly. After much thought, the colonies decided to be independent, or free, from Great Britain. The Declaration explained their reasons.

Thomas Jefferson wrote most of the Declaration of Independence. It said that people have certain rights. One of these is the right to change an unfair government.

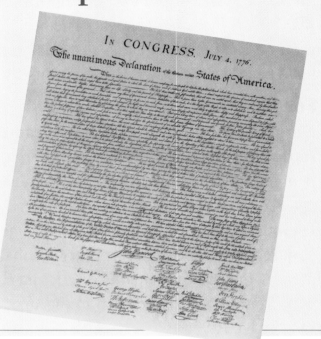

Biography

Betsy Ross

Betsy Ross lived in Philadelphia when the Declaration of Independence was signed. She may have been the first person to make an American flag with stars and stripes.

- - - - - - - - - -

Uncle Sam *(right)*, like the Liberty Bell, is a symbol of the United States. You might see him on the Fourth of July!

Celebration in Washington, D.C.

Focus *How does Washington, D.C., celebrate the whole country on the Fourth of July?*

Far to the east of Rapid City lies Washington, D.C. This city is the capital of the United States. Independence Day in Washington, D.C., celebrates the heritage of the whole nation, rather than just one community.

The celebration has a serious side. To remind people of what the holiday is about, the Declaration of Independence is read aloud. You can read more about this important document at the top of the page.

The celebration is also fun, and people from many parts of the country share in that fun. A colorful parade marches through the streets of the capital. Bands from all around the country march in the parade.

National Pride

After the parade, there are concerts. Musicians and singers perform for the crowds. Their music comes from many cultures. Do you like jazz, blues, or country and western songs? You'll hear them all in Washington on the Fourth of July.

The celebration ends with a fireworks show. Brilliant explosions of red, yellow, green, and other colors fill the night sky with light.

All Fourth of July celebrations have one thing in common. They celebrate pride in the United States. On this holiday, we take pride in this country's freedoms. We remember an important day in this nation's history, too.

Fireworks light up the night in Washington, D.C., on Independence Day. **Cultures:** *What are some ways you celebrate special days?*

Lesson Review

❶ **Key Vocabulary:** Use the following words in sentences: **independent, Independence Day, heritage, fossil.**

❷ **Focus:** How do people celebrate the Fourth of July in Rapid City, South Dakota?

❸ **Focus:** How does Washington, D.C., celebrate the whole country on the Fourth of July?

❹ **Critical Thinking: Compare** How does Washington, D.C.'s Fourth of July celebration differ from Rapid City's?

❺ **Theme: Traditions** How does your community honor the Fourth of July? Are your traditions like those in Rapid City? Why or why not?

❻ **Citizenship/Arts Activity:** Choose a symbol for your community. Make a poster about your community using it. Explain what the symbol means.

Using Inset Maps

What's in That Box?

There you are at the Washington Monument on the Fourth of July. You want to walk to the Capitol to see the fireworks. So you look at your map. It shows the whole Washington area — including major highways and nearby towns. There's no Capitol, no street names. Wouldn't it be great to put this part of the map under a magnifying glass and see it close up?

Using an inset map, you can do just that. An **inset map** gives a close-up view of part of a map. Let's see how it works.

1 Here's How

The maps on the next page show two views of Washington, D.C. — a large view and a close-up view.

- Study the large map of the District of Columbia. What state names are on this map? The box in the center marks the District of Columbia. What other places appear on the map? Do you see the Capitol?

- The inset map gives a close-up view of the District of Columbia. Find the Capitol on the inset map. What other places appear only on the inset map? What places appear on both maps?

- Now look at the scale in the large view. What distance does one inch stand for? On the inset map, what distance does one inch stand for?

- Find the distance from the White House to the Washington Monument. Which map did you use?

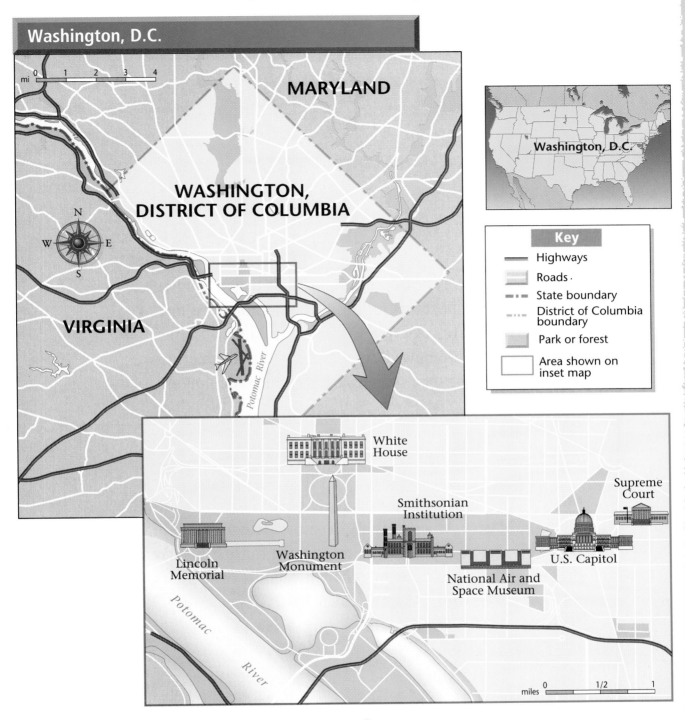

Washington, D.C.

MARYLAND

WASHINGTON, DISTRICT OF COLUMBIA

VIRGINIA

Washington, D.C.

Key
- Highways
- Roads
- State boundary
- District of Columbia boundary
- Park or forest
- Area shown on inset map

Potomac River

White House

Smithsonian Institution

Supreme Court

Lincoln Memorial

Washington Monument

National Air and Space Museum

U.S. Capitol

Potomac River

miles 0   1/2   1

2 Think It Through

What would happen if you tried to show all the places on the inset map on the map of the larger area? Could you read the names? Could you measure distances between the places? Why?

Washington, D.C., contains many monuments to American heroes of the past. In the photograph to the left, you can see parts of the Lincoln Memorial, the Washington Monument, and the Capitol Building.

3 Use It

Different maps are good for different things. Which map would you use to answer these questions?

1. How do you get from the White House to the Capitol?

2. What states lie east and west of Washington, D.C.?

3. How far is it from the Lincoln Memorial to the Supreme Court?

4. Which museum is closest to the White House?

★ CITIZENSHIP ★

Participating

Do Traditions Change?

Traditions are ways of doing things that began long ago. Holidays are important traditions. Some holidays, like Thanksgiving, are very old. Others, like Martin Luther King, Jr., Day, are new. Powwow is a Native American tradition, but the way people celebrate it has changed.

Case Study

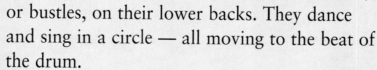

Powwow

On a warm summer night near the Black Hills of South Dakota, Native Americans and visitors gather to celebrate powwow. Some people wear traditional outfits: buckskin dresses and leather breechcloths with bands of feathers, or bustles, on their lower backs. They dance and sing in a circle — all moving to the beat of the drum.

Recently, some dancers have begun wearing brightly dyed feathers, sequins, and streamers in neon colors. These "fancy dancers" now leap and spin and compete for prizes.

Native Americans have always danced at powwows to honor their war heroes. They also dance to honor friends and changes in people's lives. Powwow dancing is one of the oldest traditions in the United States.

Take Action

Have some parts of your traditions changed over time, and some parts stayed the same? Think about traditions in your school, like the first and last days of school, or sports days, or graduations. You also have traditions at home and in your neighborhood—birthdays, holidays, picnics, and so on. Make a class book that shows your traditions!

1 As a class, decide whether you want your book to have many different traditions or whether everyone should pick the same tradition to think about.

2 Write a description of how you celebrate the tradition you choose. Draw a picture of it.

3 Interview an older person to find out how people used to celebrate your tradition. Write down what you learn. Draw a picture of it.

4 Combine your descriptions and drawings on one page. Design your page so it shows how the tradition is the same and/or different over time.

5 Put all the pages together. Give your book a title. Read it. Discuss how and why the traditions have changed and stayed the same.

Tips for Participating

- Listen to others' ideas. Ask questions when you don't understand.
- When group members can't agree, see if you can figure out what needs to change so more people can agree.
- Learn about your subject so you have more to offer to the group.

Research Activity

Interview an adult in your school or community to find out how a tradition involving many people has changed. Has the celebration changed? How? Why? How might you change one of your traditions to reflect your changing times?

A Rice Festival

Main Idea People in the Cajun area of Louisiana celebrate a natural resource and their cultural heritage.

Add some chopped onions. Shake on a little bit of hot pepper. Juicy, fresh tomatoes might make it yummy.

It's hard to think of new ways to fix food. But that's exactly what a lot of young cooks did. They dreamed up delicious rice dishes for a contest. The winners are . . . Danielle Leger, Dayle Chatagnier, and Kori Meyers!

The cooking contest is part of the Crowley International Rice Festival. That festival is held every October in Crowley, Louisiana. Rice is grown in the area. Rice is an important natural resource to the community.

Above (left to right): Danielle Leger, Dayle Chatagnier, and Kori Meyers with their prizewinning rice dishes. *Below:* Crowds come to the Crowley International Rice Festival every October.

Greetings from

Crowley

- The Crowley International Rice Festival was first held in 1927. Its parade is in the picture.
- The population of Crowley is 14,375.
- The community was named after Pat Crowley, a railroad worker.

A Harvest Celebration

Focus *How do the people of Crowley celebrate the natural resource of rice?*

All over the world, people hold festivals at harvest time. A **harvest** is the bringing in of crops. In 1621, the Pilgrims held a Thanksgiving feast to give thanks for their harvest. The Crowley International Rice Festival is also a harvest festival. It celebrates a food crop — rice.

In Crowley, many people's jobs depend on rice. Farmers in the community grow the rice. Other people ship the rice to buyers. Still others cook it in restaurants. So the festival honors a way of earning a living.

At the Festival

If you go to the festival, get ready for a good time. People in Crowley get together to have fun. Bundles of rice stalks decorate the lampposts. Rice also decorates floats in parades. Schoolchildren help decorate some of the floats. Just as you'd expect, there's great food — and a lot of it. People eat rice with other foods from the region, such as crawfish. A spicy sausage called boudin (boo DAN) is made from rice and ground meat.

Curious Facts

Every year, the community of Rayne, Louisiana, has a Frog Festival. Frog-racing, frog-jumping, and — yikes! — frog-eating contests are among the events at the Frog Festival.

Cajun Louisiana

Focus *How do Cajuns share their heritage at the Rice Festival?*

Many Cajuns live in southern Louisiana, as shown in the map below. But Cajuns aren't the only people who live in that area. Other ethnic groups live there, too. **Map Skill:** *Is Shreveport in the Cajun region? Is Lafayette? What about New Orleans?*

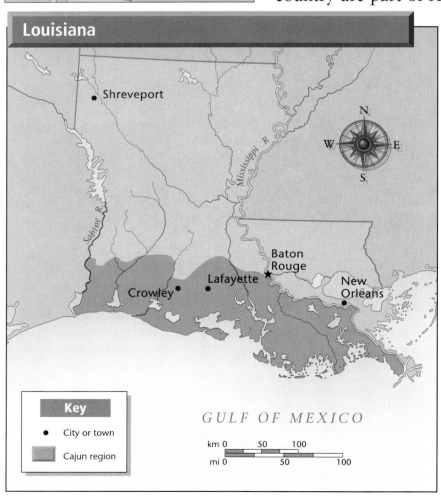

Boudin and other foods at the festival are part of Cajun tradition. A **Cajun** (CAY juhn) is a person who is descended from a large group of French-speaking people who moved to Louisiana in the 1700s. They moved from a part of Canada that was called *Acadie* in French. The people from that area were called *Acadien*. Sometimes people shortened the word to *'Cadien*. Over time the word turned into Cajun. The large map shows the area of Louisiana in which many Cajuns live today.

The Cajuns and other ethnic groups in this country are part of American culture. They celebrate national holidays like Independence Day. Each ethnic group also has its own special heritage.

Music is an important part of Cajun heritage. Bands at the festival play Cajun music on instruments like accordions and fiddles. Craftspeople show how to make the instruments in the traditional way.

Karlo Broussard (BROO sahrd), who is 13 years old, plays the accordion. His band won first prize in the Rice Festival accordion contest.

The band is called *Karlo et Amis,* which is French for "Karlo and Friends." Karlo says,

"**M**y dad's sure proud. . . . After my dad taught me to play some songs, I learned to play by ear. I only play Cajun music. Cajun music is fun to dance to."

Karlo Broussard is a young Cajun musician. He plays the accordion, shown above.
Cultures: *How is Karlo sharing his heritage with others?*

Karlo loves to listen to all the other bands at the Rice Festival. That's one reason that community festivals are special. They bring people together to have fun and to celebrate their heritage.

Lesson Review

1. **Key Vocabulary:** Write a paragraph about the Rice Festival. Use the words **harvest** and **Cajun.**

2. **Focus:** How do the people of Crowley celebrate the natural resource of rice?

3. **Focus:** How do Cajuns share their heritage at the Rice Festival?

4. **Critical Thinking: Interpret** Some festivals have a serious mood. Others are lively and even funny. What is the mood of the International Rice Festival? What about the festival shows this mood?

5. **Geography:** Why do people from many cultures celebrate harvests from their land?

6. **Theme: Traditions/Writing Activity** Write an advertisement for the Crowley International Rice Festival.

Environment and Society

How Did Swedish Settlers Build Their New Lives?

Some immigrants to the United States from Sweden ended up in Minnesota. In their letters home they told about a land and climate much like that in Sweden. Soon more Swedish families arrived in America. In time, Minnesota had large communities of Swedish settlers.

Many of the newcomers became farmers. Others worked in mines or lumber mills. They lived in a new land, but many people in Minnesota recalled their Swedish roots. They still celebrate Swedish holidays such as Midsummer Day. If you were to visit, you might hear Swedish music, eat Swedish foods, and see buildings that look Swedish.

Hilma Swenson Anderson (center), her brother, and her friend emigrated from Sweden to the United States in 1910.

The store to the left, from a Swedish community, looks like a nineteenth century American store, but has signs in Swedish and some Swedish goods. Why might Swedish settlers choose to shop there?

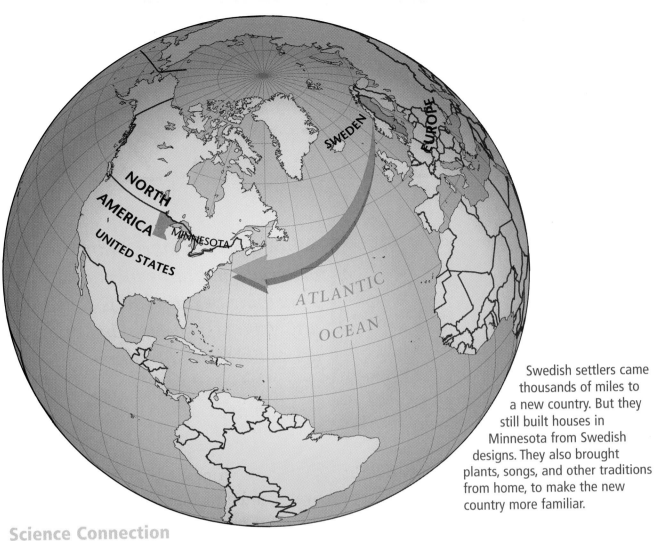

Swedish settlers came thousands of miles to a new country. But they still built houses in Minnesota from Swedish designs. They also brought plants, songs, and other traditions from home, to make the new country more familiar.

Science Connection

Many parts of Sweden have snowy winters. People there enjoy outdoor activities, like skiing. Swedish settlers found that Minnesota had snowy winters too. How do you think this made the settlers feel?

Research Activity

1 Think about the food, clothing, homes, transportation, plants, and animals in your area.

2 Write a short paragraph showing how the climate in your area affects these parts of life.

Swedish communities in Minnesota still make ginger cookies as they did in Sweden. What foods would you want to have if you moved somewhere else?

from *National Geographic World* May 1992

ZENY'S ZOO

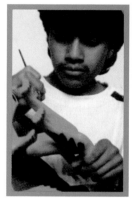

When a person takes ordinary materials and turns them into something beautiful, it is called folk art. Making a special kind of folk art can become a tradition in a community or in a family.

How did the zebra get its stripes? Zeny Fuentes (above) painted them. . . just as he painted pink fur on the coyote in his hands and polka dots on the armadillo (right). Zeny lives in Oaxaca (wuh-HAHK-uh), a state in Mexico. Woodcarvers there are famous for their art — colorful creatures in bold shapes. At school Zeny, 17, didn't study art, but he is already a well-known artist. He has traveled to the United States to show his work at a gallery in Kansas City, Missouri.

"I learned how to carve from my father and grandfather," Zeny says. He uses simple tools such as a pocket knife and a larger knife called a machete (muh-SHET-ee). Zeny started carving

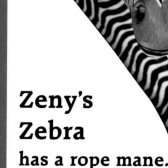

Zeny's Zebra has a rope mane.

when he was 8. "At first my pieces looked stiff and rough," he recalls. "Now I can give the animals more personality." Zeny carves animals he has seen in his village, in books, or on television. But he paints most of them in colors that, he says, are "pure fantasy."

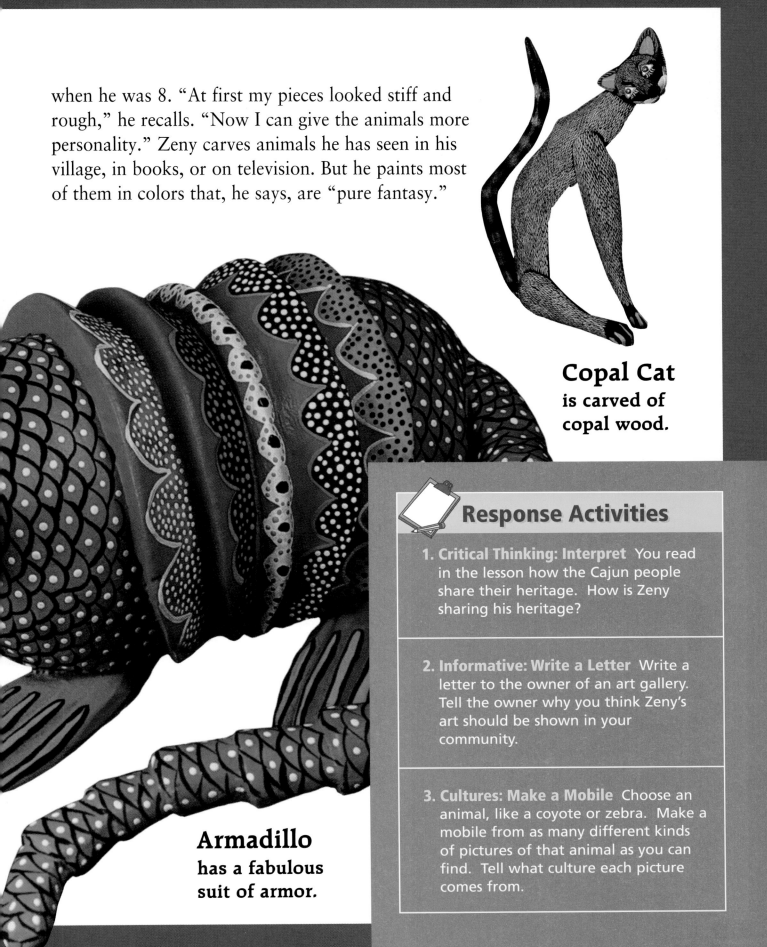

Copal Cat
is carved of
copal wood.

Armadillo
has a fabulous
suit of armor.

Response Activities

1. **Critical Thinking: Interpret** You read in the lesson how the Cajun people share their heritage. How is Zeny sharing his heritage?

2. **Informative: Write a Letter** Write a letter to the owner of an art gallery. Tell the owner why you think Zeny's art should be shown in your community.

3. **Cultures: Make a Mobile** Choose an animal, like a coyote or zebra. Make a mobile from as many different kinds of pictures of that animal as you can find. Tell what culture each picture comes from.

Chapter Review

Summarizing the Main Idea

1 Copy and fill in the chart below. Show what people celebrate and how they celebrate it.

What People Celebrate and How			
	Fourth of July, Rapid City, South Dakota	Fourth of July, Washington, D.C.	Rice Festival Crowley, Louisiana
What People Celebrate		The United States	
How They Celebrate			

Vocabulary

2 Write sentences using each word below. Write about what people celebrate and how they celebrate.

independent (p. 233)   **heritage** (p. 235)   **harvest** (p. 243)

Independence Day (p. 233)   **fossil** (p. 235)   **Cajun** (p. 244)

Reviewing the Facts

3 What do people in the United States celebrate on Independence Day?

4 What things make the celebration of Fourth of July in Rapid City, South Dakota, special?

5 Why is the Declaration of Independence read aloud on the Fourth of July in Washington, D.C.?

6 What do all Fourth of July celebrations have in common?

7 How do people in Crowley, Louisiana, celebrate the harvest?

8 How do Cajuns share their heritage at the Rice Festival?

Use the maps on page 239 for questions 9 and 10.

9 Would you use the main map or the inset map to find a path from the White House to the U.S. Capitol? Why?

10 Suppose you were making a main map and an inset map of your school. What information would you put on each map? Why? Sketch your maps. Make sure you include a map key.

Critical Thinking

11 **Comparing Then and Now** How do you think early celebrations of Independence Day were different from those today?

12 **Conclude** Why do you think that the culture and heritage of different groups are part of Fourth of July celebrations?

13 **Interpret** Why are celebrations important to a community?

Writing: Citizenship and Cultures

14 **Citizenship** Look again at the Pledge of Allegiance and National Anthem on pages 64-65. How do the pledge and anthem reflect the ideas of an Independence Day celebration?

15 **Cultures** Suppose your community were going to hold a cultural festival. What traditions from your family would you choose to share? Write a proposal that tells what you will do to share your culture.

Activities

Geography/Research Activity
You have read that many people have festivals at harvest time. Do research to find out about harvest festivals around the world. How do people celebrate? When? Where?

Citizenship/Art Activity
Uncle Sam is one symbol of the United States. Find some more American symbols. Make a coloring book that tells what each symbol means.

Internet Option

Check the **Internet Social Studies Center** for ideas on how to extend your theme project beyond your classroom.

THEME PROJECT CHECK-IN

Think about the play you are writing and answer these questions:
• Have you included any symbols that are important in your community's history?
• Have you included stories about how your community started?
• Have you included a description of the natural resources in your community? Does your community celebrate those resources?

CHAPTER 10

A World of Celebrations

Chapter Preview: *People, Places, and Events*

1935	1950	1965

City Lights

You'll find more than you expected in this city. *Lesson 1, Page 254*

Dance With Us!

These people are sharing their culture. Find out how. *Lesson 1, Page 254*

Feel the Beat

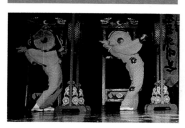

Listen to all the sounds of Festival Caravan in Toronto, Canada. *Lesson 1, Page 255*

Celebrating Cultures

Main Idea In the festival called Caravan, Canadians celebrate their cultural diversity.

Take a trip around the world. Travel to countries in Asia or visit islands in the Caribbean.

For nine days in June in Toronto, Canada, you can do all that at a festival called Caravan. This festival celebrates many cultures. You can learn about 40 different countries — without ever leaving Toronto!

When you travel to another country, you usually need a passport. A real **passport** is a government document that lets you leave your own country to visit others. You use another kind of passport in Toronto. It isn't a real passport. It's a ticket to Caravan. Are you ready? Let's go!

Here's your passport for Toronto's Festival Caravan!

◀ This dancer is sharing her cultural heritage at Festival Caravan.

| 1980 | 1995 | 2010 |

Sailing Into a New Year

Let's visit a celebration in Vietnam!
Lesson 2, Page 264

Surprise Package

What do you think is waiting inside this present? *Lesson 2, Page 265*

Dragons Dancing!

Would you like to meet a dragon? You can see them in a New Year parade! *Lesson 2, Page 266*

Greetings from

Toronto

- Toronto, with more than 3,000,000 people, is the largest city in Canada.
- The two official languages of Canada are English and French.
- The word Toronto meant "much," "many," or "land of plenty" in the language of the Huron people.

These people are sharing customs from Greece and Ukraine (yoo KRAYN). **Cultures:** *Why do people wear special clothes for celebrations?*

A Community's Traditions

Focus *How does Toronto celebrate its many cultures?*

What would you take with you if you went to another country? You would take more than your clothes or your passport. You'd take your culture too! People have moved to Toronto from countries all over the world. When they moved, they brought their cultures with them.

At one time, each ethnic group had its own festival to celebrate its own culture. In 1969, people began Festival Caravan to combine the festivals. Caravan celebrates Toronto's **cultural diversity,** its mixture of many cultures.

Music and dance groups from countries like South Korea and Finland have made special trips to Toronto. People in these countries wanted to take part in Caravan. This festival connects communities all around the world.

Let's use our special passport. As we walk around Toronto, we see that Caravan is divided into 40 separate exhibits. The exhibits are called pavilions (puh VIL yuhnz). Each pavilion is named for a city in a different country. It shows examples of that country's culture. Below is a map of Caravan pavilions. Let's take a trip to Athens, Greece!

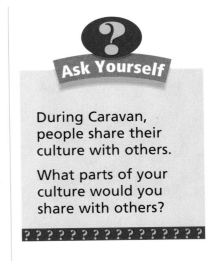

Ask Yourself

During Caravan, people share their culture with others.

What parts of your culture would you share with others?

The map shows the Caravan pavilions in Toronto. **Map Skill:** *Start at the Athens pavilion and walk west. Which pavilion do you come to first?*

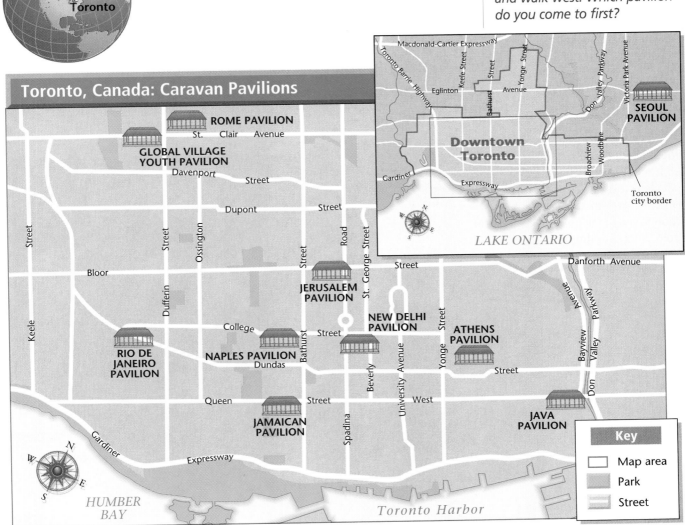

Jane Jacobs

When people planned new, bigger buildings for Toronto in 1968, Jane Jacobs said no! She had written a book that said that cities need places for people to meet, have fun, and make friends. Many city planners now know that she was right.

Holding On to Tradition

Focus *How do people in Toronto pass on their traditions?*

People keep traditions alive by teaching them to others. During Caravan, Toronto's ethnic groups share their traditions with the whole community. Families keep their traditions alive by passing them on to their children.

If you lived in Toronto, you could take classes to learn about Greek culture and traditions. On Saturday mornings in Toronto, many children do just that! They learn about the history and people of Greece. They study the language.

What else could you learn about other cultures? Jerry Jerome would answer "music." Music is part of Jerry's heritage. You read about some kinds of heritage in the last chapter. Your heritage can be many different things. It can be something you can touch, like a picture of your great-grandmother. It can be a custom, like playing steel drum music.

These children are all from different pavilions at the Festival Caravan. Though they may be from different ethnic groups, they are all part of Canada.

Jerry moved to Toronto from the island of Trinidad. Jerry teaches children how to play the steel drum. He always invites children to join him on-stage at Caravan. Jerry says,

Jerry Jerome passes on a tradition by teaching others to play the steel drum. Below are a steel drum and mallets.

> **"I**n my family, there is always music or steel drums. It just became a part of me. Kids enjoy my music and I share my culture.**"**

What do you know about other cultures in your community? What do you know about your own culture? Whatever your ethnic group is, learning about your culture is an important part of growing up.

Lesson Review

1 **Key Vocabulary:** Use **passport** and **cultural diversity** in a paragraph about a visit to Festival Caravan.

2 **Focus:** How does Toronto celebrate its many cultures?

3 **Focus:** How do people in Toronto pass on their traditions?

4 **Critical Thinking: Interpret** Why is Caravan important to the community of Toronto?

5 **Citizenship:** It is important to respect the traditions of other cultures and communities. Explain why.

6 **Geography/Arts Activity:** Suppose your community was having a festival. Draw a map that shows how it could be set up around your city. Choose symbols that stand for any hospitals, police or fire stations, schools, or other buildings found in the area. Draw the symbols on a map key.

Skills Workshop

Using Maps to See Cause and Effect

Why There?

The Caravan festival celebrates the different people who live in Toronto. Today, people move to Toronto to find jobs in offices, stores, and factories. But what brought people to Toronto before it was a big city?

1 Here's How

People move to places for many reasons. Some places have natural features or resources that make life easier. Some places have good farmland. Others have good climates. The map on this page shows the natural features around Toronto. It can help us understand why it became a city.

- Find Toronto on the map. What bodies of water do you see? On what body of water is Toronto located?

- Before people built good roads, they often traveled by water. Do you see any water routes to Toronto?

- Find Lake Simcoe. Trace water routes from Lake Simcoe to other parts of Canada. Long ago, fur traders used these routes to hunt and to bring furs to market.

- Toronto, on the shore of Lake Ontario, is between Lake Ontario and Lake Simcoe. How did this location help fur traders?

- Study the land around Toronto. Is the land flat? Are there mountains? Would the land be easy to farm? How would Toronto's location help farmers? What other ways could people make a living here?

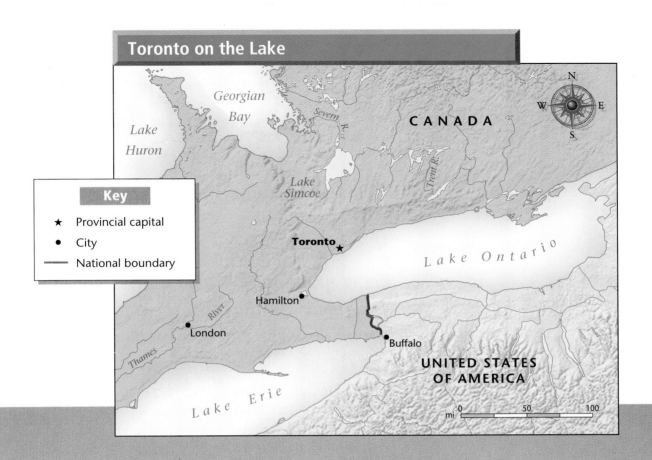

Toronto on the Lake

Georgian Bay

Lake Huron

Severn R.

Lake Simcoe

CANADA

Trent R.

Key
★ Provincial capital
● City
— National boundary

Toronto ★

Lake Ontario

Hamilton ●

London ●

River

Thames

Buffalo ●

UNITED STATES OF AMERICA

Lake Erie

mi 0   50   100

2 Think It Through

Suppose Lake Simcoe did not exist. Do you think Toronto would be in the same place? Why?

3 Use It

Why did people decide to settle in Toronto? List five reasons. Then, think about the natural features of your own city or town. List 5 reasons for people to decide to move there.

Realistic Fiction

SITTI'S SECRETS

by Naomi Shihab Nye, illustrated by Nancy Carpenter

What would it be like to visit a grandmother you had never met, a grandmother who didn't even speak your language? And what if she lived so far away that it took almost a full day flying in an airplane to get there? The girl in this story takes a trip and learns about a culture different from her own.

Once I went to visit my grandmother.

My grandmother and I do not speak the same language. We talked through my father, as if he were a telephone, because he spoke both our languages and could translate what we said.

I called her *Sitti*, which means Grandma in Arabic. She called me *habibi*, which means darling. Her voice danced as high as the whistles of birds. Her voice giggled and whooshed like wind going around corners. She had a thousand rivers in her voice.

A few curls of dark hair peeked out of her scarf on one side, and a white curl peeked out on the other side. I wanted her to take off the scarf so I could see if her hair was striped.

Soon we invented our own language together. Sitti pointed at my stomach to ask if I was hungry, I pointed to the door to ask if she wanted to go outside. We walked to the fields to watch men picking lentils. We admired the sky with hums and claps.

lentils
small flat seeds that people cook and eat like beans

We crossed the road to buy milk from a family that kept one spotted cow. I called the cow *habibi*, and it winked at me. We thanked the cow, with whistles and clicks, for the fresh milk that we carried home in Sitti's little teapot.

Every day I played with my cousins, Fowzi, Sami, Hani, and Hendia from next door. We played marbles together in their courtyard. Their marbles were blue and green and spun through the dust like planets. We didn't need words to play marbles.

My grandmother lives on the other side of the earth. She eats cucumbers for breakfast, with yogurt and bread. She bakes the big, flat bread in a round, old oven next to her house. A fire burns in the middle.

She pats the dough between her hands and presses it out to bake on a flat black rock in the center of the oven. My father says she has been baking that bread for a hundred years.

My grandmother and I sat under her lemon tree in the afternoons, drinking lemonade with mint in it. She liked me to pick bunches of mint for her. She liked to press her nose into the mint and sniff.

Some days we stuffed little zucchini squash with rice for dinner. We sang *habibi, habibi* as we stacked them in a pan. We cracked almonds and ate apricots, called *mish-mish*, while we worked.

One day Sitti took off her scarf and shook out her hair. She washed her hair in a tub right there under the sun. He hair surprised me by being very long. And it was striped! She said it got that way all by itself. I helped her brush it out while it dried. She braided it and pinned the braid up before putting on the scarf again.

zucchini

a green squash that looks like a cucumber

I felt as if I knew a secret.

Meet the Author

Naomi Shihab Nye has written many poems and one other book for children called *Benito's Dream Bottle*. You might also like to read poems she collected into a book called, *The Same Sky: A Collection of Poems from around the World*.

Additional Books to Read

Carlos, Light the Farolito
by Jean Ciavonne
The story of a Christmas tradition.

Our National Holidays
by Karen Spies
Why Americans celebrate special days.

Response Activities

1. **Critical Thinking: Problem Solving** The narrator and Sitti don't speak the same language. Not all the people at Caravan do, either. How can they share their cultures?

2. **Descriptive: Write a Thank-You Note** Suppose you visited the grandmother in this story. Write her a thank-you note. Tell her what you did and what you liked best.

3. **Cultures: Make a Collage** Make a collage from pictures of the food, clothes, people, and animals that are part of Sitti's culture. Don't forget to label the pictures!

Celebrating a New Year

Main Idea The New Year's celebration is the most important yearly festival in Vietnam.

China

VIETNAM

Happy New Year! Some people say that on January 1. For other people, New Year's Day falls at a different time. Vietnam is one place where that happens.

Vietnam is a country in Southeast Asia. There, people use a **lunar** calendar, one based on the moon. On this calendar, the New Year begins sometime between January 21 and February 19. The day changes from year to year.

The New Year in Vietnam welcomes the return of spring. It begins the farming season. Many holidays around the world happen when seasons change.

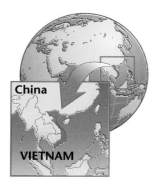

People visit flower markets to buy decorations for the New Year.

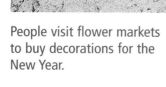

Everyone comes out into the streets to celebrate, visit friends, and go to the homes of family members.

Greetings from Nha Trang

- Nha Trang is on the southern coast of Vietnam. It has a harbor and a popular beach.
- More than 200,000 people live in Nha Trang.
- There are towers near Nha Trang that were built more than 1000 years ago!

Preparing For a New Year

Focus *How do people prepare for the New Year in Vietnam?*

For two weeks in January, Vietnamese people in communities everywhere plan for the New Year. It is the year's biggest holiday. People clean and decorate their homes. They buy new clothes and gifts. They buy special foods like sweet rice cakes.

Some families decorate altars. An **altar** is a table or raised place that is used during religious services. They use altars to honor their ancestors. An **ancestor** is a relative, like a great-grandparent, who has died. Families put flowers, fruit, and coins on the altar for luck. They place pictures of their ancestors and a *bai vi* (by vee) on the altar. A *bai vi* is a piece of wood with ancestors' names on it.

The New Year's festival began as an important religious holiday. It still is for many people. People decorate temples and churches as they prepare for the New Year.

This Vietnamese family wraps rice cakes to give as gifts for the New Year.

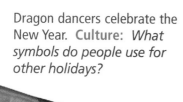

Dragon dancers celebrate the New Year. **Culture:** *What symbols do people use for other holidays?*

Days of Celebration

Focus *Why are some activities especially important during the New Year's celebration in Vietnam?*

The full name for the New Year's holiday means "Festival of the First Morning of the Year." Most people call it *Tet.* For many Vietnamese, the New Year is a new beginning.

On New Year's Eve, people set up an altar outdoors. They do this to remember their ancestors. At midnight, the old year melts into the new. Firecrackers explode! Gongs clash! People go to temples, churches, or other religious places. There, they will pray for a good year ahead.

On the first morning of the New Year, families give children gifts of money. They put the money in red envelopes. Some children save the money for things they want to buy in the future. The Vietnamese believe that red is the color of happiness. Grownups give their parents gifts of tea or candy or some other special food.

If you lived in Vietnam, you would want to get the New Year off to a good start. So be on your very best

Red is a happy color. People wear it to bring a good year. If you don't have your own smile, masks like the ones below will give you one.

behavior! Wear a bright, happy color, like red. Invite a cheerful person to your home. An unfriendly visitor can bring a bad year.

The New Year's festival celebrates a new beginning. It is also a time to celebrate the past. People visit graves of family members. They leave gifts of flowers, candles, and other special things.

During the festival, the people of Vietnam try to set a happy mood for the New Year. After people celebrate the festival, they return to work. They plan to make the rest of the year match the bright new beginning.

Lesson Review

1. **Key Vocabulary:** Use **ancestor**, **altar**, and **lunar** in sentences about celebrations in Vietnam.

2. **Focus:** How do people prepare for the New Year in Vietnam?

3. **Focus:** Why are some activities especially important during the New Year's celebration in Vietnam?

4. **Critical Thinking: Interpret** The New Year in Vietnam is at the beginning of the farming year. Why might this be a good time to start the year?

5. **Theme: Traditions** What colors or decorations do people use to celebrate holidays in your community?

6. **Citizenship/Music Activity:** Read or listen to the songs "America the Beautiful" and "The Star-Spangled Banner." On which holidays would these songs be important? Why?

Chapter Review

Summarizing the Main Idea

1 Copy and fill in the table below. For each event, show what is celebrated and how it is celebrated.

Celebrations		
	Caravan in Toronto, Canada	New Year in Vietnam
What Is Celebrated	*Toronto's cultural diversity*	
How It Is Celebrated		

Vocabulary

2 Write paragraphs about Festival Caravan in Toronto and the New Year in Vietnam. Use the words below to describe these celebrations.

passport (p. 253)   **lunar (p.264)**   **ancestor (p. 265)**
cultural diversity   **altar (p. 265)**
(p. 254)

Reviewing the Facts

3 What does Festival Caravan in Toronto, Canada, celebrate?

4 What are some things that you might see at the pavilions at Festival Caravan?

5 What are some examples of heritage that can be passed down in families?

6 What is the most important yearly festival in Vietnam?

7 When do people in Vietnam celebrate the New Year?

8 What symbols do Vietnamese people use in the New Year's celebration?

9 What do Vietnamese families do on the first morning of the New Year?

10 How do people in Vietnam celebrate the past on New Year's?

Use the map on page 259 to answer questions 11 and 12.

11 Which is bigger, Lake Ontario or Lake Simcoe? How do you think that affected the location of Toronto?

12 What would be another good place for a city near Toronto? Why?

Geography Skills

Use the maps of Festival Caravan on page 255 for questions 13 and 14.

13 Start at the Jamaican Pavilion. Which direction would you walk to get to the Rio de Janeiro Pavilion?

14 Will these maps show you how to walk from the Naples Pavilion to the Seoul Pavilion? Why or why not?

15 Create a map of a festival that your community might have.

Writing: Citizenship and Cultures

16 Citizenship Suppose you were planning a festival to celebrate the cultures in your community. What would you include? Write an editorial for the newspaper explaining your plan. Suggest activities for students your age.

17 Cultures Suppose you were in Nha Trang for the New Year. Write a letter to a friend describing all the things you did and saw.

Activities

History/Research Activity
Why do people in the United States celebrate the New Year on January 1? Do research to find out. Make a short presentation to your class to explain what you learned.

Cultures/Arts Activity
Make signs advertising Festival Caravan. What events do you think would be the most fun and interesting? Make sure you include many cultures on your signs.

Internet Option

Check the **Internet Social Studies Center** for ideas on how to extend your theme project beyond your classroom.

THEME PROJECT CHECK-IN

Think about your play and answer these questions:
• Have you represented the cultures of the people in your community?
• Have you described the heritage of the people who founded your community?

Governing Ourselves

". . . proclaim liberty throughout all the land unto all the inhabitants thereof."

These words from the Bible are on the Liberty Bell

The Book of Leviticus 25:10

· THEME ·

Cooperation

" Cooperating helps people in a community get along and work together. If people didn't work together there wouldn't be enough food or clothing for all of us. "

Jeffrey Rodriguez, San Antonio, Texas

People in a community share rules. Rules tell people how to behave in their communities. Rules also help prevent disagreements. When there is a disagreement, rules can help solve it. Who are the leaders in your community? What kind of rules do you have there? How do these rules help people in your community get along? This unit explains ways people use rules to work together.

Theme Project

Plan a Government Day

Invite people from your town's government to visit your class. Ask them to tell you about some of the important rules in your town. Then prepare reports and displays about your town government to share with other classes.

- List some important rules and laws in your community.
- Find out about the people who make laws in your community. How are they chosen? What do they do?
- Make posters showing the rights and responsibilities of people in your community.

◄ Monuments and buildings are symbols of government.

WHEN & WHERE
ATLAS

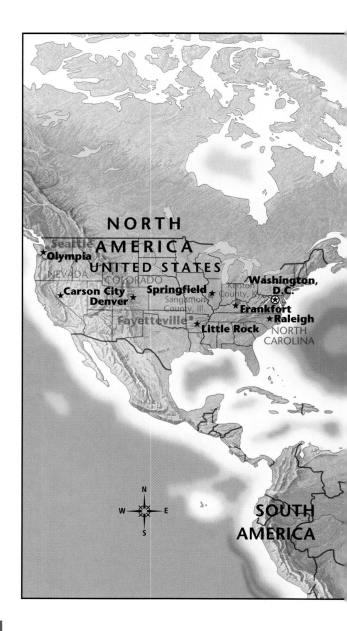

The countries on this world map all have governments. The states, counties, and cities on this map also have governments. Governments create rules for people in a community.

In this unit, you will learn about government. You will read about state, county, and national government in the United States. You will also read about the governments of other countries. Finally, you will learn how people work together to solve disagreements between countries.

Unit 6 Chapters

Unit Timeline

1750	1800	1850

Local Parks

What does local government do for you? *Chapter 11, Lesson 1*

Oink Oink

What does county government have to do with raising pigs? *Chapter 11, Lesson 2*

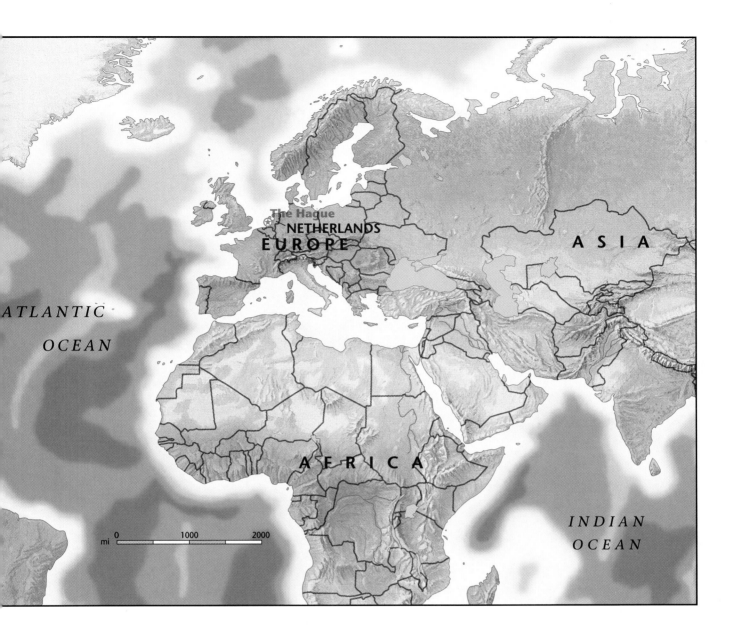

The Hague
NETHERLANDS
EUROPE
ASIA
ATLANTIC OCEAN
AFRICA
INDIAN OCEAN

mi 0   1000   2000

1900   1950   2000

You're in Another State

Welcome
COLORADO
Mountains and Much More!

What happens when you cross from one state to another? *Chapter 11, Lesson 3*

In the Netherlands

Who helps you get around in the Netherlands? *Chapter 12, Lesson 1*

People Come Together

What brings people from all over the world together? *Chapter 12, Lesson 2*

Government in the United States

We the Peo[ple]

insure domestic Tranquility provide for

and our Posterity, do ordain and establ[ish]

Article I

Chapter Preview: *People, Places, and Events*

1760   1810   1860

Local Government Services

What is this woman doing?
Lesson 1, Page 276

Local Parks

This sign stands for fun! Where can you find a sign like this? *Lesson 1, Page 277*

County Government

What can you do at a county fair?
Lesson 2, Page 284

Our Local Governments

Main Idea Local government helps people in communities.

Key Vocabulary

local

citizen

public

private

tax

The bell rings. School is out! You grab your books and lunch box. Out the door you go. You've worked hard all day. Now it's time to play. After school, many children go to parks to do just that.

Parks are for everyone. People use them in different ways. Some like the swings and jungle gyms best. They swing and climb and hang by their knees. Others sit quietly in the sun. They feed the birds or gaze at the flowers. Some people play games like baseball. Others jog down paths or walk their dogs.

Do you play in a park? Neighborhood parks are one thing that many local governments do for communities.

Parks are for everyone to enjoy.

◀ This 1787 document is the plan for America's government and laws.

1910	1960	2010

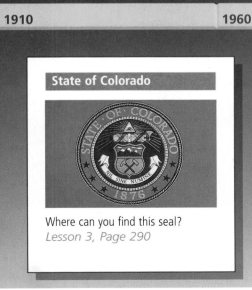

State of Colorado

Where can you find this seal? *Lesson 3, Page 290*

North Carolina

How does Sergeant McMurray help people in his state? *Lesson 3, Page 291*

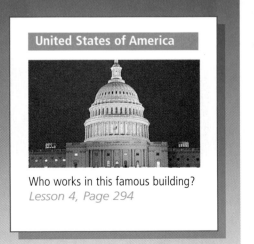

United States of America

Who works in this famous building? *Lesson 4, Page 294*

Government in Communities

Focus *What services does local government provide?*

A local government serves the people of a town or a city. Local means part of one community.

People choose local leaders to make decisions for their town or city. Citizens of the United States can vote for government leaders. A **citizen** is an official member of a country, state, or community. People born in this country are citizens of the United States. Other people can become citizens, too. Among other things, they must live here for several years and then swear loyalty to the country.

Remember from Chapter 2 that Austin has a mayor and a city council. Mayors and city council members are community leaders. So are town managers and city managers. These leaders help people in their community.

Local government provides public places for the people of a town or city. A **public** place can be used by everyone. One example is a public park. Everyone has the right to

Local government repairs roads and puts in traffic lights to help people travel safely.
Citizenship: *How does local government help people in your community?*

Firefighters provide protection against fires for everyone in a community.

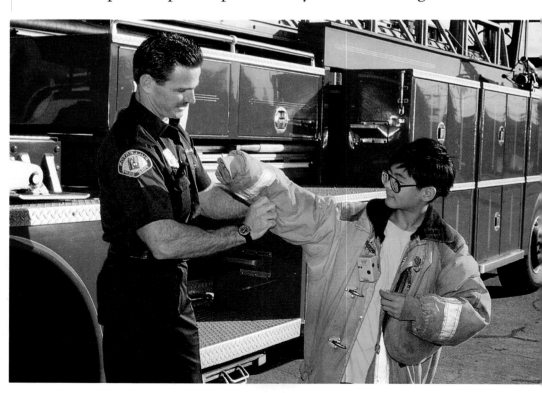

use a public park. There are private places that may look similar to parks, but not everyone may use them. **Private** places belong to one person or one group. To use a private place, you must have permission from the owner. What public and private places can you think of?

How do communities pay for public places? Governments raise money through taxes. A **tax** is money people pay to the government. All people in a community pay some taxes. With tax money, local governments can buy things that most people can't afford on their own. Taxes pay for public libraries, parks, and schools. They also pay for important services like firefighting.

The public places and services that local government provides are important. People choose leaders who they hope will make good decisions for their community.

Local government hires trash collectors like this one to keep the community clean.

· **Tell Me More** ·

Rights and Responsibilities at a Public Park

Public parks are public places. That means everyone has the right to use and enjoy them. A right is something that is guaranteed by law.

Everyone has responsibilities in a public park, too. A responsibility is something that it is your duty to do. In this case, it means everyone has a responsibility to follow the park rules.

Can you think of other rights and responsibilities people have in parks?

Local Governments at Work

Focus *How are people involved in their local government?*

As you have learned, local government helps people by providing public services and public places. Governments don't work alone. People help, too. Very often, government and citizens work together to get things done. Let's look at two examples.

In Fayetteville, Arkansas, the local government and citizens work together to recycle some kinds of trash. When trash is recycled, it isn't thrown away. Instead, it is used again in some way. People in Fayetteville didn't want to waste all their trash. They talked to the mayor and city council. Soon, the city council started a recycling program.

Now people in Fayetteville save newspapers, cans, glass, and some types of plastic. They put these things in a special recycling bag. Then, once a week, people place their bags on the curb. Trucks pick up the bags for recycling. Does your community have a recycling program? How could you help to make it work?

In Fayetteville, people worked with the mayor and city council to start curbside recycling.

Many public libraries get tax money from local government. In Seattle, Washington, some libraries offer a program for kids after school. The program is called SPLASH. SPLASH stands for Seattle Public Library After School Happenings. Instead of going home or to the park after

Then & Now

Long ago, in 1731, Benjamin Franklin started the first library from which people could check out books. People paid to belong to it. With the money that its members paid, the library bought new books. Almost 100 years later, the first free public library opened in Dublin, New Hampshire. It was open to everyone in the community.

school, some students go to the public library. There they can get help with their homework. They can also do craft activities or science experiments. Of course, they can also take out books.

Local government works with citizens in many ways. It helps to make life better for people in the community. What services does your local government provide?

Lesson Review

1 Key Vocabulary: Write about your community's government, using **local**, **citizen**, **public**, **private**, and **tax**.

2 Focus: What services does local government provide?

3 Focus: How are people involved in their local government?

4 Critical Thinking: Cause and Effect What happens when people don't follow the laws of a community? How does this affect the community?

5 Theme: Cooperation How do the people in Fayetteville cooperate with their city council?

6 Citizenship/Research Activity: Find out about a public building in your community, such as a library or town hall. Who uses it? What services does it offer? Make a poster to tell people about the public building you chose.

★ CITIZENSHIP ★

Resolving Conflicts

How Can People Agree?

Not everyone agrees on everything. Some people want to do one thing. Others don't like the idea. There are ways to solve these conflicts, though. Read the case study below to see how people in Ohio worked together for a bike path.

Case Study

Community Members Listen to Each Other

In Toledo, Ohio, many people wanted to build a bike path on an old railroad bed. The path was to go from the university into town and then out into the woods. Lots of people were excited. The path would be safe and fun for runners, hikers, bikers, rollerbladers, and people in wheelchairs.

Five organizations came together to plan and build the path. Some other people were not happy, though. They had yards right next to the path. They thought there would be crowds and noise. The five groups realized these people were right. They hired special patrols to make sure everything was peaceful. They built a parking lot to control entry. They added benches for people to sit on. The path is open now, and many people love it. When new problems come up, people work to solve them.

Take Action

Design a whole new classroom! First think of a favorite spot in the new room where everyone will like to sit. How will you decide who sits there? How will you arrange the classroom seating? Will you have a library? a math corner? a place for building models or doing science experiments? an art studio with cupboards for art supplies?

1 With a partner, write down your ideas. For every idea you give, your partner should give an idea, too. Draw a plan combining your ideas.

2 Get together with other sets of partners. Share your plans.

3 Come up with a new plan you can all agree on. Adjust your plan until everyone is satisfied with at least one part of it.

4 Build a model of your new classroom in the bottom of a box. Use cardboard or wood or clay. Present your model to the class. What did your group have the hardest time agreeing on? How did you solve the disagreements?

Tips for Resolving Conflicts

- When people disagree in a group, vote to see what most people think.
- Give those who disagree a chance to explain their side of the story. You might want to vote again.
- Stay open-minded. Listening to others might make you think differently.

Research Activity

Learn about a park or building that was built in your community to serve a group of people. Find the person who was in charge and ask: Who was the space designed for? What were the difficulties in deciding the design? How were the problems resolved?

Our County Governments

Main Idea County government helps state government and the people who live in that county.

Where could you find a huge pumpkin and a giant Ferris wheel? The answer is a county fair. In the summer and fall, many counties hold fairs. A **county** is an area within a state that has its own government. Counties often contain many communities.

County fairgrounds buzz with activity. Farmers show plants and animals they have raised. There are often contests. People receive prizes for things like the tallest sunflower, the juiciest tomato, or the biggest calf.

County governments run fairs for fun. They also provide services for people. Counties do important work for people and their state.

Many county fairs have contests in which people show animals they have raised — like this pig. Others show delicious homemade pies. **Economics:** *How can county fairs help farmers?*

FIRST PLACE

Government in Counties

Focus *What is a county?*

Most states are divided into counties. Counties often include several communities. For example, Springfield, Buffalo, and other towns are in Sangamon County, Illinois.

County governments help their state government. One job of county government is to keep records for the state. For example, county government keeps track of voters. People vote for candidates for government. A **candidate** is someone who wants to be elected to a government job. The candidates voters choose become government leaders. Counties keep track of voters for all levels of government.

In some places, county government provides police protection. Other counties provide public schools and airports. Let's look at some county governments at work.

Curious Facts

Forty-eight of fifty states have counties. Two states use different names for the areas or districts within the state. Louisiana has parishes. Alaska has boroughs.

· Tell Me More ·

Rights and Responsibilities of Voters

People in the United States vote to choose their leaders. Voting is an important right that Americans have. By voting, Americans exercise the right to choose their government. Voting is a responsibility, too. Running a government is a big job. It is every voter's responsibility to help choose the best leaders.

Candidates are people running for a government job. Usually several people run for the same job, but only one is elected.

Voters are citizens who are 18 years or older. They vote on candidates and questions.

County Governments at Work

Focus *How does county government help people?*

County government helps people in many ways. Kenton County is in Kentucky. The Kenton County Extension Service offers many programs to help people who live in Kenton County. Some programs help farmers. Experts who work for the county teach farmers how to raise healthier crops and cattle. The County Extension Service also offers 4-H, a club where kids do projects. Kids raise animals and learn woodworking. They also do projects that make their community a nicer place to live.

Each year, Kenton County has a fair. At the fair, farmers in the county can show off the animals and crops they have raised. The fair is a chance to have some fun.

John Mains, Danita Scherder, and John Scherder are all in 4-H. They work on projects all year long. They each entered contests in the county fair. Danita sewed a pair of shorts. Her brother grew tomatoes.

John Mains lives on a farm. He raised a pig and a lamb to show at the fair. He had to get up early in the

The fair is a good place for people to sell the animals they raise. Below, 4-H members get a pig and a goat ready to show at the county fair.

morning to feed and care for his animals. At the fair, John washed his pig before he showed it. It isn't easy to give a pig a bath. "They really don't want to get washed," John says. "They just jump in the puddles they make."

County governments keep a record of the births in the county. If you were born in Sangamon County, Illinois, that county would give your parents a copy of your birth certificate. A **certificate** is an official document that can prove an event or fact. A birth certificate tells when and where you were born. It can prove that you're old enough to start school. Later, you would need it to get other important papers such as a driver's license.

What county do you live in? Find out about what your county government does. Learn how it helps people in your community and in your state. Does it have programs for children?

Counties keep records like birth certificates for the state. **Geography:** *In which state and county were you born?*

Lesson Review

1 **Key Vocabulary:** Write a paragraph, using the words **county**, **candidate**, and **certificate**.

2 **Focus:** What is a county?

3 **Focus:** How does county government help people?

4 **Critical Thinking: Conclude** How does a county fair help bring people together? Why is that important?

5 **Citizenship:** How does county government help state government?

6 **Geography/Research Activity:** Find your county on a state map. Where is it in relation to the center of the state? Where is it in relation to the state capital?

THINK LIKE A
GEOGRAPHER

Environment and Society

How Do People Change the Environment?

People have polluted the water in the Chesapeake Bay, but now they are trying to clean the bay. The pollution comes from chemicals that people use on farms, in factories, and even on their lawns. It makes the water unsafe for the wildlife and sealife there.

Bernie Fowler noticed that the Patuxent River, which flows into the Chesapeake Bay, was polluted. Fowler and other citizens are working to get local, state, and national laws to clean and protect the bay.

Science Connection

Water usually flows from streams to rivers and from rivers into the ocean. How could pollution in streams far from the bay hurt the bay?

Research Activity

1. Using a map, follow one river away from the Chesapeake Bay. List the communities you find.

2. How might these communities affect the bay? List some of the ways.

Bernie Fowler and some friends walk chest-deep into the Patuxent River each June. They hope some day the water will be so clear that they can see their toes.

The Chesapeake Bay

You can read this satellite photograph as you would a map. The dark blue areas are water. The others are land. Can you see any other features?

1 Chesapeake Bay

Sunset on the Bay
A bay is a part of the ocean that reaches into the land. The Chesapeake Bay reaches into Virginia and Maryland. What other bodies of water can you see on this photo?

2 Potomac River

Washington from the River
The Potomac flows through several states before it reaches the Chesapeake Bay. Pollution from those states harms the fish, shellfish, birds, and animals in the bay.

Blue crabs live in the Chesapeake Bay.

Our State Governments

Main Idea State government works with county and local governments to make life better for the people in that state.

You're riding down a highway in Nebraska. Suddenly, you see a sign: WELCOME TO COLORADO. As you cross the line where one state ends and another begins, you cross the **border**. The highway may look the same in both states, but there is a difference. Each state has its own government and its own laws. For example, laws about speeding differ from state to state. It's a good idea to read the signs.

What other differences are there among the 50 states? Each state has its own flag, state flower, and state animal or bird. Look at the sign below. What can you learn about Colorado from it?

Colorado's state sign lets travelers know they're entering a new state.

Welcome

COLORADO
Mountains and Much More!

WELD COUNTY

Government in States

[Focus] *What does state government do?*

Fifty states make up the United States of America. Each state has its own laws and government. State laws help people in the state live together safely and peacefully.

State government is elected by the voters in the state. The head of state government is called the **governor**. The group that makes state laws is called the **legislature**. The governor and legislature are chosen by the voters in each state. Who is the governor of your state?

State government helps people and communities. For example, many states have state hospitals and state police.

States raise money through taxes. Some tax money pays for state programs. Other money goes to communities in the state. State money helps build new buildings and roads. Read on to learn more about state tax money.

Biography

Thomas Jefferson

Jefferson was born in 1743 in Virginia. He was a leader who helped shape our country. He was the third President of the United States. Jefferson designed the buildings at the University of Virginia. He was state governor for two years.

· Tell Me More ·

Rights and Responsibilities of Taxpayers

People who live in a state have a responsibility to pay state taxes. State tax money pays for the services that states provide. People have the right to those services.

- State taxes pay for things that keep people safe, like state police.

- State taxes pay for health services to keep people well.

- State tax money pays for new buildings, like schools.

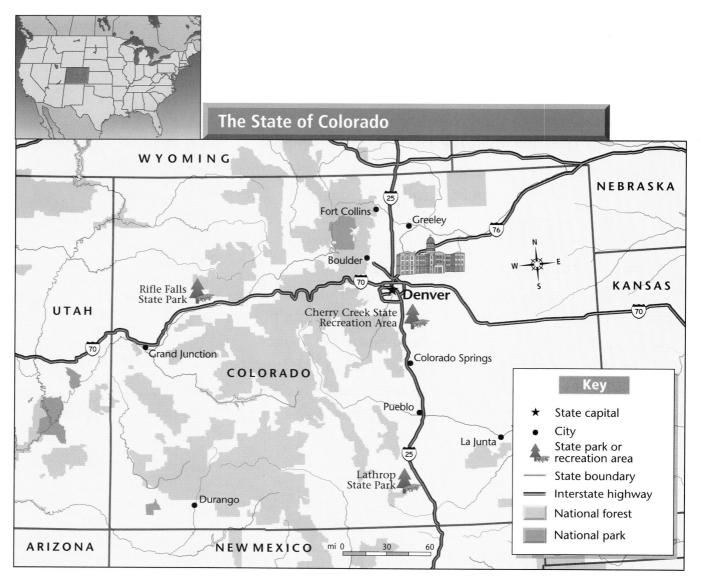

The State of Colorado

WYOMING

NEBRASKA

Fort Collins

Greeley

76

Boulder

70

Denver

KANSAS

Rifle Falls
State Park

UTAH

Cherry Creek State
Recreation Area

70

Grand Junction

COLORADO

Colorado Springs

Pueblo

La Junta

25

Lathrop
State Park

Durango

ARIZONA

NEW MEXICO

mi 0   30   60

Key

★   State capital

●   City

🌲   State park or
     recreation area

—   State boundary

━   Interstate highway

▢   National forest

▢   National park

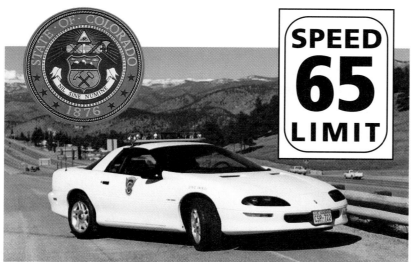

State highway laws and state highway
patrols help prevent injuries on the road.

SPEED 65 LIMIT

State laws affect all the people in the
state. On highways, laws like speed limits
help make sure people drive safely. State
road crews also build and repair highways.

Each state has a capital where the
government meets. States also offer state
parks for people to enjoy. **Geography:**
*What can you learn about Colorado by
looking at this map?*

State Government at Work

Focus *What services does state government provide to people in the state?*

State government provides many services for people. Do you go to a public school? State money helps pay for new school buildings. There are many state colleges and universities. States have programs to help people who are sick or needy. Are you careful about using water? Many states work to protect water resources.

Sergeant David McMurray works for the North Carolina State Highway Patrol. He is a Traffic Safety Information Officer. Part of his job is going to schools to talk to students. He teaches them about safety. McMurray teaches students to obey North Carolina's seat belt law. He thinks teaching students to wear seat belts makes parents safer, too. He says, "Parents will tell me, 'My kids get after me if I don't buckle up.'" North Carolina's seat belt law — and Sergeant McMurray — help make traveling safer.

Sergeant David McMurray teaches people about North Carolina's safety laws. He wears a badge like the one above to show that he's a member of the North Carolina State Highway Patrol.

Like all the third graders in Nevada, third graders at Mark Twain Elementary School in Carson City study citizenship. **Citizenship:** *What do you think every third grader should learn about citizenship?*

Someone in your state government may be talking about you right now! That's because many states decide what will be taught in school. Schools are a big responsibility of the states.

Nevada has a state curriculum. That means that the state decides what all students should study in each grade. In Nevada, all third grade students learn about respecting the rights of others. Citizenship is an important part of Nevada's social studies program.

Find out what your state government does for your school. What other services does your state offer to people?

Lesson Review

1. **Key Vocabulary:** Write a paragraph about your state. Use the words **border**, **governor**, and **legislature**.

2. **Focus:** What does state government do?

3. **Focus:** What services does state government provide to people in the state?

4. **Critical Thinking: Conclude** Why is going to school both a right and a responsibility?

5. **Theme: Cooperation** What can people do to show that they respect the rights of others?

6. **Geography/Arts Activity:** Make a map of your state. Show the capital city where the state government meets. Show where you live, too.

Our National Government

Main Idea The three branches of our national government work together to make life better for people in the United States.

Key Vocabulary
President
Congress
court
Supreme Court
Constitution

Moving vans crowd the streets around Washington, D.C. It's January, and people are moving in. The vans bring furniture and boxes from all over the country. Airplanes carry men and women and their families. People are moving to the nation's capital to begin their new jobs.

In November, voters in each state chose these men and women to be part of their national government. Now the new members of government must move to Washington, D.C. That's where the national government meets. Let's explore the capital city and our national government.

People who are elected to our national government go to Washington, D.C., to do their jobs.

National Government

Focus *What does each branch of government do to help people?*

Our national government makes decisions and passes laws to help people in the United States. The United States government has three parts, or branches. You can learn about each branch on the map of Washington, D.C., below.

Can you find the White House? That's where the President lives and works. The **President** is the leader of our country and head of the first branch of government.

The map also shows the building where Congress, the second branch of government, meets. **Congress** makes the laws for our country. It is the national legislature. Like the President, members of Congress are chosen by voters.

Washington, D.C.

Three important buildings are shown on the map of Washington, D.C., below. **Map Skills:** *The mapmaker chose to show only certain parts of the city. How does that help you read the map?*

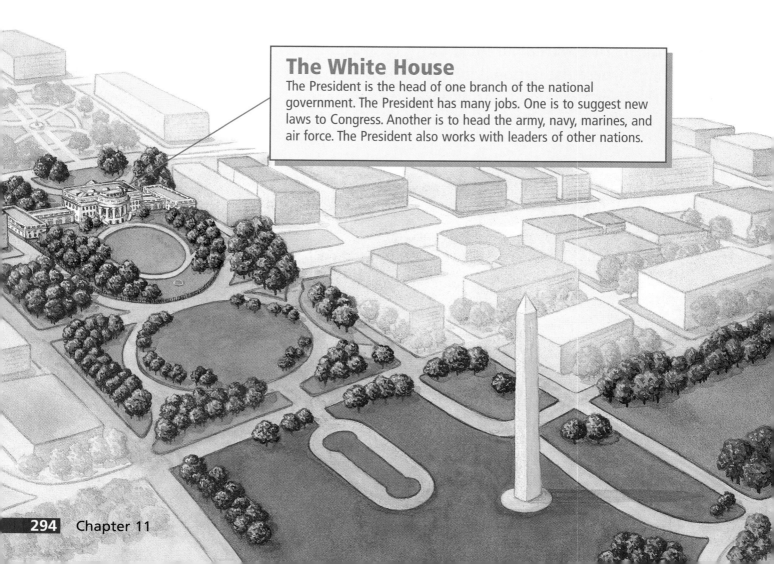

The White House
The President is the head of one branch of the national government. The President has many jobs. One is to suggest new laws to Congress. Another is to head the army, navy, marines, and air force. The President also works with leaders of other nations.

A **court** is a place where questions about the law are answered. The **Supreme Court** is the head of the third branch of the national government. The Supreme Court is the most powerful court in our country.

Three branches of government work for the people of this country. They provide services for people and states.

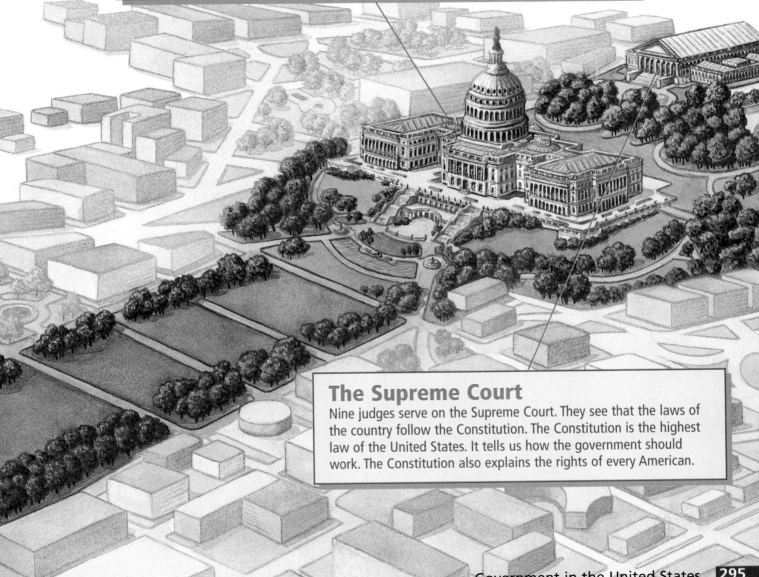

The Capitol

Congress meets in the Capitol building. The main job of Congress is to make laws. The Senate and the House of Representatives make up the Congress. The Senate has two members from each state. The House of Representatives has members from each state, too. The number of representatives from each state depends on the number of people who live in that state. **Math:** *How many people are in the Senate?*

The Supreme Court

Nine judges serve on the Supreme Court. They see that the laws of the country follow the Constitution. The Constitution is the highest law of the United States. It tells us how the government should work. The Constitution also explains the rights of every American.

Voting is one way for a group of people to make a decision.

Have you ever voted before? Maybe you voted for a kickball team captain or a class president. What did you think about when making your decision?

? ? ? ? ? ? ? ? ? ? ? ? ?

Four levels of government work together in our country. People in towns or cities must follow local laws. People in every community in the county must follow county laws. People in every county in the state must follow state laws. People in every state in the United States must follow national laws. **Map Skill:** *What state is Litchfield in?*

Governments Work Together

Focus *How do the different levels of government in our country work together?*

You have read about different levels of government — local, county, state, and national. Americans vote for their leaders at each of these levels. Someday, you may too. You already follow the laws of many levels of government. Each level is important.

Many levels of government work together to provide services people need. For example, local and county governments may work together to run a landfill. National and state governments work together to build safe highways. When the national government makes laws, people in every part of the country must follow them.

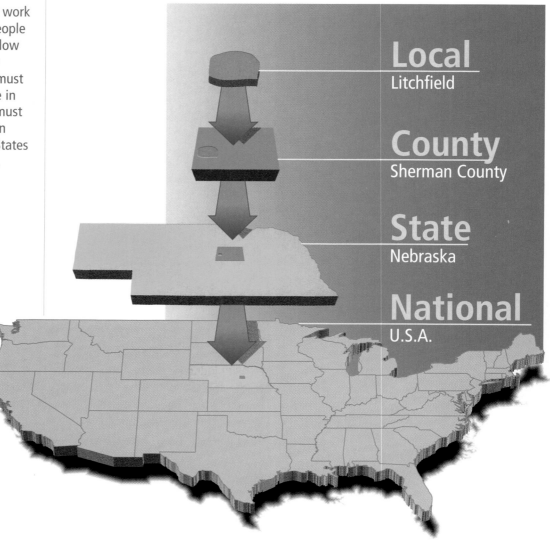

Local
Litchfield

County
Sherman County

State
Nebraska

National
U.S.A.

Rights and Responsibilities

Americans in every town, county, and state have rights. Some of these rights are stated in the Bill of Rights. The Bill of Rights is a part of the Constitution. The **Constitution** is the basic laws and ideas that our national government follows. All new laws must agree with the Constitution.

People use their rights all the time. For example, the Bill of Rights says that Americans have freedom of speech. This means that they are free to speak out on things that matter to them.

When people have rights, they also have responsibilities. If you speak out, you have the responsibility not to hurt others unfairly with your words. People need to know their rights. But it is just as important for them to remember their responsibilities.

Many levels of government help Americans. They make laws and help keep us safe. Many levels of government protect our rights. Having rights also means having responsibilities. What responsibilities do you have?

Americans can write to their representatives in Congress to ask for changes in the laws in our country.

Lesson Review

1. **Key Vocabulary:** Write sentences that describe the work of the President, Congress, a court, the Supreme Court, and the Constitution.

2. **Focus:** What does each branch of the national government do to help people?

3. **Focus:** How do the different levels of government in our country work together?

4. **Critical Thinking: Conclude** Why is working for the government an important job?

5. **Geography:** What are the names of your community, county, state, and nation? Who are the leaders at each level of government?

6. **Citizenship/Literature Activity:** Read a story about the early days of the United States. How are rights and responsibilities important in the story?

Workshop

Comparing Tables and Graphs

How Much? How Many?

Can you compare important features of Colorado and Arkansas? How about their geographical size? It's easy. Look at a map! How about their populations? Comparing that information is more difficult — unless you use one of two important tools. **Bar graphs** let you see information quickly and help you compare how much or how many of something. **Tables** often show very detailed information.

Population Table

	1989	1990	1991	1992	1993
Colorado	3,276,000	3,294,000	3,370,000	3,456,000	3,586,000
Arkansas	2,346,000	2,351,000	2,371,000	2,394,000	2,424,000

1 Here's How

- Look at the table. It lists exact population numbers. In 1992, how many people lived in Colorado?

- Look at the graph. Bar graphs are good for making quick comparisons. Without looking at the numbers, find which state had a larger population in 1993.

- Compare the tables and the graphs. Both show population information, but in different ways. When you need to show information, think about whether it's more important to make quick comparisons or to show exact numbers.

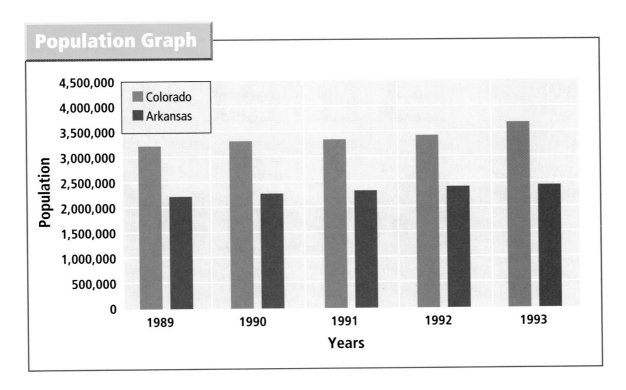

Population Graph

Population graph showing Colorado and Arkansas populations for years 1989–1993.

Legend:
- Colorado
- Arkansas

Y-axis (Population): 0, 500,000, 1,000,000, 1,500,000, 2,000,000, 2,500,000, 3,000,000, 3,500,000, 4,000,000, 4,500,000

X-axis (Years): 1989, 1990, 1991, 1992, 1993

② Think It Through

Suppose you wanted to show how many times the people in your class went to the movies last year. Would you use a table or a graph? Why?

③ Use It

1. Find out some information about your class — the numbers of boys and girls, or the numbers of left-handed and right-handed students. Make either a table or a bar graph to show what you found.

2. Tell why you chose a table or graph.

3. Make it the other way. What's different?

Government in the United States **299**

America the Beautiful

by Katharine Lee Bates

People in all parts of the world express a love for their country through patriotic songs. For Americans, "America the Beautiful" is one of the favorites.

Oh beautiful for spacious skies,
for amber waves of grain;
For purple mountain majesties
above the fruited plain;
America! America!
God shed His grace on thee;
And crown thy good
with brotherhood
from sea to shining sea!

spacious
having a lot of space

amber
golden-brown colored

majesty
grand; like royalty

fruited plain
A plain is a large area of flat land. Here, a fruited plain is a plain on which grain is growing.

shed
send out

Response Activities

1. Conclude
What is described in this song?

2. Expressive: Write a Patriotic Song
America the Beautiful describes things that Bates thought were special about the United States. Write a song that describes the things that you think are special about the United States.

3. Geography: Draw a Map
Where can you find mountains or growing grain in the United States? Do research to find out. Then draw a map of the United States that shows the features mentioned in *America the Beautiful*. Add to your map other features that you think are important.

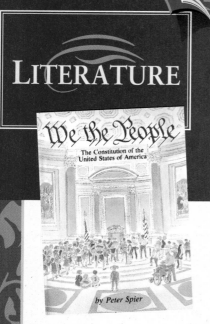

Nonfiction

We the People
The Constitution of the United States of America

by Peter Spier

Think how hard it would be to play a game of checkers if players could change the rules whenever they wanted to. The game would be more fair if one set of rules was written down so everyone could obey them. Countries need rules, too. The rules that were used to set up the government of the United States are written down. They are called the Constitution. This first sentence of the United States Constitution tells how the government is supposed to help all the people of the country.

union
something that joins many people or parts

We the People of the United States,
in Order to form a more perfect Union,

establish Justice,

insure domestic Tranquility,

provide for the common defence,

promote
to help something improve

promote the general Welfare,

Freedom of Speech

Freedom of the Press

secure
to get

and secure the Blessings of Liberty

posterity
future generations

to ourselves and our Posterity,

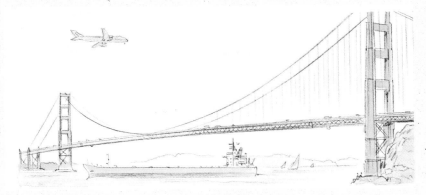

Minute Man, Concord, Massachusetts

Golden Gate Bridge, San Francisco, California

do ordain and establish this Constitution for the United States of America.

ordain
to decide by law

Meet the Author

Peter Spier was born in Amsterdam, the Netherlands, in 1927. He came to the United States in 1951 and became a U.S. citizen in 1958. He has written and illustrated over 30 books for children. If you like his artwork, be sure to look for his book *People*.

Additional Books to Read

Kate Shelley and the Midnight Express
by Margaret K. Wetterer
How a brave girl saves her community.

Our National Symbols
by Linda Carlson Johnson
The American eagle, Uncle Sam, and more.

Response Activities

1. Conclude
What's an example of something the national government does that fits the goals of the Constitution?

2. Descriptive: Use Your Own Words
The Constitution was written in 1787. That's why some of the words seem strange. With a group, rewrite its first sentence. Use modern language that means the same thing as the original words.

3. Citizenship: Make a Poster
Peter Spier's illustrations show what the Constitution means. Make a poster that shows what you think is special about our country.

Chapter Review

Summarizing the Main Idea

1 Copy and fill in the chart below. Show how different levels of government help people.

How Government Helps People			
Local	County	State	National
	helps state government to keep records		

Vocabulary

2 Use at least ten of the words below to write a paragraph about local, county, state, and national government.

local (p. 276)	**county (p. 282)**	**legislature (p. 289)**
citizen (p. 276)	**candidate (p. 283)**	**President (p. 294)**
public (p. 276)	**certificate (p. 285)**	**Congress (p. 294)**
private (p. 277)	**border (p. 288)**	**court (p. 295)**
tax (p. 277)	**governor (p. 289)**	**Supreme Court (p. 295)**

Reviewing the Facts

3 Who does local government serve?

4 How are public places different from private places?

5 How does the county government of Kenton County, Kentucky, help farmers who live there?

6 What are some things that the state does with the tax money it collects?

7 What do we call the legislature of our national government?

8 If you wanted to know the exact population of the state of Colorado, would you use the table or the graph from pages 298 and 299?

9 In a report, how might you use tables and graphs to help people understand your information?

Critical Thinking

10 Generalize In what ways are all local governments the same?

11 Problem Solving Suppose people in a town wanted a new park. How could they work with the local government to get it?

12 Classify If you thought that a law was not fair, which branch of the national government would be able to help you? Why?

Writing: Citizenship and Economics

13 Citizenship: People who are born in countries other than the United States can become United States citizens. How do you think that might feel? Write what a new citizen might write in a journal.

14 Economics: Suppose your state government is making decisions about spending tax money. They need to choose between giving more money to the schools or the police. Write a letter to your state lawmakers explaining where you think the money should go.

Activities

History/Literature Activity
Many citizens have fought for their civil rights. Read about someone in the United States who fought for civil rights. Who was it and what rights did he or she fight for?

Geography/Art Activity
Make a chart like the chart on page 296. It should show your community, county, and state within the United States. Compare the location of your state to the location of other states in the United States of America.

Internet Option

Check the **Internet Social Studies Center** for ideas on how to extend your theme project beyond your classroom.

THEME PROJECT CHECK-IN

Look at your Government Day plan and answer these questions:
• Have you included a display of the laws in your community?
• Do you show the rights and responsibilities of people in the community?

CHAPTER 12 Our Nation and the World

Chapter Preview: *People, Places, and Events*

1960	1970	1980

Gouda, the Netherlands

Where does local government in the Netherlands meet? *Lesson 1, Page 310*

Netherlands Post Office

What do governments do to help the people in their countries? *Lesson 1, Page 311*

Coins of the World

What do coins from another country look like? *Lesson 1, Page 314*

Looking at Governments

Main Idea Every country in the world has a government.

Men and women gather in a government building in the Netherlands. These 150 lawmakers are discussing the laws that they will decide upon today.

Off the coast of Africa is a country made up of more than 100 islands. There, 25 lawmakers of the island nation of Seychelles (say SHEHL) are gathering too. Today they will discuss a new law that will help the people of their country.

The United States Congress has 535 lawmakers. These men and women represent the citizens of our country.

Countries all over the world have governments. Governments make laws that help people live together.

Key Vocabulary

parliament
dike
ambassador

Lawmakers in the Netherlands meet in this building in the city of The Hague.

◀ There are many nations in the world. Each nation has its own flag.

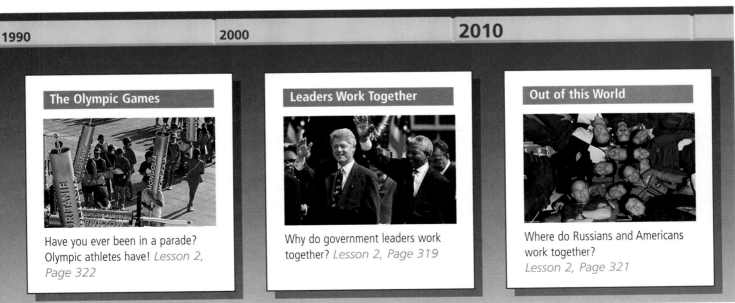

1990	2000	2010

The Olympic Games

Have you ever been in a parade? Olympic athletes have! *Lesson 2, Page 322*

Leaders Work Together

Why do government leaders work together? *Lesson 2, Page 319*

Out of this World

Where do Russians and Americans work together? *Lesson 2, Page 321*

The Netherlands is a country in Europe. The capital is Amsterdam, but the government meets in The Hague. **Map Skill:** *Find both cities on the map.*

Government in the Netherlands

[Focus] *In what ways is the government of the Netherlands like the government of the United States?*

The Netherlands is a small country in Europe. It's about two times the size of New Jersey. The Netherlands has many people for its small size. Even though people live close together in the Netherlands, they get along with one another. That's because national and local governments there make laws to keep order.

Like the United States, the Netherlands has a branch of government that makes laws. In the United States, the lawmaking branch is called Congress.

The Netherlands

FRISIAN ISLANDS

Waddenzee

GRONINGEN

Harlingen

FRIESLAND

Den Oever

Barrier Dam

DRENTHE

IJsselmeer (Zuider Zee)

NORTH HOLLAND

NORTH SEA

FLEVOLAND

OVERIJSSEL

Amsterdam

NETHERLANDS

The Hague

SOUTH HOLLAND

UTRECHT

GELDERLAND

Gouda

GERMANY

ZEELAND

NORTH BRABANT

LIMBURG

BELGIUM

mi 0 25 50

Key

— National boundary

— Provincial boundary

⊛ National capital

• City

The Netherlands has a queen, Queen Beatrix. She helps the government.

The Netherlands has a **parliament** that makes laws. Sari van Heemskerck is a member of the parliament in the Netherlands. That's like being a member of Congress in the United States. Heemskerck says citizens in the Netherlands choose lawmakers differently than citizens in the United States do. "The Netherlands has one national government. We lawmakers are national representatives. We are elected by citizens in the whole country to represent everyone, not just people from one area." Whom do lawmakers represent in the United States? How is that different from the Netherlands?

The Netherlands has a leader called the prime minister, whose job is like that of the President of the United States. Unlike the United States, the Netherlands also has a queen. Queen Beatrix helps the government. She gives the government ideas on how to solve the problems it is facing.

Curious Facts

Many people call the Netherlands *Holland*. That comes from the names of two of the provinces, North Holland and South Holland. In English, people and things from the Netherlands are called *Dutch*.

Public transportation in the Netherlands is run by the government. **Citizenship:** *What public transportation is there in your community?*

The government of the Netherlands has built over 11,000 miles of bike paths. The paths have their own stoplights so people can travel safely. **Citizenship:** *How can people tell that the light is for bicycles?*

What Governments Do

Local governments also help the people of the Netherlands. The Water Control Boards are a very important part of local government. The Netherlands was once a much smaller country than it is now. Long ago, people found that they could make land by filling in the sea with earth. They built **dikes** of mounded earth around the new land to keep the water out. Windmills powered pumps that pumped water out. If one of the dikes were to break, water from the sea would flood the land. Many people would lose their homes. Farmers would lose their crops. Water Control Boards make sure that the land does not flood. They keep the people of the Netherlands safe.

The government of the Netherlands also works with other governments. Sari van Heemskerck says, "In the Netherlands you are always thinking about the other countries in Europe. When we turn on the television, we see stations from the Netherlands, England, and Germany."

Dikes and windmills like those below help the Dutch make land where there was once water. **Geography:** *How might the Netherlands change as it gets new land?*

The Countries of Europe

ARCTIC OCEAN

Key

SPAIN   European Union Countries, 1995

ICELAND

ATLANTIC OCEAN

NORWAY   SWEDEN   FINLAND

RUSSIA

ESTONIA

NORTH SEA   DENMARK   LATVIA   LITHUANIA   RUSSIA

IRELAND   UNITED KINGDOM   BELARUS

NETHERLANDS   POLAND

BELGIUM   GERMANY

LUXEMBOURG   CZECH REPUBLIC   SLOVAK REPUBLIC   UKRAINE

LIECHTENSTEIN   AUSTRIA   HUNGARY   MOLDOVA

SWITZERLAND   SLOVENIA   ROMANIA

FRANCE   SAN MARINO   CROATIA

MONACO   SERBIA & MONTENEGRO   BULGARIA   BLACK SEA

ANDORRA   BOSNIA & HERZEGOVINA   VATICAN CITY   ALBANIA   TURKEY

PORTUGAL   SPAIN   ITALY   MACEDONIA   GREECE

MALTA

MEDITERRANEAN SEA

mi   0   300   600

You can see the continent of Europe on the map above. It is made up of large and small countries. Each country has its own laws and government. Fifteen of those countries have also agreed to work together as a group. They call themselves the European Union. You can see the member nations on the map. Some people in the European Union are French, some are Dutch, some are Spanish, and so on. They are all Europeans. The European Union represents them all.

The continent of Europe has many countries. Large or small, each country has a government that makes laws. Some of the countries in Europe have joined what's called the European Union. **Map Skill:** *Use the key to find the countries in the European Union. Make a list of the countries that belong to it.*

National Governments

Focus *What do governments throughout the world have in common?*

Governments differ from country to country, but most governments have several things in common. That's because most governments have a similar job to do. For example, governments have a national flag, issue passports, and print money and postage stamps.

Every country has is its own flag, too. A flag has special meaning to the citizens of that country. The United States flag tells about our country. The stripes represent the number of states there were when our nation began. The stars represent the number of states in our nation today. Flags are important symbols.

If you travel to another country, you might need a passport. Passports are issued by the government. They show that you are a citizen of that country.

The money a government provides often has pictures of people or buildings that are important to the country. The money on this page comes from countries around the

Here is some brightly colored money from other countries. Countries all over the world make bills and coins that people use to pay for things. **Art:** *If you had to design money, what would it look like?*

world. Which countries can you identify from the money?

Most governments print postage stamps. The pictures on stamps often tell you about the country. Those pictures make stamps so interesting that many people collect stamps as a hobby.

In order to help governments work together, many nations send representatives to other countries. A representative from the government of another country is called an **ambassador**. The President of the United States sends United States ambassadors to countries all over the world. Ambassadors can speak for the President and help make agreements between countries.

No matter what their size, countries all over the world have governments. They have leaders and laws for their citizens to follow.

Postage stamps say you have paid for mail delivery. They also show a country's important symbols or leaders.
Citizenship: *What important symbol or leader might appear on stamps from the Netherlands?*

Lesson Review

1. **Key Vocabulary:** Write a paragraph about a trip to another country, using parliament, dike, and **ambassador**.

2. **Focus:** In what ways is the government of the Netherlands like the government of the United States?

3. **Focus:** What do governments throughout the world have in common?

4. **Critical Thinking: Problem Solving** What kinds of skills do you think an ambassador should have? Why?

5. **Theme: Cooperation** Why is it important for world governments to cooperate?

6. **Geography/Art Activity:** Design a postage stamp for a European country based on what you can tell from the map of Europe.

Using the Media

What's New?

Current events are things that are happening now. The news tells us about current events. We get the news from media like newspapers and television. The **media** are forms of communication. They connect the world by sending information quickly from one place to another. They help you know what is happening. Different kinds of media teach us different things.

● **Newspapers** are printed daily or weekly. Headlines tell you what the story is about. The dateline, under the headline, tells when and where the story was written.

● **Radio** is often first to tell about something that is happening, for example a hurricane or a traffic jam. But radio doesn't have pictures to help show you what is going on.

● **Magazines** can have articles on all kinds of subjects — news, cultural events, and people. They can also be on just one subject, like sports or the environment.

Television can tell you about something and show it to you at the same time. Television shows people or things in action.

The Internet is a new kind of media. Using computers and the Internet, people can share information with people all over the world. Pictures, video, printed words, and sound can all be sent over the Internet.

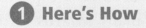

1 Here's How

Use the media when you are writing a report.

- Think about some subjects that interest you. Read newspapers and magazines often and look for stories on those subjects. At the library, you can find copies of old newspaper and magazine articles that give you more information.

- Listen to the radio to find out up-to-the-minute news.

- When you watch television, pay attention to programs or articles about your subjects.

2 Think It Through

Why is it useful to have several different forms of media? What can you learn from different media sources?

3 Use It

1. Find an article or news story that interests you in the media.

2. Write about what you learned.

3. Try to find something about the same subject in a different media source. How are they different?

Working Across Borders

Main Idea People, governments, and organizations all over the world work together.

Kristi Yamaguchi was an Olympic ice skater. She won a gold medal for the United States in the 1992 Olympics.

It is early in the morning. The sun is not yet up. An alarm goes off, and a young girl tumbles out of bed. Quickly, she dresses and eats breakfast. Then she grabs her ice skates and heads for the rink. With luck, she can fit in several hours of practice before school.

This girl is like young athletes in many other countries. She hopes someday to compete in world sporting events. First she must practice long hours.

Like the young girl above, Kristi Yamaguchi of California spent many years practicing her skating. She began at age six. Since then she has skated in many national and international events. As a top skater, Kristi has won many awards for the United States, including an Olympic gold medal.

The sporting events that athletes compete in are one way that people from around the world come together. Governments from countries around the world can come together to work too.

Governments Work Together

Focus *In what ways does the United States government work with other governments in the world?*

Many governments around the world work together. Many work together through the United Nations. The United Nations is made up of almost all the nations in the world. The government of each member nation sends ambassadors to the United Nations headquarters in New York City. The ambassadors work together to try to make the world a better place. For example, the countries in the United Nations work to improve world health, farming, housing, and relations between nations.

Helping Around the World

One part of the United Nations works specifically to help children. It is called UNICEF, the United Nations Children's Fund. This organization works with different governments in the world to make the lives of children there better. With the money it raises, UNICEF helps governments provide food, health care, and education to children in their countries. UNICEF is one organization that helps those in need.

At the 50th anniversary of the United Nations, leaders of member nations posed for a photograph together.

Biography

Andrew Young

As a boy, Young fought with the children who called him names. As he got older, he learned to compromise instead of fight. He worked for civil rights with Dr. Martin Luther King, Jr. Later, he became the U.S. ambassador to the United Nations. He also was mayor of Atlanta, Georgia, and head of the 1996 Atlanta Olympics organizing committee.

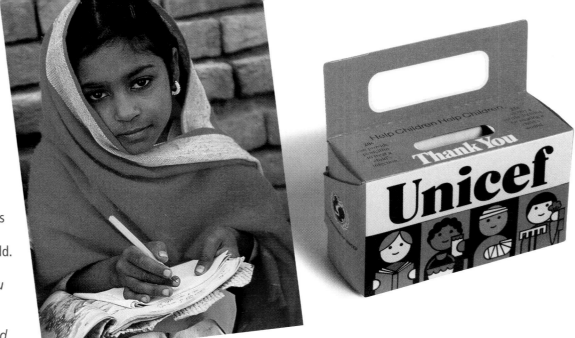

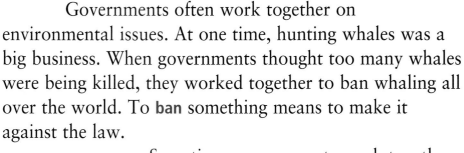

UNICEF is part of the United Nations. It works to help children all over the world. **Citizenship:** *What could you do to help children in the world who need food or medicine?*

World leaders often work together. Here, President Clinton and Nelson Mandela, president of South Africa, meet and talk about their countries.

Governments often work together on environmental issues. At one time, hunting whales was a big business. When governments thought too many whales were being killed, they worked together to ban whaling all over the world. To **ban** something means to make it against the law.

Sometimes governments work together on special projects. For example, the United States and Russia are cooperating on a space program. Working together in space helps both countries save money.

One difficulty of working with governments of other nations is that not everyone speaks the same language. That makes it hard to talk to one another. Translators can help because they speak more than one language. A **translator** listens to what someone says in one language, then repeats it in another language. It's a difficult job. Translators need to know the languages that they use very well. As you might guess, many translators are needed to help governments work together!

Nations Work Together

Russians and Americans Meet in Space

For many years, the United States sent astronauts into space while Russia sent up cosmonauts. Each nation had its own space program — and its own cookies! The American astronauts brought butter cookies. Russian cosmonauts brought *Vostok* (vah STOHK) cookies.

Then, in 1994, the two countries began working together. An American astronaut, Dr. Norman Thagard, started special space training in Russia. A year later, Dr. Thagard and two Russian cosmonauts were launched into space. After about two days, they docked with a Russian space station called *Mir*. Dr. Thagard was the first American to visit *Mir*. He and the Russian cosmonauts lived and worked on the space station for more than three months. Together, they performed many science experiments and shared their test results. They also shared their cookies.

An American astronaut in space.

Russian cosmonauts and American astronauts meet in the space shuttle *Atlantis.*

People Coming Together

Focus *What kinds of organizations bring people in the world together?*

More than 10,000 athletes proudly march in a long parade. They wear official uniforms and follow their country's flag. Hundreds of thousands of people are there to watch the opening ceremonies of the Olympics. About three billion people see the parade on television. At this moment, people around the world are linked by one event. In the following days, athletes from all over the world compete. When athletes win an award in the Olympics, they bring honor to themselves and to their country.

Organizations like the World Association of Girl Guides and Girl Scouts help people from different parts of the world get to know one another. In over 100 countries, girls work and learn together. There are world centers in India, England, Mexico, and Switzerland where Girl Scouts and Girl Guides from all over the world can meet.

Gymnasts compete for their country in the Olympics.

At the start of the Olympic Games, athletes walk in a parade. Then the host nation puts on a show. In Spain, performers wore bright costumes.

These girls belong to the World Association of Girl Guides and Girl Scouts. They live in the United Arab Emirates.

In an **exchange program,** students live and study in another country. Sari van Heemskerck came to the United States on an exchange program in 1958. She says that Louisiana was so different from the Netherlands that "it felt partly like stepping into another world." Exchange programs help people in different parts of the world get to know one another. When people learn about other cultures they can understand and accept what others say and do. Often, people find out that they share beliefs and values.

You have learned that all countries have governments. In this past year, you have taken a trip to many communities around the world. You have seen that they all have some things in common, yet every community has its own way of doing things.

Then & Now

The Olympic Games began in ancient Greece. Every four years, people gathered to compete. For hundreds of years, there were no Olympic Games. Then, in 1896, the Olympic Games began again.

Lesson Review

1. **Vocabulary:** Write sentences using the words **translator, ban,** and **exchange program.**

2. **Focus:** In what ways does the United States government work with other governments in the world?

3. **Focus:** What kinds of organizations bring people in the world together?

4. **Critical Thinking: Interpret** In what ways are the members of an Olympic team "ambassadors" to other countries?

5. **Theme: Cooperation** In what ways do people all over the world help one another?

6. **Geography/Science Activity:** Pollution does not stop at national borders. Find out how governments are working together to fight pollution. Share your findings with the class.

Chapter Review

Summarizing the Main Idea

1 Copy and fill in the table below. Show what governments in the world do for their citizens.

Governments in the World			
	Government in the Netherlands	Government in the United States	Governments Throughout the World
What the Government Does For Citizens			

Vocabulary

2 Write a sentence for each word or phrase below.

parliament (p. 311)   **ban (p. 320)**   **exchange program (p. 323)**

dike (p. 312)   **translator (p. 320)**

ambassador (p. 315)

Reviewing the Facts

3 What does Parliament do in the Netherlands?

4 How is the government of the Netherlands different from the government of the United States?

5 What do Water Control Boards do in the Netherlands?

6 Why do the people in the Netherlands often think about the other countries of Europe?

7 What is the European Union?

8 How do sporting events help countries?

9 Why do countries in the United Nations work together?

10 What are some of the organizations that help bring people in the world together?

Skill Review: Using the Media to Get Information

You have read that newspapers, magazines, radio, and television provide information. Your textbook is also a source of information. Reread the first paragraph on page 323 to answer questions 11 and 12.

11 What is the main idea of the paragraph?

12 Which information in the paragraph is fact? Which information is nonfact? Why do you think this?

Geography Skills

Use the map on page 313 to answer these questions.

13 Which countries share a border with the Netherlands?

14 Why did the people of the Netherlands make new land by filling in the sea with earth?

Writing: Citizenship and Cultures

15 **Culture** Suppose a student from the Netherlands was going to come to your community on an exchange program. Make a handbook that gives information to the student to help him or her live in the United States.

16 **Citizenship** Write a letter to someone in another country describing the government where you live.

Activities

Cultures/Research Activity
Choose a country to which you would like to go on an exchange. Do research to find out something special about the heritage of that country. Present what you find to the class.

History/Science Activity
How has the American space program changed since it began? Do research to find out. Write a short report on what you find.

THEME PROJECT CHECK-IN

Look at your Government Day plan and answer these questions:
- Have you invited a visitor from the government who helps to make laws?
- Have you included a display that shows how lawmakers in your community are chosen?

Internet Option

Check the **Internet Social Studies Center** for ideas on how to extend your theme project beyond your classroom.

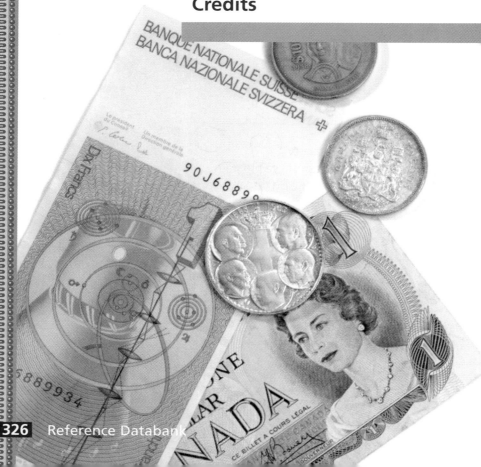

Reference Databank

Handbook for Learners

Reading this book is like traveling. As you go through the chapters, you visit many places. You drop in around your country. You see lands far away from you on the other side of the world.

To go from one place to another you need two things. First of all, you need directions and information. So you must have maps, globes, charts, and graphs. You also need to think about how to get around in the area you are visiting. This handbook will show you what you need to know for this trip.

Contents

Reviewing Map and Globe Skills

Comparing Maps and Globes

You know that the earth is round. A globe is a map of the earth, so it is round too. But sometimes we need a flat map of the round globe. How much of the world does this picture of the globe show? The World Map shows the whole world.

Suppose you are on the continent of South America. You want to go to North America. You have a map. You can use its compass rose to find out which way to travel. In what direction will you go? In what direction should you go to get from South America to Europe?

ASIA

PACIFIC
OCEAN

INDIAN
OCEAN

AUSTRALIA

Scale

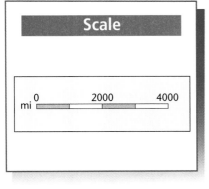

The map scale shows distances. One inch stands for 3,000 miles on real land.

Compass Rose

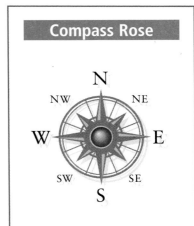

A compass rose is a drawing showing the directions on a map. It shows north, south, east, and west.

ARCTIC
OCEAN

NORTH
AMERICA

UNITED
STATES

EUROPE

ASIA

ATLANTIC
OCEAN

AFRICA

In what direction are you heading if you're moving between north and west? Northwest. The directions between the cardinal points are northwest, southwest, southeast and northeast. By using them you can describe directions more precisely.

SOUTH
AMERICA

INDIAN
OCEAN

N
NW   NE
W   E
SW   SE
S

mi 0   2000   4000

ANTARCTICA

Use it

The seven main bodies of land on the earth are called continents. Find these continents on the World Map: Africa, Antarctica, Asia, Australia, Europe, North America, and South America.

Going Further

Plan a trip that will take you from home to Holland, in Europe, and then to Chile, in South America. Use a wall map or globe. Describe the directions in which you will be traveling.

Reading Maps

Suppose you are standing on a corner in Charleston, South Carolina. You have never been there before. Of course, you are lost. What you need is a map. A map can show you where you are and how to get where you want to go.

The map to the right was made from the photograph below. How are this photograph and the map the same? How are they different?

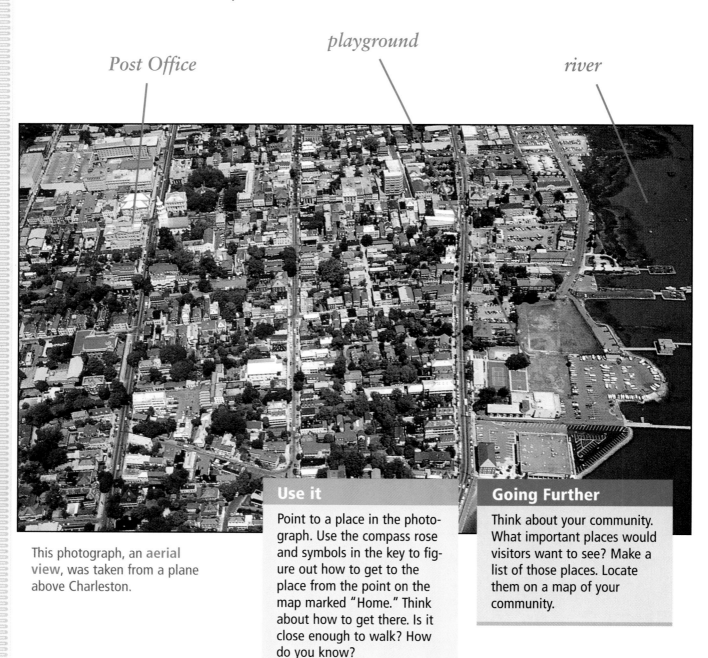

Post Office

playground

river

This photograph, an **aerial view**, was taken from a plane above Charleston.

Use it

Point to a place in the photograph. Use the compass rose and symbols in the key to figure out how to get to the place from the point on the map marked "Home." Think about how to get there. Is it close enough to walk? How do you know?

Going Further

Think about your community. What important places would visitors want to see? Make a list of those places. Locate them on a map of your community.

Locator maps show you where the area on the main map is in the country or on the earth. They help you see how large or small the area on the main map is.

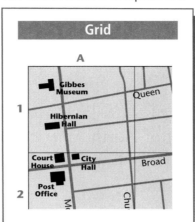

Locator Map

Maps sometimes have a **grid** of lines on them to help locate places. Letters run across the top, and numbers go down the side. The Court House is in square 2A.

Grid

The **key** lists the symbols on the map. These symbols stand for real things such as streets, rivers, parks, buildings, or monuments.

Key

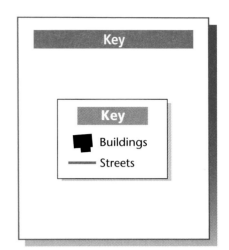

Key

■ Buildings
— Streets

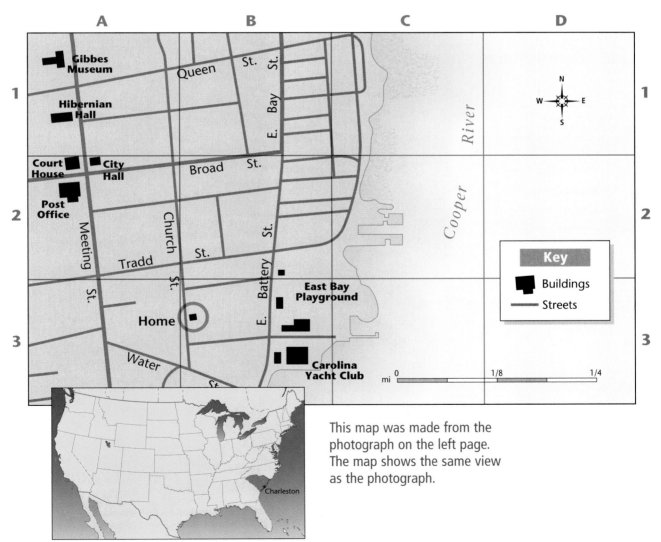

This map was made from the photograph on the left page. The map shows the same view as the photograph.

Reading a United States Map

You live in the country called the United States of America. It is on the continent of North America. As you can see on the map, 48 of the states are all linked together. The states of Alaska and Hawaii are separate. Which state do you live in?

Canada, the United States, and Mexico are all countries on the continent of North America. Look at the lines that divide the countries. How are they different from the lines that divide the states?

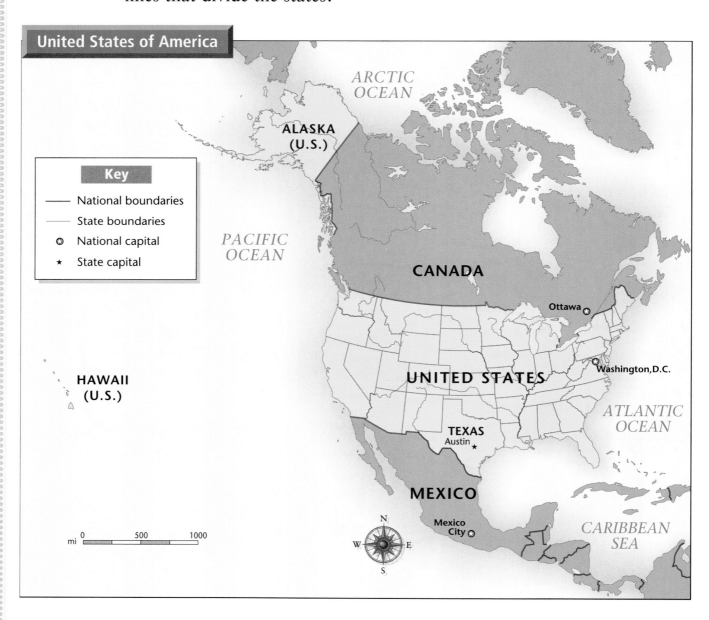

United States of America

ARCTIC OCEAN

ALASKA (U.S.)

Key
— National boundaries
— State boundaries
⊙ National capital
★ State capital

PACIFIC OCEAN

CANADA

Ottawa ⊙

Washington, D.C. ⊙

HAWAII (U.S.)

UNITED STATES

ATLANTIC OCEAN

TEXAS
Austin ★

MEXICO

Mexico City ⊙

CARIBBEAN SEA

mi 0   500   1000

N
W E
S

Global Address

Your town is one of many towns in your county. The county is one of many in your state. The state is one of the fifty of the United States. The United States is on the continent of North America. This is your global address. Your global address shows you how you and your community relate to everyone else on the earth.

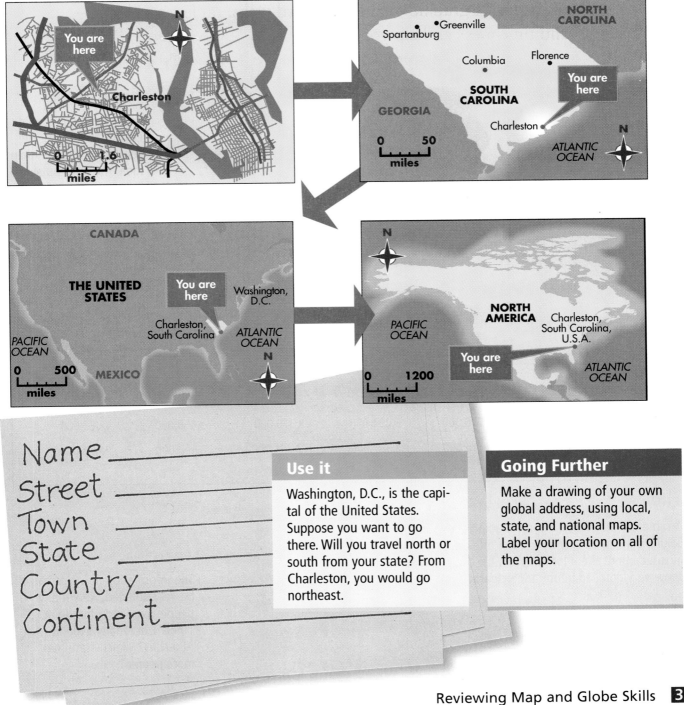

Name _____

Street _____

Town _____

State _____

Country_____

Continent_____

Use it

Washington, D.C., is the capital of the United States. Suppose you want to go there. Will you travel north or south from your state? From Charleston, you would go northeast.

Going Further

Make a drawing of your own global address, using local, state, and national maps. Label your location on all of the maps.

Reviewing Visual Learning Skills

Graphic Organizers

Sometimes the best way to show information is in a kind of picture, a graphic organizer. Word webs, tables, graphs, and timelines can help you out.

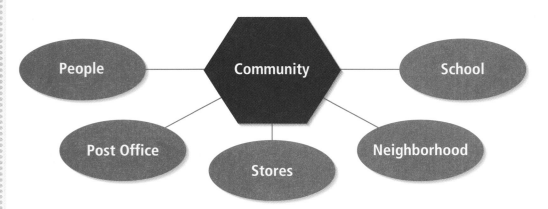

Word Webs

Word webs show related words or ideas. The center word is the main idea. The ones outside are the related ideas. Word webs can help you think of questions for reports or answer questions about other topics.

Population Table

	1989	1990	1991	1992	1993
Colorado	3,276,000	3,294,000	3,370,000	3,456,000	3,586,000
Arkansas	2,346,000	2,351,000	2,371,000	2,394,000	2,424,000

Tables

A table has information in rows going across and columns going up and down. The title and the headings tell about the information in the table. Tables can show very detailed information clearly.

Use it

The information in tables can be very detailed. How many people lived in Colorado in 1993? How many lived in Arkansas? Which state had more people?

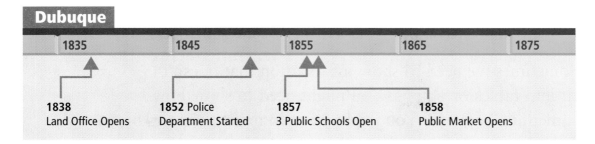

Dubuque

| 1835 | 1845 | 1855 | 1865 | 1875 |

1838
Land Office Opens

1852 Police
Department Started

1857
3 Public Schools Open

1858
Public Market Opens

Timelines

A timeline places things that have happened onto a line. That way it's easier to see when things happened, and how different events fit together. On this timeline you can see that the Dubuque Police Department was started 14 years after the Land Office opened.

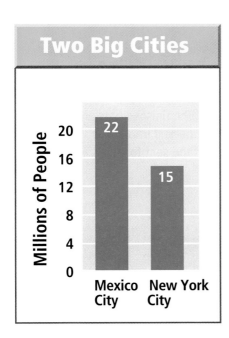

Two Big Cities

Millions of People

| | 22 | 15 |

Mexico City — New York City

Bar Graphs

A bar graph shows information quickly. It can help you compare how much or how many of something. Which city had more people in 1992, Mexico City or New York City? To the right is a photograph of Mexico City—it certainly is a big city!

Mexico City, Mexico

Going Further

Have your classmates vote for a favorite trip—to a dinosaur museum, a baseball game, or a concert. Show the results in a bar graph. Which was the most popular trip? The least?

Charts and Diagrams

Sometimes we need to show information that doesn't fit into tables or graphs. You might need to show how something happens. You might want to make the parts of something clear. Then the tools you would use are charts and diagrams.

1 An ash tree is cut down.

2 The tree is cut into smaller pieces.

4 The finished bats are packed into boxes and sent to stores.

3 The baseball bat is shaped on a special machine.

Flow Charts

Flow charts are diagrams with arrows that show the flow from one stage to the next. The arrows make the order of events or stages clear. Here we see how a tree becomes a baseball bat.

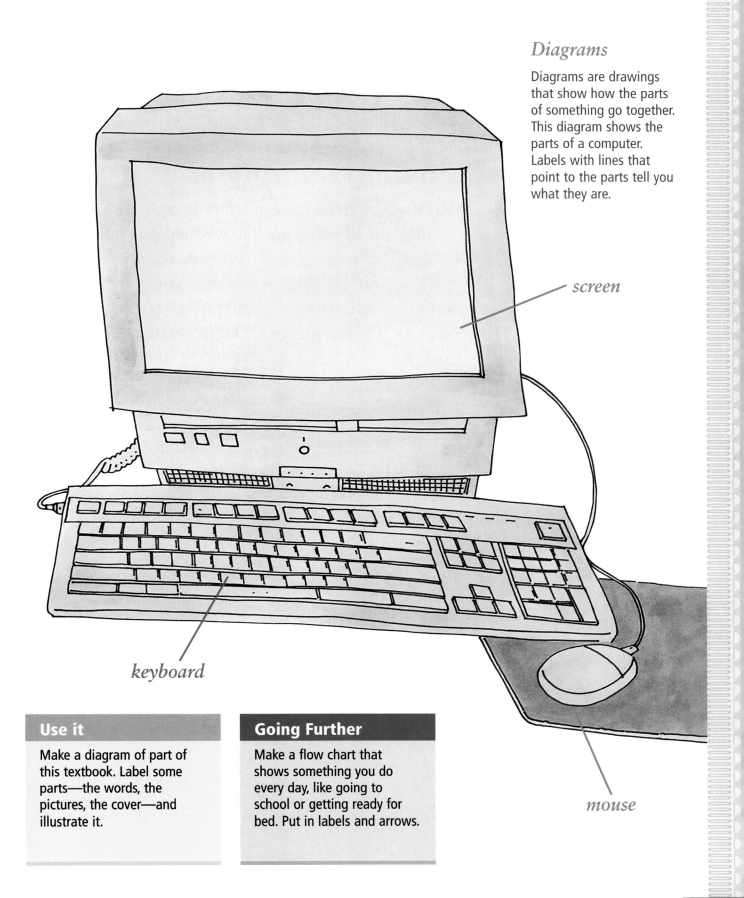

Diagrams

Diagrams are drawings that show how the parts of something go together. This diagram shows the parts of a computer. Labels with lines that point to the parts tell you what they are.

screen

keyboard

mouse

Use it

Make a diagram of part of this textbook. Label some parts—the words, the pictures, the cover—and illustrate it.

Going Further

Make a flow chart that shows something you do every day, like going to school or getting ready for bed. Put in labels and arrows.

Reviewing Social Studies Research Skills

Gathering Information

What if you wanted to plan a family trip? How would you find out where to go? How would you figure out the best way to get there? You and your friends can probably come up with some good ideas. But there are other ways to gather information. You could take a survey. You could interview people to find out where they've gone. You could also write a letter.

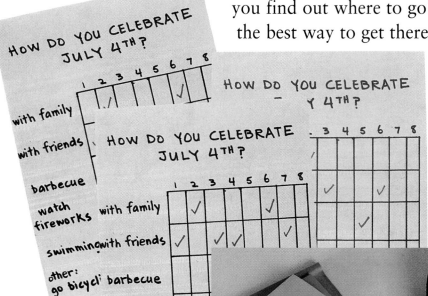

Surveys

In a survey you ask a number of people a series of questions about a topic. Surveys can offer a choice of questions: How long did you visit—less than a week, more than a week? Would you go again—yes or no? When you're done, add up the answers you got for each question. The information can help you decide where to go.

Interviews

In an interview you ask someone questions about a topic. Interview people who know about special places. They can give you information about their favorite places. Write down the questions you want to ask first. Record or write the answers as you get them. Remember to thank the person after the interview.

Have you ever taken a trip on a jet plane?

Where did you go?

...e is another place ...would like to

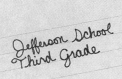

Letter

You can write a letter to ask for information from someone who is too far away to interview. Keep the questions organized and end with a thank you. This letter is asking about dude ranches.

Jefferson School
Third Grade

Dude Ranchers Association
Box 471
La Porte, CO 80535

Dear Association Members:

We are studying great trips. We found your address in a book. It looks interesting to us. Could you please send us some information?

First of all we would like... ranch is. What happens... have fun?

We would like a list of d... with our families. We... there. We also want t... to stay at a dude ra...

Thank you,
The Jefferson School
Third Grade

Use it

Design a survey card you would use if you wanted to find out where people went on vacation, and what their favorite places to visit are.

Going Further

Find someone to interview about a trip they have taken. Remember to write your questions down before the interview, to make sure you find out what you want to know.

Using the Library

The best place to get written information is the library. The library has reference books like encyclopedias, dictionaries, and atlases. It also has books on every subject, magazines, newspapers, and other media. Tell the librarian what you want to find out. The librarian will be able to tell you which books or media will have the information.

There are many resources available in the library— books, reference books, the computer, and other people.

Dictionary

A dictionary can tell you the meaning of a word and how it is pronounced. If you are looking up something in an encyclopedia or other book, and come across a word you don't know, the dictionary will help you out. The guide words at the top of the page show what words are on the page. Since the words in the dictionary are in alphabetical order, it's easy to find the word you want.

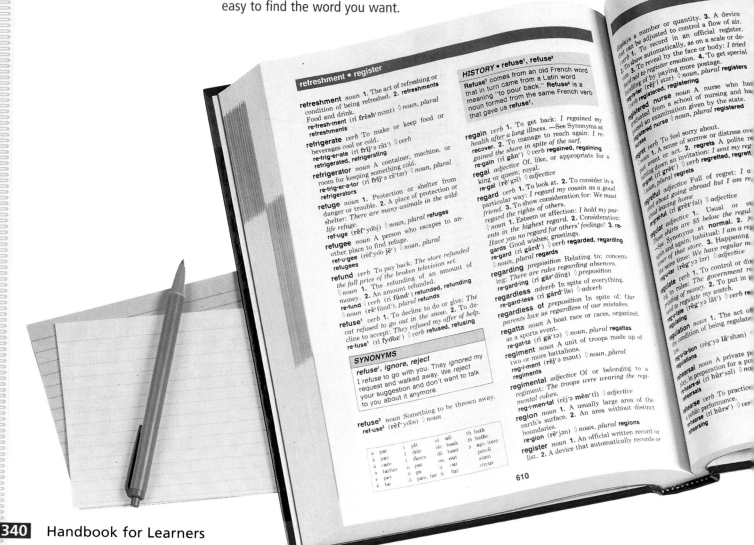

Encyclopedia

An encyclopedia can give you information about any trip you want to take. You can look on the backs of the volumes for the one which contains your topic. The back of each volume shows the letter or letters covered in that volume. The articles are in alphabetical order. They also list related topics. Turn to an article on a related topic for even more information.

346 **Bird**

Birds of Europe and Asia

Europe and Asia have many of the same species of birds. The two continents form one land mass called *Eurasia*. Many birds have extended their range across Eurasia from western Europe to eastern China and Siberia. However, differences in climate have restricted the spread of species in a north-south direction.

Most of Eurasia lies in the North Temperate Zone. This region has many of the same kinds of habitats—including grasslands and needleleaf and broadleaf forests—as temperate North America. Some birds of the region are the European bee-eater, European cuckoo, European roller, nightingale, wall creeper, and white stork. The region also has many kinds of buntings, ducks, finches, larks, sandpipers, tits, warblers, and woodpeckers. Extreme northern Eurasia lies in the Arctic. Many of the same species of birds nest there as in the North American Arctic. Most birds of Arctic and temperate Eurasia fly south for the winter.

Most of Arabia, India, and Southeast Asia lie in the tropics. Each of these regions has its own species of birds. The rain forests of India and Southeast Asia have the greatest variety. The pink-necked fruit dove and rhinoceros hornbill are typical Southeast Asian species. The golden-fronted leafbird lives in both India and Southeast Asia. The Himalaya, the great mountain range on India's northern border, hinders the spread of species between India and lands to the north. The northern and eastern foothills of the Himalaya have a number of birds that are found nowhere else. These birds include the Himalayan monal and Lady Amherst's pheasant.

European bee-eater
Merops apiaster
About 11 inches
(28 centimeters)

Himalayan monal
Lophophorus impejanus
23 to 28 inches
(58 to 71 centimeters)

Pink-necked fruit
Ptilinopus porphyrea
About 12 inches
(30 centimeters)

Lady Amherst's pheasant
Chrysolophus amherstiae
About 50 inches
(127 centimeters)

Wall creeper
Tichodroma muraria
About 6½ inches
(16.5 centimeters)

Nightingale
Luscinia megarhynchos
6 to 6½ inches
(15 to 16.5 centimeters)

---

registered nurse • rejoice

n **1.** The power or rule of a monThe time when a monarch rules.
To rule as a monarch. **2.** To be
ad: *Silence reigned in the forest.*
(rān) ◊ *noun, plural* **reigns** ◊ *verb*
, **reigning**
sound alike: **reign, rain, rein**

oun **1.** Often **reins** A long, narrow,
r strap attached to the bit of a bridle
eld by the rider or driver to control an
al. **2.** A restraining influence: *The
her kept the class under a tight rein.*
eins Power to control or guide.
erb To guide or control by or as if by reins.
n (rān) ◊ *noun, plural* **reins** ◊ *verb* **reined,**
ining
These sound alike: **rein, rain, reign**
indeer *noun* A deer of Arctic regions of Europe and Greenland that has large, spreading
antlers in both the male and female.
rein-deer (rān'dir') ◊ *noun, plural*
reindeer

g or
ie or

ural

as of a
rmance.

ration for

ed,

▲ reindeer

R

reinforce *verb* To make stronger with more
material, help, or support.
re-in-force (rē'in fôrs') ◊ *verb* **reinforced,**
reinforcing
reject *verb* To refuse to accept or consider:
The school paper rejected my article. —See
Synonyms at **refuse.**
re-ject (ri jĕkt') ◊ *verb* **rejected, rejecting**
rejoice *verb* To feel or express joy.
re-joice (ri jois') ◊ *verb* **rejoiced, rejoicing**

611

Use it

Make a list of the topics you would look up in an encyclopedia to get information for a family trip. Think of places you would like to go or things you would like to do.

Going Further

Plan a vacation! Decide where to go. Find out about it. Write down what you'll see there. Make a map of the place you plan to visit. Show the route you will take to do the things you want to do.

Atlas

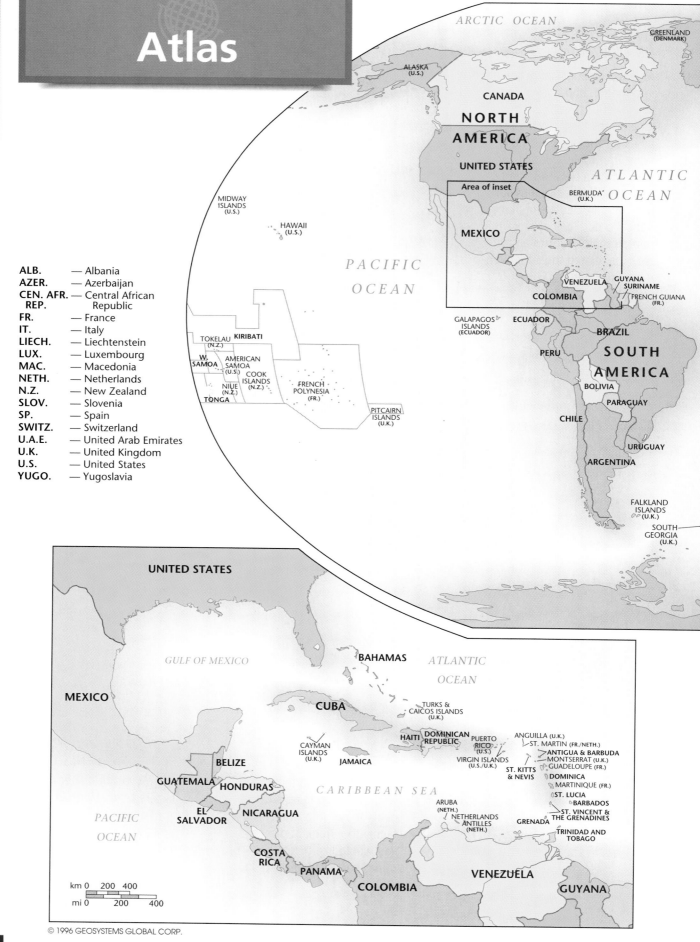

ALB. — Albania
AZER. — Azerbaijan
CEN. AFR. REP. — Central African Republic
FR. — France
IT. — Italy
LIECH. — Liechtenstein
LUX. — Luxembourg
MAC. — Macedonia
NETH. — Netherlands
N.Z. — New Zealand
SLOV. — Slovenia
SP. — Spain
SWITZ. — Switzerland
U.A.E. — United Arab Emirates
U.K. — United Kingdom
U.S. — United States
YUGO. — Yugoslavia

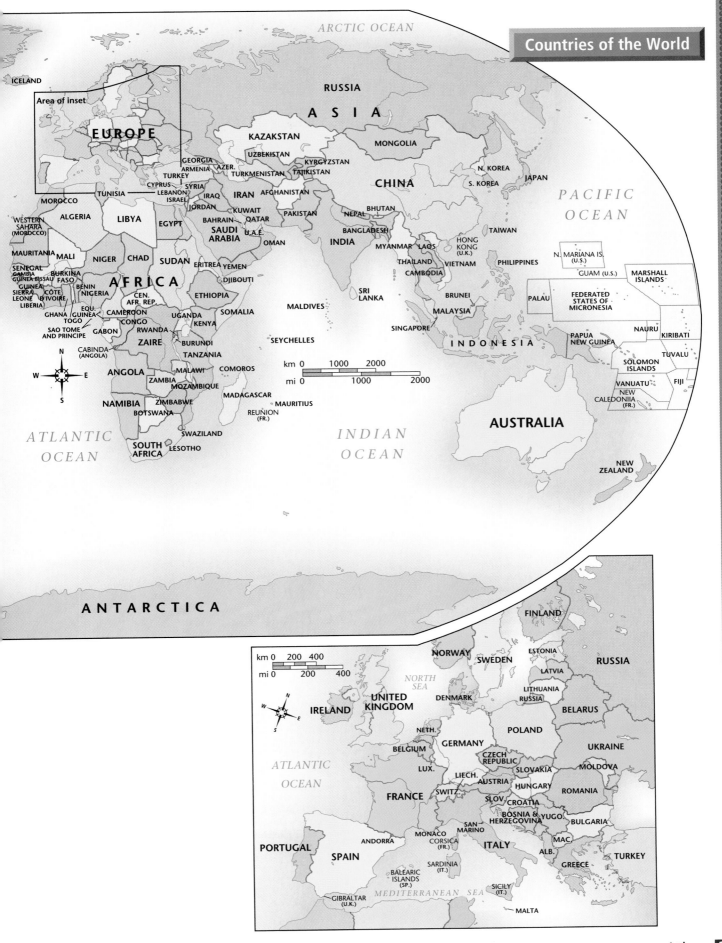

ARCTIC OCEAN

ICELAND

Area of inset

EUROPE

RUSSIA

A S I A

KAZAKSTAN

UZBEKISTAN

MONGOLIA

GEORGIA
ARMENIA   AZER.
TURKEY   KYRGYZSTAN
TURKMENISTAN   TAJIKISTAN

CHINA

N. KOREA
S. KOREA   JAPAN

PACIFIC
OCEAN

TUNISIA
CYPRUS
LEBANON   SYRIA
ISRAEL

IRAQ   IRAN   AFGHANISTAN

JORDAN   KUWAIT   PAKISTAN   NEPAL   BHUTAN

TAIWAN

MOROCCO

BAHRAIN   QATAR
SAUDI   U.A.E.
ARABIA   OMAN

BANGLADESH

HONG
KONG
(U.K.)

N. MARIANA IS.
(U.S.)

WESTERN
SAHARA
(MOROCCO)   ALGERIA   LIBYA   EGYPT

INDIA

MYANMAR   LAOS

GUAM (U.S.)

MARSHALL
ISLANDS

MAURITANIA   MALI   NIGER   CHAD   SUDAN   ERITREA   YEMEN

THAILAND   VIETNAM
CAMBODIA

PHILIPPINES

PALAU

FEDERATED
STATES OF
MICRONESIA

NAURU

KIRIBATI

SENEGAL
GAMBIA   BURKINA
GUINEA-BISSAU   FASO
GUINEA   BENIN
SIERRA   CÔTE   NIGERIA
LEONE   D'IVOIRE
LIBERIA

AFRICA

DJIBOUTI

CEN.
AFR. REP.   ETHIOPIA

SRI
LANKA

BRUNEI

MALDIVES

MALAYSIA

TUVALU

GHANA   EQU.
TOGO   GUINEA
SAO TOME   CAMEROON
AND PRINCIPE   GABON

UGANDA
CONGO
RWANDA

SOMALIA
KENYA

SINGAPORE

INDONESIA

PAPUA
NEW GUINEA

SOLOMON
ISLANDS

FIJI

CABINDA
(ANGOLA)

ZAIRE

BURUNDI

TANZANIA

SEYCHELLES

VANUATU   NEW
CALEDONIA
(FR.)

N
W   E
S

ANGOLA

MALAWI

COMOROS

ZAMBIA
MOZAMBIQUE

NAMIBIA   ZIMBABWE

MADAGASCAR

MAURITIUS

AUSTRALIA

BOTSWANA

REUNION
(FR.)

km 0   1000   2000
mi 0   1000   2000

ATLANTIC
OCEAN

SOUTH
AFRICA

SWAZILAND
LESOTHO

INDIAN
OCEAN

NEW
ZEALAND

ANTARCTICA

FINLAND

NORWAY   SWEDEN   ESTONIA   RUSSIA
LATVIA

km 0   200   400
mi 0   200   400

NORTH
SEA   LITHUANIA   BELARUS
RUSSIA

N
W   E
S

IRELAND   UNITED
KINGDOM   DENMARK

NETH.   POLAND   UKRAINE

ATLANTIC
OCEAN

BELGIUM   GERMANY

LUX.   CZECH
REPUBLIC   SLOVAKIA   MOLDOVA

LIECH.   AUSTRIA   HUNGARY   ROMANIA

FRANCE   SWITZ.   SLOV   CROATIA

MONACO   SAN   BOSNIA &   YUGO   BULGARIA
MARINO   HERZEGOVINA

PORTUGAL   ANDORRA   CORSICA
(FR.)   ITALY   MAC
ALB.   TURKEY

SPAIN   BALEARIC
ISLANDS
(SP.)   SARDINIA
(IT.)   GREECE

GIBRALTAR
(U.K.)   SICILY
(IT.)

MEDITERRANEAN SEA   MALTA

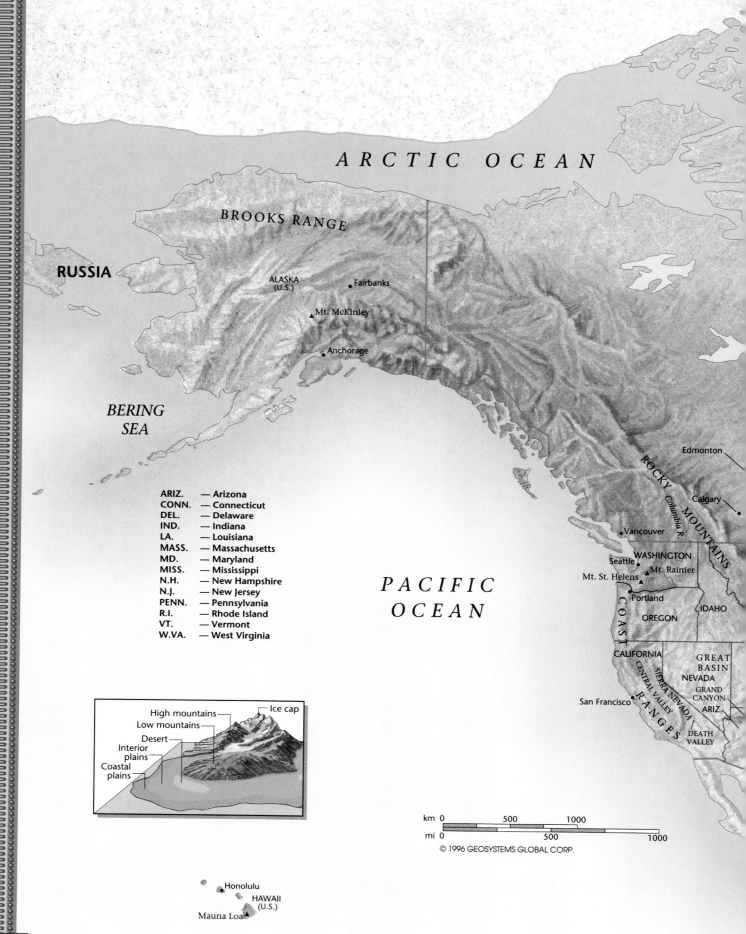

ARCTIC OCEAN

BROOKS RANGE

RUSSIA

ALASKA
(U.S.)

Fairbanks

▲ Mt. McKinley

● Anchorage

BERING
SEA

ARIZ.	— Arizona
CONN.	— Connecticut
DEL.	— Delaware
IND.	— Indiana
LA.	— Louisiana
MASS.	— Massachusetts
MD.	— Maryland
MISS.	— Mississippi
N.H.	— New Hampshire
N.J.	— New Jersey
PENN.	— Pennsylvania
R.I.	— Rhode Island
VT.	— Vermont
W.VA.	— West Virginia

PACIFIC
OCEAN

Edmonton

Calgary

ROCKY MOUNTAINS

Columbia R.

● Vancouver

WASHINGTON
Seattle ●   ▲ Mt. Rainier
Mt. St. Helens ▲
● Portland   IDAHO

OREGON

COAST

CALIFORNIA

GREAT
BASIN

NEVADA

SIERRA NEVADA

CENTRAL VALLEY

GRAND
CANYON

ARIZ.

San Francisco ●

R A N G E S

DEATH
VALLEY

High mountains — Ice cap
Low mountains
Desert
Interior
plains
Coastal
plains

km 0   500   1000
mi 0   500   1000

© 1996 GEOSYSTEMS GLOBAL CORP.

Honolulu
●
HAWAII
(U.S.)
Mauna Loa ▲

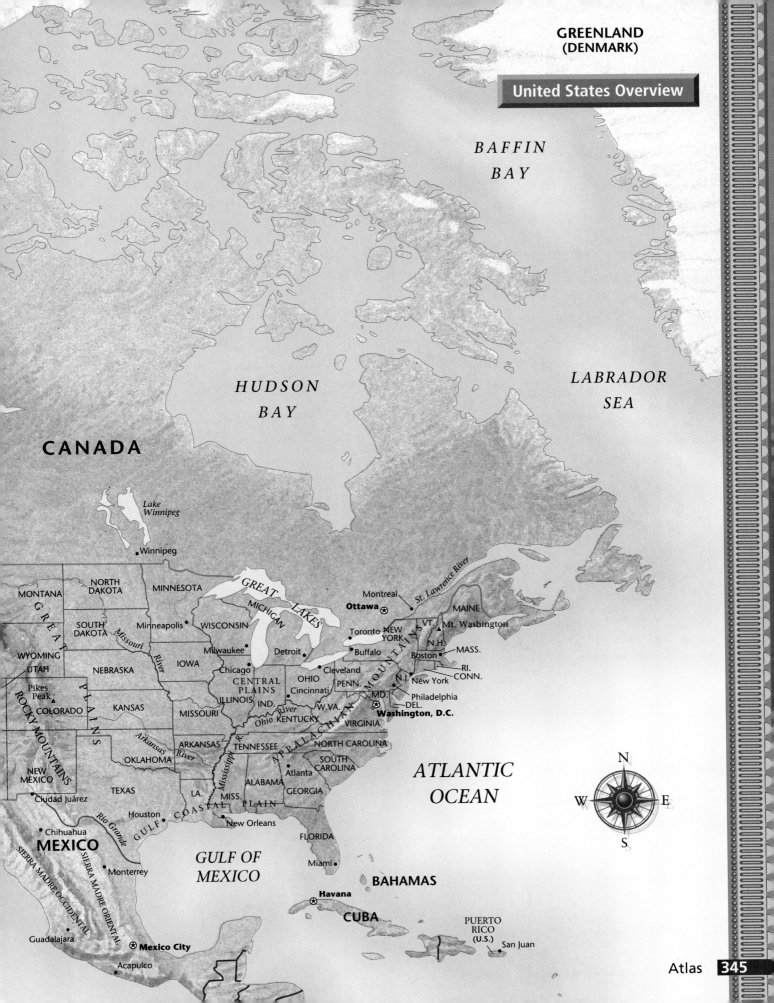

GREENLAND
(DENMARK)

BAFFIN
BAY

LABRADOR
SEA

HUDSON
BAY

CANADA

Lake Winnipeg

• Winnipeg

MONTANA

NORTH DAKOTA

MINNESOTA

GREAT LAKES

MICHIGAN

Montreal

St. Lawrence River

⊛ Ottawa

MAINE

▲ Mt. Washington

VT.

N.H.

SOUTH DAKOTA

• Minneapolis

WISCONSIN

Missouri River

Toronto

NEW YORK

Buffalo

Boston

MASS.

RI.

CONN.

WYOMING

UTAH

NEBRASKA

IOWA

Milwaukee •

• Detroit

Chicago

CENTRAL
PLAINS

OHIO

Cleveland

Cincinnati

IND.

N.J.

New York

PENN.

Philadelphia

MD.

DEL.

Pikes
Peak ▲

COLORADO

KANSAS

MISSOURI

ILLINOIS

Ohio River

W.VA.

KENTUCKY

⊛ Washington, D.C.

VIRGINIA

ROCKY MOUNTAINS

GREAT PLAINS

Arkansas River

ARKANSAS

Mississippi R.

TENNESSEE

NORTH CAROLINA

APPALACHIAN MOUNTAINS

NEW
MEXICO

OKLAHOMA

SOUTH
CAROLINA

ATLANTIC
OCEAN

Ciudad Juárez •

TEXAS

LA.

MISS.

ALABAMA

Atlanta •

GEORGIA

N

Rio Grande

Houston •

GULF COASTAL PLAIN

New Orleans

W

E

• Chihuahua

MEXICO

FLORIDA

S

SIERRA MADRE OCCIDENTAL

SIERRA MADRE ORIENTAL

• Monterrey

GULF OF
MEXICO

Miami •

BAHAMAS

⊛ Havana

Guadalajara •

⊛ Mexico City

CUBA

PUERTO
RICO
(U.S.)

• San Juan

Acapulco •

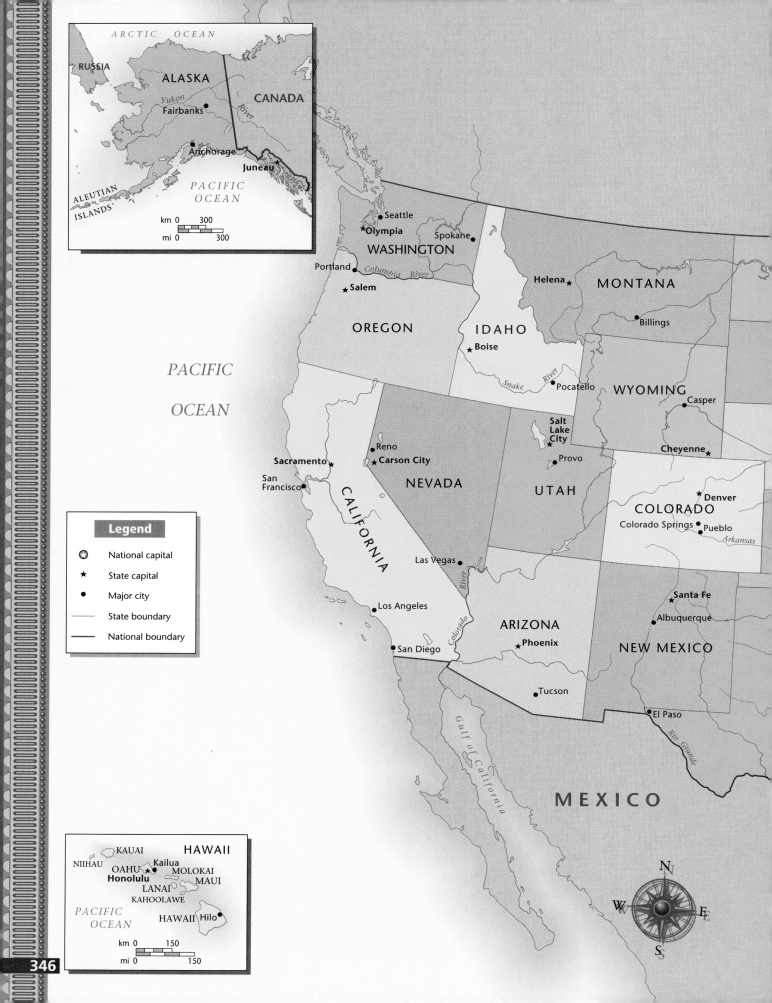

ARCTIC OCEAN

RUSSIA

ALASKA

CANADA

Yukon

Fairbanks

River

Anchorage

Juneau ★

PACIFIC
OCEAN

ALEUTIAN
ISLANDS

km 0   300
mi 0   300

PACIFIC

OCEAN

Seattle

★ Olympia

Spokane

WASHINGTON

Portland   *Columbia River*

★ Salem

OREGON

Helena ★

MONTANA

Billings

IDAHO

★ Boise

Snake   River

Pocatello

WYOMING

Casper

Salt
Lake
City

Provo

Cheyenne ★

Reno

Sacramento ★ Carson City

San
Francisco

NEVADA

CALIFORNIA

UTAH

COLORADO

★ Denver

Colorado Springs   Pueblo

Arkansas

Legend

◎ National capital

★ State capital

● Major city

...... State boundary

—— National boundary

Las Vegas

Los Angeles

San Diego

ARIZONA

★ Phoenix

Tucson

*Colorado
River*

Santa Fe ★

Albuquerque

NEW MEXICO

El Paso

Rio Grande

Gulf of California

MEXICO

HAWAII

KAUAI

NIIHAU

OAHU   Kailua

Honolulu ★   MOLOKAI

LANAI   MAUI

KAHOOLAWE

PACIFIC
OCEAN

HAWAII   Hilo

km 0   150
mi 0   150

N
W   E
S

CANADA

NORTH DAKOTA
Bismarck
Fargo

SOUTH DAKOTA
Pierre
Sioux Falls

MINNESOTA
St. Paul
Minneapolis

Lake Superior

MICHIGAN

Lake Huron

Lake Michigan

MAINE
Augusta

NEW HAMPSHIRE
Burlington
Montpelier
VERMONT
Portland
Concord
Manchester

Albany
Rochester
NEW YORK
Buffalo

Boston
MASSACHUSETTS
Hartford
Providence
New Haven
Bridgeport
RHODE ISLAND
Newark
CONNECTICUT
New York

WISCONSIN
Madison
Milwaukee

Mississippi River

Grand Rapids
Lansing

Detroit

Lake Ontario

Lake Erie
Cleveland

PENNSYLVANIA
Harrisburg
Pittsburgh

Trenton
Philadelphia
NEW JERSEY
Wilmington
Dover
DELAWARE

IOWA
Cedar Rapids
Des Moines

Chicago

Fort Wayne

OHIO
Columbus

NEBRASKA
Omaha
Platte River
Lincoln

ILLINOIS
Springfield

Indianapolis
INDIANA

Cincinnati
Ohio River

WEST VIRGINIA
Charleston

Baltimore
Annapolis
Washington, D.C.
MARYLAND

Richmond
VIRGINIA
Norfolk

Missouri River

Kansas City
KANSAS
Topeka
Kansas City
Wichita

St. Louis
Jefferson City
MISSOURI

Frankfort
Louisville

Evansville

KENTUCKY

Greensboro
Raleigh
NORTH CAROLINA
Charlotte

OKLAHOMA
Tulsa
Oklahoma City

ARKANSAS

Nashville
TENNESSEE

Memphis

SOUTH CAROLINA
Columbia
Charleston

Fort Smith
Little Rock

Birmingham

Atlanta
GEORGIA
Columbus
Savannah

Dallas

TEXAS

LOUISIANA

ALABAMA
Montgomery

Jackson
MISSISSIPPI
Mobile

Jacksonville

Tallahassee
FLORIDA

Austin
San Antonio

Houston

Baton Rouge
New Orleans

ATLANTIC OCEAN

Tampa

Miami

GULF OF MEXICO

BAHAMAS

km 0   200   400
mi 0   200   400

© 1996 GEOSYSTEMS GLOBAL CORP.

CUBA

St. Lawrence River

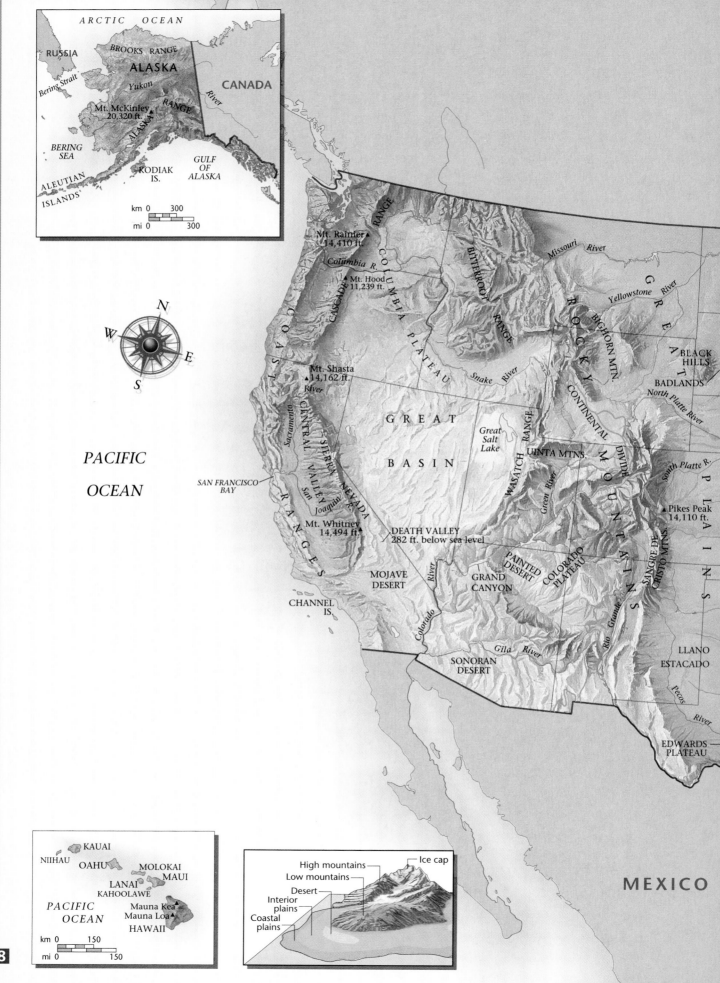

ARCTIC OCEAN

RUSSIA

BROOKS RANGE

ALASKA

CANADA

Bering Strait

Yukon

River

BERING SEA

Mt. McKinley
20,320 ft.

RANGE

ALASKA

GULF
OF
ALASKA

KODIAK
IS.

ALEUTIAN

ISLANDS

km 0   300

mi 0   300

Mt. Rainier
14,410 ft.

Columbia R.

Mt. Hood
11,239 ft.

RANGE

CASCADE

COLUMBIA   PLATEAU

BITTERROOT

RANGE

Missouri   River

Yellowstone   River

GREAT

BIGHORN MTN.

ROCKY

BLACK
HILLS

BADLANDS

Snake   River

North Platte River

Mt. Shasta
14,162 ft.

COAST

River

Sacramento

CENTRAL   VALLEY

SIERRA   NEVADA

San

Joaquin

River

GREAT

BASIN

Great
Salt
Lake

WASATCH   RANGE

UINTA MTNS.

CONTINENTAL   DIVIDE

MOUNTAINS

Green River

South Platte R.

Pikes Peak
14,110 ft.

PLAINS

PACIFIC

OCEAN

N
W   E
S

SAN FRANCISCO
BAY

RANGES

Mt. Whitney
14,494 ft.

DEATH VALLEY
282 ft. below sea level

River

PAINTED
DESERT

COLORADO   PLATEAU

SANGRE DE

CRISTO MTNS.

MOJAVE
DESERT

Colorado

GRAND
CANYON

Gila   River

Rio   Grande

LLANO
ESTACADO

CHANNEL
IS.

Pecos

River

SONORAN
DESERT

EDWARDS
PLATEAU

MEXICO

KAUAI

NIIHAU   OAHU

MOLOKAI

MAUI

LANAI

KAHOOLAWE

PACIFIC
OCEAN

Mauna Kea

Mauna Loa

HAWAII

km 0   150

mi 0   150

High mountains

Low mountains

Desert

Interior
plains

Coastal
plains

Ice cap

CANADA

MESABI RANGE

Lake Superior

Lake Michigan

Lake Huron

Lake Ontario

Lake Erie

Mississippi

Missouri

Des Moines River

SAND HILLS

Platte River

Mississippi River

CENTRAL PLAINS

Wabash R.

Ohio River

River

St. Lawrence River

ADIRONDACK MTS.

Hudson River

Connecticut R.

Mt. Washington 6,288 ft.

WHITE MTS.

CATSKILL MTS.

NANTUCKET
MARTHA'S VINEYARD
LONG ISLAND

Susquehanna River

Delaware River

ALLEGHENY PLATEAU

DELAWARE BAY

CHESAPEAKE BAY

Arkansas River

OZARK PLATEAU

CUMBERLAND PLATEAU

APPALACHIAN MOUNTAINS

BLUE RIDGE MOUNTAINS

Mt. Mitchell 6,684 ft.

FALL LINE

ATLANTIC COASTAL PLAIN

OUACHITA MOUNTAINS

Mississippi River

Tennessee River

Cumberland River

Chattahoochee R.

Tombigbee R.

Savannah River

Altamaha River

Brazos River

Sabine River

Pearl River

Alabama R.

GULF COASTAL PLAIN

ATLANTIC OCEAN

Colorado River

GALVESTON BAY

MOBILE BAY

PENSACOLA BAY

TAMPA BAY

EVERGLADES

BAHAMAS

Rio Grande

GULF   OF   MEXICO

FLORIDA KEYS

CUBA

km 0   200   400

mi 0   200   400

© 1996 GEOSYSTEMS GLOBAL CORP.

349

Gazetteer

Geographic Glossary

bay
part of a lake or ocean extending into the land

coast
the land next to the ocean

desert
a dry area where few plants grow

▼ **forest**
a large area of land where many trees grow

▲ **harbor**
a protected body of water where ships can safely stop

highland
land that is higher than most of the surrounding land

1 hill
a raised mass of land, smaller than a mountain

island
a body of land with water all around it

2 lake
a body of water with land all around it

lowland
land that is lower than most of the surrounding land

3 mountain
a steeply raised mass of land, much higher than the surrounding country

4 mountain range
a row of mountains

ocean or sea
a salty body of water covering a large area of the earth

▲ **plain**
a broad flat area of land

prairie
a large level area of grassland with few or no trees

5 **tree line**
on a mountain, the area above which no trees grow

▲ **river**
a large stream of water that runs into a lake, ocean or another river

sea level
the level of the surface of the ocean

shore
the land along the edge of a lake, sea, or ocean

▼ **valley**
low land between hills or mountains

Community Populations

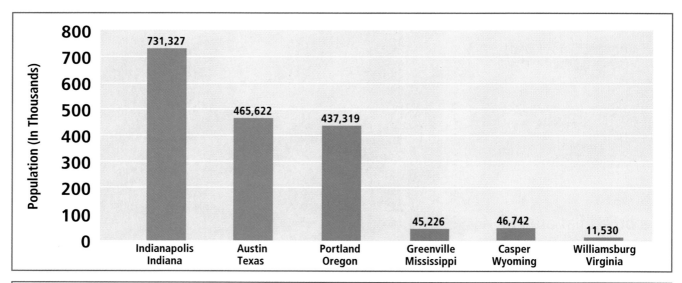

Population (In Thousands)

City	Population
Indianapolis, Indiana	731,327
Austin, Texas	465,622
Portland, Oregon	437,319
Greenville, Mississippi	45,226
Casper, Wyoming	46,742
Williamsburg, Virginia	11,530

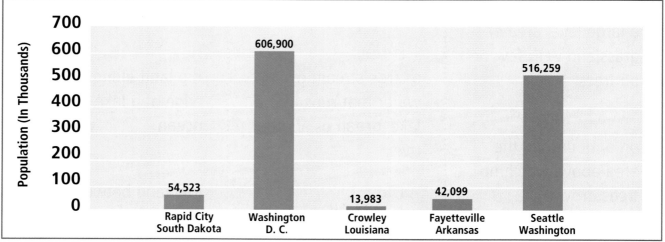

Population (In Thousands)

City	Population
Rapid City, South Dakota	54,523
Washington, D.C.	606,900
Crowley, Louisiana	13,983
Fayetteville, Arkansas	42,099
Seattle, Washington	516,259

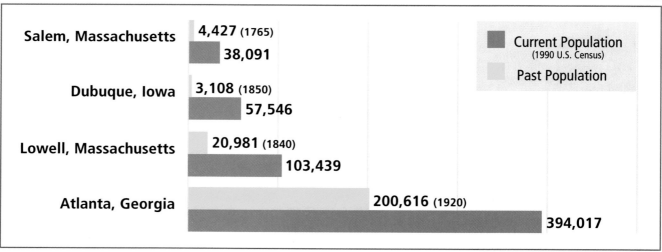

Current Population (1990 U.S. Census)
Past Population

City	Past Population	Current Population
Salem, Massachusetts	4,427 (1765)	38,091
Dubuque, Iowa	3,108 (1850)	57,546
Lowell, Massachusetts	20,981 (1840)	103,439
Atlanta, Georgia	200,616 (1920)	394,017

Glossary

A **adapt** (uh DAPT) To learn to use your surroundings. (p. 74)

agriculture (AG rih kuhl chur) Farming. (p. 151)

air pollution (air puh LOO shuhn) Dirt and chemicals in the air that can harm people. (p. 173)

altar (AWL tur) A table or raised place used during religious services. (p. 265)

ambassador (am BAS uh dur) A representative from the government of another country. (p. 315)

ancestor (AN ses tur) A relative, like a great-grandparent, who has died. (p. 265)

architecture (AHR kih tehk chur) The design of a building. (p. 42)

B **ban** (ban) To make something against the law. (p. 320)

bargain (BAHR gihn) When buyers and sellers discuss the price of an item to reach an agreement. There is no set price. (p. 217)

bar graph (bahr graf) A graph that uses bars of different heights to compare how much or how many of something. (p. 298)

border (BAWR dur) The line where one state or country ends and another begins. (p. 288)

C **Cajun** (KAY juhn) A person who is descended from a large group of French-speaking people who moved to Louisiana in the 1700s. (p. 244)

canal (kuh NAL) A waterway built by people. (p. 17)

candidate (KAN dih dayt) Someone who wants to be elected to a government job. (p. 283)

capital (KAP ih tuhl) The center of an area's government. (p. 172)

car-pool (KAHR pool) To form groups in which people take turns driving. (p. 35)

cargo (KAHR goh) The things a ship carries. (p. 91)

certificate (sur TIHF ih kiht) An official document that can prove an event or fact. (p. 285)

citizen (SIHT ih zuhn) An official member of a country, state, or community. (p. 276)

city council (SIHT ee KOWN suhl) A group of people that makes plans for a city. (p. 59)

climate (KLY muht) The kind of weather that a place has over a long time. (p. 167)

climate map (KLY miht map) A map that shows the climates of different places. (p. 176)

colonial (kuh LOH nee uhl) Related to a colony. (p. 195)

colony (KAHL uh nee) A group of people from one country who settle in another country. (p. 85)

commerce (KAHM urs) The buying and selling of goods. (p. 220)

community (kuh MYOO nih tee) People who live together in the same area. (p. 14)

Congress (KAHNG grihs) A branch of the government of the United States. It makes the laws for the United States. (p. 294)

Constitution (kahn stih TOO shuhn) The basic laws and ideas that the national government of the United States follows. (p. 297)

county (KOWN tee) An area within a state that has its own government. (p. 282)

court (kawrt) A place where questions about the law are answered. (p. 295)

crop (krahp) A plant that is grown to be used, eaten, or sold. (p. 151)

crossroad (KRAHS rohd) A place where two or more roads meet. (p. 23)

cultural diversity (KUHL chur uhl dih VUR sih tee) A mixture of many cultures. (p. 254)

culture (KUHL chur) Everything that makes up the way of life of people in a community. (p. 25)

custom (KUHS tuhm) A way of doing things. (p. 26)

D **demand** (dih MAND) The wish to buy or use something. (p. 188)

diagram (DY uh gram) A picture that shows how to do something or the order of events. (p. 156)

dictionary (DIHK shuhn ehr ee) A reference book that tells you what words mean and how to say them. (p. 200)

dike (dyk) Mounded earth that keeps water out of new land. (p. 312)

E **economics** (ehk uh NAHM ihks) The study of how things are made, bought, sold, and used. (p. 48)

economist (ih KAHN uh mihst) A person who studies how businesses change an economy. (p. 48)

elect (ih LEHKT) To choose a person for an office or a job by voting. (p. 59)

employment (ehm PLOY muhnt) Work people do for a living. (p. 190)

encyclopedia (ehn sy kluh PEE dee uh) A reference book with short articles about many subjects. (p. 200)

environment (ehn VY ruhn muhnt) The natural world around us. (p. 139)

ethnic group (EHTH nihk groop) People who share the same culture. (p. 117)

exchange program (ihks CHAYNJ PROH gram) A program in which students live and study in another country. (p. 323)

export (EHK spawrt) To send things to other countries. (p. 210)

expressway (ihk SPREHS way) A wide highway built to help traffic move quickly. (p. 122)

F **factory** (FAK tuh ree) A building where people use machines to make things. (p. 111)

folklife (FOHK lyf) A community's special music, stories, arts, crafts, and other customs. (p. 53)

folklorist (FOHK lawr ihst) A person who studies the folklife of a community. (p. 54)

fort (fawrt) An area or building surrounded by walls for protection. (p. 85)

fossil (FOHS uhl) The remains of a living thing that died long ago. (p. 235)

G **geography** (jee AHG ruh fee) The study of people, places, and the earth. (p. 32)

geographer (jee AHG ruh fur) A person who studies people, places, and the earth. (p. 32)

global market (GLOH buhl MAHR kiht) Goods from one part of the world can be sold in another part. (p. 210)

goods (gudz) Things that are made or grown that can be sold. (p. 188)

government (GUHV urn muhnt) An organization that keeps a community, state, or nation in order. (p. 58)

governor (GUHV ur nur) The head of a state's government. (p. 289)

H **habitat** (HAB ih tat) A place where a plant or animal lives. (p. 35)

harvest (HAHR vist) The bringing in of crops. (p. 243)

hemisphere (HEHM ih sfihr) One half of the earth. (p. 222)

heritage (HEHR ih tihj) A people's language, customs, and beliefs that have been passed down from parents to children. (p. 235)

high tech (hy tehk) Having to do with up-to-date machines like computers. (p. 50)

historian (hih STAWR ee uhn) A person who studies the past. (p. 39)

history (HIHS tuh ree) The study of the past. (p. 39)

I **immigrant** (IHM ih gruhnt) A person who comes into a new country after leaving his or her home country. (p. 114)

import (IHM pawrt) To bring something in from another country. (p. 95)

Independence Day (ihn dih PEHN duhns day) July 4th, which is the day that people in the United States celebrate their freedom. (p. 233)

independent (ihn dih PEHN duhnt) Ruling yourself. (p. 233)

interview (IHN tur vyoo) To ask someone questions. (p. 43)

inset map (IHN seht map) A map that gives a close-up view of part of another map. (p. 238)

Internet (IHN tur neht) A way for people to share information using computers. (p. 317)

irrigation (ihr ih GAY shuhn) Bringing water to fields. (p. 167)

L **landmark** (LAND mahrk) A place or building that is important to a community. (p. 41)

law (law) A rule that people must follow to keep order. (p. 14)

legislature (LEHJ ih slay chur) The group of people that makes state laws. (p. 289)

levee (LEHV ee) A bank of dirt that has been raised to prevent a river from overflowing. (p. 153)

license (LY suhns) Written permission to do something. (p. 121)

local (LOH kuhl) Part of one community. (p. 276)

long house (lawng hows) A home built by the Iroquois where ten or more families lived. (p. 74)

lunar (LOO nur) Based on the moon. (p. 264)

M **magazine** (MAG uh zeen) A printed form of media that can have lots of different articles. It can also have articles on just one subject. (p. 316)

maize (mayz) Corn. (p. 171)

manufacture (man yuh FAK chur) To make things by using machines. (p. 50)

map (map) A drawing of a place that shows where things are. (p. 18)

market (MAHR kiht) A place where people buy and sell things they need. (p. 168)

mayor (MAY ur) The chief government official in some communities. (p. 59)

media (MEE dee uh) Forms of communication, like newspapers, radio, magazines, television, and the Internet. (p. 316)

merchant (MUR chuhnt) A person who buys and sells things to make money. (p. 91)

mill (mihl) A factory where people make cloth. (p. 111)

mine (myn) To dig something out of the earth. (p. 104)

mineral (MIHN ur uhl) A nonliving thing in the earth or in water. (p. 104)

N **natural resource** (NACH ur uhl REE sawrs) Anything found in the environment that people use. (p. 140)

negotiate (nih GO shee ayt) To discuss the price of an item in order to reach an agreement. (p. 217)

newspaper (NOOZ pay pur) A daily or weekly printed form of communication. (p. 316)

P parliament (PAHR luh muhnt) A branch of government that makes laws. (p. 311)

passport (PAS pawrt) A government document that lets you leave your home country to visit other countries. (p. 253)

petition (puh TIHSH uhn) A written request. (p. 60)

pollution (puh LOO shuhn) Things in the water, soil, or air which harm plants, animals, and people. (p. 34)

population (pahp yuh LAY shuhn) The number of people who live in a place. (p. 166)

port (pawrt) A place on a river, lake, or ocean where boats can dock. (p. 141)

President (PREHZ ih dehnt) The leader of the United States and head of one branch of the government. (p. 294)

private (PRY viht) Belonging to one person or one group. (p. 277)

product (PRAHD uhkt) Something that people make. (p. 143)

public (PUHB lihk) Able to be used by everyone. (p. 276)

pueblo (PWEHB loh) A group of houses built by the Hopi. (p. 78)

R radio (RAY dee oh) A form of communication that uses sound but not pictures to tell you what is happening. (p. 316)

rapid transit (RAP ihd TRAN ziht) A system of high-speed trains, buses, and expressways. (p. 124)

reference book (REHF ur uhns buk) A book that gives information on many subjects. (p. 200)

religion (rih LIJ uhn) The way people show their beliefs. (p. 26)

research (rih SURCH) To study a subject very carefully. (p. 40)

resource map (REE sawrs map) A map that shows where different resources are. (p. 177)

road map (rohd map) A map that shows routes between different places. (p. 130)

route (root) A road or street. (p. 15)

rural (RUR uhl) In the country, far from cities. (p. 112)

S service (SUR vihs) Work that someone does for other people. (p. 194)

settler (SEHT lur) A person who moves to a new place to make a home. (p. 20)

silt (sihlt) Fine dirt particles that floodwater carries. They make the soil fertile. (p. 151)

sister city (SIHS tur SIHT ee) A city that shares its ways of living and doing business with another city. (p. 25)

slavery (SLAY vuh ree) When people are forced to work for others without pay. (p. 89)

suburb (SUHB urb) A community just outside a city. (p. 121)

Supreme Court (su PREEM kawrt) The head of a branch of the national government and the most powerful court in the United States. (p. 295)

T **tax** (taks) Money people pay to the government. (p. 277)

technology (tehk NAHL uh jee) The use of science to make something. (p. 120)

television (TEHL uh vihzh uhn) A form of media that uses sound and pictures to tell and show what is happening. (p. 317)

territory (TEHR ih tawr ee) Land that is an official part of another country. (p. 104)

timeline (TYM lyn) A drawing that shows events in history in the order in which they happened. (p. 96)

trade (trayd) To give something away to get something in return. (p. 87)

tradition (truh DIHSH uhn) A custom or belief that is passed down from parents to children. (p. 55)

translator (TRANZ lay tur) A person who listens to what someone says in one language, then repeats it in another language. (p. 320)

transportation (trans pur TAY shuhn) What people use to travel from one place to another. (p. 22)

U **urban** (UR buhn) In a city. (p. 112)

W **wampum** (WAHM puhm) Beads made of pieces of shells. (p. 76)

wharf (hwawrf) A landing place where ships tie up to load and unload their cargoes. (p. 93)

worship (WUR shihp) To take part in religious services. (p. 26)

Index

Chapter Reviews

Credits

Acknowledgments: American Voices

3 Blackfoot Chief; *Touch the Earth: A Self-Portrait of Indian Existence*, by T.C. McLuhan, Outerbridge and Dienstfrey, 1971. **4** Emma Lazarus; Found in *Familiar Quotations*, by John Bartlett, Little, Brown and Company, 1980. **5** Abraham Lincoln; "The Address at Gettysburg," November 19, 1863, found in *Familiar Quotations*, by John Bartlett, Little, Brown and Company, 1980. **6** Frederick Douglass; *Frederick Douglass: The Clarion Voice*, by John W. Blassingame, 1976.

Unit Opener Quotes

Unit 1 Ruth Delong Peterson; Every attempt has been made to locate the rightsholder of this work. If the rightsholder should read this, please contact Houghton Mifflin Company, School Permissions, 222 Berkeley St., Boston, MA 02116-3764. **Unit 2** Emma Lazarus; *The Women Poets in English*, Ann Stanford, ed., McGraw-Hill. **Unit 3** Eve Merriam; Selection from "Landscape," from *Finding a Poem*, by Eve Merriam. Copyright © 1970 by Eve Merriam. Reprinted by permission of Marian Reiner for the author. **Unit 4** Dylan Thomas; *The Macmillan Dictionary of Quotes*, Macmillan, 1987. **Unit 5** Chippewa Indian Song; *The Riverside Anthology of Children's Literature*, Judith Saltman, ed., Houghton Mifflin, 1985. **Unit 6** *Leviticus*; *Celebrating America*, compiled by Laura Whipple, Philomel Books, 1994.

Permissioned Material

Selection from *Amelia Earhart: Pioneer of the Sky*, by John Parlin, illustrated by Wayne Alfano. Text copyright © 1962 by John Parlin. Illustrations copyright © 1991 by Wayne Alfano. Reprinted by permission of Chelsea House Publishers, a division of Main Line Book Company, 1-(800)362-9786. "America the Beautiful," by Katharine Lee Bates, arranged by Samuel Ward. "Anno's Find-It Game" from *Anno's Math Games*, Vol. 1 by Mitsumasa Anno, as reprinted in *Spider* magazine, January 1994, Vol. 1, No. 1. Copyright © 1994 by Leah Palmer Preiss. Reprinted by permission of Philomel Books, a division of the Putnam & Grosset Group. Cover copyright © 1994 by Leah Palmer Preiss. Reprinted by permission of *Spider* magazine and the Carus Publishing Company. "Counting in Swahili," illustrated by Barbara Knutson, as reprinted in *Spider* magazine, June 1994, Vol. 1, No. 6. Text copyright © 1994 by Carus Publishing Company. Cover copyright © 1994 by Robert Byrd. Reprinted by permission of *Spider* magazine. Illustrations copyright © 1994 by Barbara Knutson. Illustrations reprinted by permission of the artist. Selection from *Home Place*, by Crescent Dragonwagon, illustrated by Jerry Pinkney. Text copyright © 1990 by Crescent Dragonwagon. Illustrations copyright © 1990 by Jerry Pinkney. Reprinted by permission of Simon & Schuster Children's Publishing Division and Curtis Brown Ltd. Cover of *National Geographic World* magazine, April 1993. Copyright © 1993 by *National Geographic World*. *World* is the official magazine for Junior Members of the National Geographic Society. Reprinted by permission. Selection from *Sitti's Secrets*, by Naomi Shihab Nye, illustrated by Nancy Carpenter. Text copyright © 1994 by Naomi Shihab Nye. Illustrations copyright © 1994 by Nancy Carpenter. Reprinted by permission of Four Winds Press, a division of Simon & Schuster Children's Publishing Division. "Sticking to Tradition," by Marty Kaminsky, from *Highlights for Children* magazine, February 1993. Copyright © 1993 by Highlights for Children, Inc., Columbus, Ohio. Reprinted by permission. Selection from *The Story of Money*, by Betsy Maestro, illustrated by Giulio Maestro. Text copyright © 1993 by Betsy Maestro. Illustrations copyright © 1993 by Giulio Maestro. Reprinted by permission of Clarion Books, a division of Houghton Mifflin Company. All rights reserved. Selection from *Three Days on a River in a Red Canoe*, by Vera B. Williams. Copyright © 1981 by Vera B. Williams. Reprinted by permission of Greenwillow Books, a division of William Morrow and Company, Inc. *USA TODAY*, November 1, 1995. Copyright © 1995 by USA TODAY/Gannett News Service. Reprinted by permission. Selection from *We the People: The Constitution of the United States of America*, by Peter Spier. Copyright © 1987 by Peter Spier. Reprinted by permission of Bantam Doubleday Dell Books for Young Readers, a division of Bantam Doubleday Dell Publishing Group, Inc., New York, New York. All rights reserved. "Zeny's Zoo," from *National Geographic World* magazine, May 1992. Copyright © 1992 by *National Geographic World*. *World* is the official magazine for Junior Members of the National Geographic Society. Reprinted by permission.

Fair Use Quotes

20 Oliver Johnson; *Log Cabin in the Woods*, by Joanne Landers Henry, Four Winds Press, 1988. **21** Ibid. **104** Blackhawk; *Dubuque on the Mississippi 1788–1988*, by William E. Wilkie, Loras College Press, 1987. **114** Elizabeth Phillips; *Ellis Island: An Illustrated History of the Immigrant Experience*, by Ivan Chermayeff, Fred Wasserman, and Mary J. Shapiro, Macmillan, 1991. **115** Paul Sturman; Ibid. **120** A.B. Steele; *Atlanta and Environs*, by Franklin M. Garrett, University of Georgia Press, 1954. **152** Mark Twain; *Life on the Mississippi*, by Mark Twain, 1883. **153** General Alexander G. Paxton; *Three Wars and a Flood*, (n.p., n.d.), p. 24; copy in Mississippi Levee Commissioner's Office, Greenville.

Photo Credits

Cover (inset) Bokelberg/The Image Bank; (bk) Donovan Reese/Tony Stone Images **Back Cover** (m) Joseph Nettis/Tony Stone Images; (br) Earth Imaging/Tony Stone Images **i** Bokelberg/The Image Bank **ii–iii** (inset) Alex S. MacLean/Landslides; (bk) Donovan Reese/Tony Stone Images; (br) Earth Imaging/Tony Stone Images **vii** (l) Susanne Page **x** (tr) Joe Viesti/Viesti Associates **xi** (tr) Courtesy of NASA **2** (m) Bokelberg/The Image Bank **2–3** (t) © David Muench 1996 **4** (all) Peter & Georgina Bowater/The Image Bank **5** (t) D. Young-Wolff/PhotoEdit **6** (m) 1994 Paul Barton/The Stock Market **6–7** (m) Russell D. Curtis/Photo Researchers, Inc. **6–7** (bk) Donovan Reese/Tony Stone Images **8–9** (bk) Jane Wooster-Scott/SuperStock **10** (ml) Jane Wooster-Scott/Superstock; (br) Conner Prairie Museum, Fishers, IN **11** (bm) Texas Folklife Reources; (br) Will Van Overbeek **12** (bk) Darryl Jones; (br) Courtesy Conner Prairie Museum, Fishers, IN **13** (tl) Courtesy of U.S. Postal Service; (bl) © Shawn Spence Photography; (bm) Courtesy of The Children's Museum; (br) T. Di Girolamo GE/Marka/Mercury Pictures **20** (bl) Indiana Historical Society, Bass Photo Collection **21** (tr) (mr), (br) Courtesy of Conner Prairie Museum, Fishers, IN **23** (t) Indiana Historical Society, Bass Photo Collection; (mr) © Shawn Spence Photography **24** (b) G. Luigi Sosio/Marka/Mercury Pictures **25** (tr) Tony Stone Images/Earth Imaging; (mr) M. Albonico/Marka/Mercury Pictures **26** (tl) M. Albonico/Marka/Mercury Pictures **27** (tl) (tr) M. Albonico/Marka/Mercury Pictures **30** (bk) Ariel Skelley/The Stock Market **31** (tl) Courtesy of U.S. Postal Service; (bm) Michael Young/Texas Folklife Resources **51** (tr) © University of Texas at Austin; (mr) © David R. Frazier Photolibrary **55** (tl) Kay Turner/Texas Folklife Resources; (tr & br) Michael Young/Texas Folklife Resources **56** (tl) (tr) Texas Folklife Resources; (bl) Michael Young/Texas Folklife Resources **60** (t) (bl) Will Van Overbeek **61** © 1990 Alan Pogue **62–63** (l) (r) Jeff Hunter/The Image Bank **64** (l) Pete Saloutos/The Stock Market; (m) Robert E. Daemmrich/Tony Stone Images **65** (t) Marc Romanelli/The Image Bank **68–69** (bk) Library of Congress **70** (ml) Library of Congress **71** (bl) Museum of the City of New York; (br) Atlanta History Center **72** (bk) © David Muench 1996; (bm) Susanne Page; (br) BETTMANN **73** (t) courtesy of U.S. Postal Service; (mr) National Museum of the American Indian; (bl) Courtesy of Jamestown-Yorktown Foundation; (bm) Peabody Essex Museum/Jeffrey Dykes; (br) Peabody Essex Museum/Mark Sexton **77** (ml & br) Courtesy of Steve Thome **78** (tl) Courtesy of Haffenreffer Museum of Anthropology, Brown University/Cathy Carver **80** (t) Susanne Page **81** (tr) Susanne Page **82** (bl) Tim Reese/The Syracuse Newspapers **83** (bl) Tim Reese/The Syracuse Newspapers **84** (ml) BETTMANN; (br) Courtesy of the Association for the Preservation of Virginia Antiquities **85** (br) The Granger Collection, New York **87** (tr) BETTMANN **88** (tm) Courtesy of the Association for the Preservation of Virginia Antiquities; (tr) Courtesy of the Association for the Preservation of Virginia Antiquities **89** (tr) Courtesy of Jamestown-Yorktown Foundation **90** (b) Peabody Essex Museum/Mark Sexton **91** (t) Peabody Essex Museum/Jeffrey Dykes; (br) Peabody Essex Museum/Jeffrey Dykes **92** (b) Peabody Essex Museum/Jeffrey Dykes **92–93** (t) Peabody Essex Museum/Mark Sexton **95** (tr) Peabody Essex Museum/Mark Sexton **96** (bl) Courtesy of the Association for the Preservation of Virginia Antiquities; (br) Peabody Essex Museum/Mark Sexton **97** (t) Peabody Essex Museum, Salem, MA; (b) Peabody Essex Museum/Mark Sexton **98** (bl) Peabody Essex

Museum/Mark Sexton **98–99** (l) (r) Jeff Hunter/The Image Bank **102** (bk) Library of Congress; (bm) Courtesy of Sturbridge Village; (br) © Stuart Dee/The Image Bank **103** (tl) Courtesy of U.S. Postal Service; (bl) Brown Brothers; (bm) Atlanta History Center; (br) © Ron Sherman/The Image Bank **104** (t) State Historical Society of Iowa — Iowa City; (l) The Warner Collection of Gulf States Paper Corporation, Tuscaloosa, Alabama **105** (l) (c) Dubuque County Historical Society **106** (tl) Museum of the City of New York; (bl) State Historical Society of Iowa — Iowa City **107** (r) Courtesy of Hallie Brown **108** (mr) Cincinnati Historical Society; (bl) Cincinnati Historical Society **111** (r) Museum of American Textile History **112** (t) Museum of American Textile History; (bl) Courtesy of Sturbridge Village **113** (tr) Bettmann Archive **114** (bl) © Stuart Dee/The Image Bank **115** (t) Library of Congress; (br) Brown Brothers **116** (t) George Eastman House **117** (t) (m) The Museum of the City of New York; (b) Library of Congress **118** (t) UPI/The Bettmann Archive; (b) © Lawrence Migdale **120** (tr) Atlanta History Center **121** Atlanta History Center **122** (bl) (br) Atlanta History Center **123** (t) Atlanta History Center; (mr) © Andrea Pistolesi/The Image Bank; (br) © David R. Frazier Photolibrary **124** (tl) © Ron Sherman/Tony Stone Images; (tr) © 95 Rob Nelson/Black Star; (bl) © Ken Biggs/Tony Stone Images **125** © Diego Goldberg/Sygma **134–135** (bk) Alex S. MacLean/Landslides **136** (ml) Alex S. MacLean/Landslides; (bm) Jon Gnass **137** (bl) Delta Design Group, Inc.; (br) Robert Frero/Tony Stone Images **138** (bk) © David Muench 1996; (bl) © David Falconer/David R. Frazier Photolibrary; (bm) © Linda J. Moore; (br) The Bettmann Archive **139** (tl) Courtesy of U.S. Postal Service; (mr) © Michael Melford/The Image Bank; (bl) Delta Design Group, Inc.; (bm) Clifton Adams/National Geographic Society Image Collection; (br) © Les Stone/Sygma **140** (t) © Barbara Filet/Tony Stone Images; (ml) © John Gnass **141** (r) The Bettmann Archive **148** (mr) Steve McCutcheon **148–149** (b) David Rhode **150** (ml) Delta Design Group, Inc.; (b) © Franke Keating **151** (t) Delta Design Group, Inc. **152** (bl) UPI/Bettmann Newsphotos **153** (tr) (bl) Clifton Adams/National Geographic Society Image Collection **154** (tl) Bill Rowe/Mercury Pictures; (tr) © Brooks Kraft/Sygma; (bl) © Warren Winter/Sygma **156–157** (b) © Tom Bean 1993 **164** (bk) © Fong Siu Nang/The Image Bank; (bl) Elizabeth Leppman; (bm) © Larry Dale Gordon/The Image Bank; (br) © Alain le Garsmeur/Tony Stone Images **165** (mr) Elizabeth Leppman; (bl) © Anne Rippy/The Image Bank; (bm) © David R. Frazier Photolibrary; (br) © Yorim Kahana/Shooting Star **166** (t) (b) Elizabeth Leppman **168** (bl) © Alain le Garsmeur/Tony Stone Images **170** © David Hiser/Photographers/Aspen **171** (t) © Anne Rippy/The Image Bank **172** (tl) TRIP/R. Powers; (m) TRIP/C. Caffrey **174** (b) © David R. Frazier Photolibrary **175** (tl) © Robert Frero/Tony Stone Images; (tr) © Yorim Kahana/Shooting Star **178** (bl) Walter Bibikow/The Image Bank **178–179** (l) (r) Jeff Hunter/The Image Bank **182–183** (bk) Lewis Hine/Avery Architectural and Fine Arts Library, Columbia University in the City of New York **184** (ml) Lewis Hine/Avery Architectural and Fine Arts Library, Columbia University in the City of New York **185** (br) Barry Brukoff **186** (bl) Langdon Clay **187** (tl) Courtesy of U.S. Postal Service; (bl) Colonial Williamsburg Foundation **190** (l) UPI/Bettmann Newsphotos **192** (bl) Marcel Isy-Schwart/The Image Bank **192–193** Jeff Hunter/The Image Bank **195** (tl) (mr) Colonial Williamsburg Foundation **196** © Langdon Clay **208** (bk) Cliff Hollenbeck; (bl) © Victor Englebert/Photo Researchers, Inc.; (bm) © David R. Frazier Photolibrary; (br) © The Stock Market/Tibor Bognar, 1994 **209** (tr) © David R. Frazier Photolibrary; (bl) (br) © David G. Houser; (bm) © Barry Brukoff, 1993 **210** (t) David A. Harvey © National Geographic Society; (l) UPI/Bettmann Newsphotos **212** (t) © David G. Houser, 1990; (bl) © Eduardo Gil **213** (tl) E. Manewal/Superstock **214** (mr) Tom Tracy/Tony Stone Images **215** (tr) Joseph Menta/Philadelphia Regional Port Authority **216** (b) TRIP/M. Jelliffe **217** (tl) © Barry Brukoff **218** (t) © Robert Frerck/Tony Stone Images **218–219** (b) © The Stock Market/Michele Burgess, 1989 **219** (tr) © Barry Brukoff, 1993 **220** (bl) © David G. Houser; (br) Wolfgang Kaehler **228–229** (bk) Daemmrich/Stock Boston **230** (ml) Daemmrich/Stock Boston; (bm) Roxanne M. Heizler/Silver Images Photography; (br) Frank Whitney/The Image Bank **231** (bm) Donald Nausbaum/Tony Stone Images; (br) Kim Naylor **232** (bk) Fred Maroon/Photo Researchers, Inc.; (bl) © Steven A. Page; (bm) The Bettmann Archive; (br) © Renato Rotolo/Gamma Liaison **234** (t) © The Stock Market/Michele Burgess, 1993; (b) © Roxanne M. Heizler/Silver Images Photography **235** (bl) Courtesy of Black Hills Heritage Festival; (br) © Roxanne M. Heizler/Silver Images Photography **236** (bl) The Bettmann Archive; (br) Frank Whitney/The Image Bank **237** (bl) Pamela Zilly/The Image Bank **238** (br) George Chan/Photo Researchers, Inc. **240** (bl) 1995 Steven A. Page/Silver Images Photography **240–241** (l & r) Jeff Hunter/The Image Bank **246** (bl) (mr) Minnesota Historical Society **252** (bk) Cliff Hollenbeck; (bl) © The Stock Market/Benjamin Rondel, 1992; (bm) (br) Courtesy of Festival Caravan, Toronto **253** (bl) © Wolfgang Kaehler; (br) © Joe Viesti/Viesti Associates **254** (t) © The Stock Market/David Barnes; (ml) © Donald Nausbaum/Tony Stone Images; (br) Courtesy of Festival Caravan, Toronto

256 (tl) © The Toronto Star/P. Gower; (b) Courtesy of Festival Caravan, Toronto **257** (tr) Courtesy of Jerry Jerome **258** (br) David R. Frazier/Photo Researchers, Inc. **258–259** (b) Larry Dale Gordon/The Image Bank **264** (bl) (br) © Joe Viesti/Viesti Associates **265** (t) © Wolfgang Kaehler; (mr) © Joe Viesti/Viesti Associates **266** (t) © Joe Viesti/Viesti Associates **267** (tl) © Joe Viesti/Viesti Associates; (tr) © Kim Naylor **270–271** (bk) Fred J. Maroon/Photo Researchers, Inc. **272** (ml) Fred J. Maroon/Photo Researchers, Inc. (bm) Jeff Greenberg/PhotoEdit; (br) Zefa-Reinhard/The Stock Market; **273** (bl) Penelope A. Pearson; (bm) Ron Giling/Lineair/Panos Pictures; (br) Gianni Giansanti/Sygma; **274** (bk) Jeff Hunter/The Image Bank; (bl) © W.B. Spunbarg/PhotoEdit; (br) © Eddie R. Sjostrum **275** (tl) Courtesy of U.S. Postal Service; (tr) © Jeff Greenberg/PhotoEdit; (bm) Courtesy of North Carolina Highway Patrol; (br) © Joseph Sohm/Tony Stone Images **276** (br) © Tony Freeman/PhotoEdit **277** (bl) Steven W. Jones/FPG International Corp., 1992 **280–281** (l) (r) Jeff Hunter/The Image Bank **282** (bl) © Zefa-Reinhard/The Stock Market, 1994 **285** © Terry Qing/FPG International Corp., 1994 **286** (br) Robert W. Madden/National Geographic Society **287** (t) Earth Satelite Corporation/Science Photo Library/Photo Researchers, Inc.; (tr) (mr) Dan Beigel **288** (bl) © Penelope A. Pearson; (br) © T. Kevin Smyth/The Stock Market **290** (ml) Courtesy of Design Center, State of Colorado; (bl) Courtesy of Colorado State Patrol **291** (b) Courtesy of North Carolina Highway Patrol **292** Courtesy of the Mark Twain Elementary School **300–301** (b) © David Muench 1996 **308** (bk) Jon Bradley/Tony Stone Images; (bl) (bm) © Ron Giling/Lineair/Panos Pictures **309** (tr) © Doris DeWitt/Tony Stone Images; (bl) © Derek Hudson/Sygma; (bm) © 1993 Sal DiMarco/Black Star; (br) Courtesy of NASA **310** (br) © SPAARNESTAD FOTOARCHIEF/NFGC **311** (bl) © John Elk/Stock Boston; (br) © Ron Giling/Lineair/Panos Pictures **312** (ml) © Charles Kennard/Stock Boston; (b) © Manfred Mehlig/Tony Stone Images **316** (br) Franklin Jay Viola/© National Geographic Society Image Collection **318** (bl) © Richard Mackson/FPG International **319** (t) © 1995 L.Q. Owen/Black Star; (mr) UPI/Bettmann Newsphotos **320** (tl) UNICEF/92-023/John Isaac; (bl) BETTMANN **321** (mr) (bl) Courtesy of NASA **322** (tl) (b) © Gianni Giansanti/Sygma **323** (tl) Courtesy of World Association of Girl Guides and Girl Scouts **330** (bl) Alex S. MacLean/Landslides **335** (r) © Anne Rippy/The Image Bank **336** (tl) © Roy Morsch/The Stock Market; (tr) (ml) © 1994 Earl Fansler/Photographers, Inc./Courtesy of Hillerich & Bradbury Co. **354** (t) © Piero Guerrini/Liaison International; (bl) Jean Pierre Pieuchot/The Image Bank **354–355** (b) James Randklev/Tony Stone Images **355** (tl) Hans Wendler/The Image Bank; (tr) Nikolas de Rohan/© 1991 Wernher Krutein/Liaison International; (br) Larry Mayer/Liaison International

Assignment Photo Credits

Kindra Clineff: 274 (bm), 276 (l); Rob Crandall: 185 (bl), 187 (br), 197 (bl) (br), 198 (t), 199 (t); Dave Desroches: 63 (background), 99 (background), 176–177 (background), 193 (background), 241 (background), 281 (background), 338 (middle), (bl), 339 (tr) (bl), 340–341 (all); FayFoto: 193 (m), 287 (bl); Max Lawrence: 221 (tl) (tr); Ken Lax: 63 (m), 277 (tl); Mark Maritado: 119 (mr); Lawrence Migdale: 231 (bl), 233 (bl) (bm) (br), 242 (ml) (bl), 243 (t) (mr), 245 (t) (tr); Rob Nelson: 124 (tl) (tr); Ilene Perlman: 95 (mr); Jeff Reinking: 277 (tr), 279 (t); Tony Scarpetta: 15 (tl), 43 (tl), 113 (tl), 154 (br), 179 (background), 185 (bm), 195–196 (b), 211 (tl) (ml) (bl), 217 (r) (mr) (br), 247 (br), 257 (m), 266 (l), 278 (b), 297 (tr), 316 (all), 317 (all); Ed Sjostrom: 184 (bl) (br), 186 (bl) (bm) (br), 189 (b), 190 (t), 191 (t) (mr); Will Van Overbeek: 11 (bl), 30 (bl) (bm) (br), 31 (bl) (br), 32 (t) (bl), 33 (tr), 34 (tl), 35, 38–39 (b), 39 (t), 40 (tl) (bl) (bm) (br), 41 (bl) (bm) (mr), 48 (b), 49 (t), 50 (tl), 52 (t), 53 (b) (m), 54 (t) (b), 57 (tr), 58 (b), 59 (t) (br), 284 (bl) (br); Tracey Wheeler: 43 (b), 49 (b), 119 (tr), 177, 201, 223, 328 (bl), 339 (tl); Joyce Wilson: vi (bl), 10 (bm), 12 (bl) (bm), 13 (mr), 14–15 (b), 16 (tr) (ml) (bl), 17 (tr) (mr)

Illustration Credits

Francis Back: 74–75; Bob Barner: 337; Joan Brancale: 19; Glasgow & Associates: 173; Carlyn Iverson: 86; Joseph McKendry: 76; Rob Schuster: 142; Wood Ronsaville Harlin, Inc.: 78, 79, 105, 110–111, 294–295

Map Credits

Joan Brancale: 19; DLF Group: 22, 109, 172, 189, 215, 310; GeoSystems Corp.: 33, 36–37, 51, 74, 78, 117, 125, 130, 141, 149, 176, 177, 211, 222, 223, 239, 244, 247, 255, 259, 290, 313, 328–329, 331, 332; © 1996 GeoSystems Global Corp.: 10–11, 70–71, 136–137, 184–185, 230–231, 272–273, 342–349; Glasgow and Associates: 333; Albert Lorenz: 94; Karen Minot: 18, 293; Ortelius Design: 85